NORTH CAROLINA

Goldboro □

Gastonia □       □ Charlotte

□ Albemarle

Fayetteville □

□ Laurel Hill

Elizabethtown □

*Cape Fear River*

□ Anderson

*Saluda River*

SOUTH

COLUMBIA ●
*Congaree River*

Wilmington □

□ Camden

CAROLINA

□ Stateburg

*Peedee River*

□ Washington

□ Aiken

Orangeburg □

*Lake Moultrie*
Santee

□ Georgetown

Augusta □

*Ogeechee River*

*Savannah River*

□ Blackville
□ Barnwell

*Edisto River*

*Santee River*

*Ashley River*

*Cooper River*

□ James Town

lle

□ Allendale

*Combahee River*

CHARLESTON □

Sullivan's Island

Ft. Sumter

□ Lawtonville
□ Furman
□ Robertville

*Broad River*

Beaufort

Edisto Island

Two Sisters'
Ferry

Port Royal

Hardeeville □

St. Helena's Island

Hilton Head Island

*Oconee River*

GIA

*Altamaha River*

SAVANNAH □

□ Fort Pulaski

Fort McAlister ▲

Darien □

*Satilla River*

Brunswick □

Sea Island
St. Simon's Island

Jekyll Island

Irwinsville □

*Okefenokee Swamp*

DA

Jacksonville □

*St. John's River*

□ Gainsville

*Suwannee River*

**Atlantic
Ocean**

South Carolina and Georgia c. 1800

# KITH AND KIN

# KITH AND KIN
## *A Portrait of a Southern Family*
## *(1630-1934)*

by
Carolyn L. Harrell

Mercer

All books published by Mercer University Press are produced
on acid-free paper that exceeds the minimum standards set by the
National Historical Publications and Records Commission.

**Library of Congress Cataloging in Publication Data**

Harrell, Carolyn L. (Carolyn Lawton), 1911-
  Kith and Kin.

  Bibliography: p. 305.
  Includes index.
  1. Furman family.    I. Title.
CT274.F87H37   1984      929'.2'0973         83-24957
ISBN 0-86554-090-X (alk. paper)

# TABLE OF CONTENTS

# DEDICATION

*For Glover*
*and our Forever Family*
*Mary and Charles*
*Lyn and Jim*
*Charlotte and Craig*
*Emily and Bill*
*and*
*Abraham, Joel, and David*

# PREFACE

When I first started writing this book, I thought I would be writing a story about the family for our children and grandchildren, and now, for great-grandchildren. I wanted to give them a true picture of one special family, their own family, who had lived in South Carolina and Georgia for three hundred years.

The basic purpose remains the same, but throughout the nine years that I have been gathering material and putting the book together, the realization has grown that the story might have a wider interest. I am indebted to Robert Coles and Flannery O'Connor for kindling an awareness that in a portrait of the everyday life of one Southern family, with all its human strengths and weaknesses, "its realities, its drama, its textures, its things,"[1] can be found the everlasting vitality of the human spirit. If that is found in *Kith and Kin*, the book is worthwhile.

Much of the basic genealogical information had been documented: births and marriages and deaths of scores of members of the family. Annie Elizabeth Miller, a distant cousin of mine, after years of correspondence,

---

[1]Coles, *Flannery O'Connor's South*, 122.

interviews, research, and compilation, published "Our Family Circle" in 1931. Robert E. H. Peeples,[2] another cousin, made corrections and additions to Annie Miller's book after careful research, and it was reprinted in 1975 with his changes. I am grateful to them both.

But the history of a family with its multifarious roots and intertwining branches cannot be written simply by stringing together Bible records, military records, newspaper obituaries, wills, and inscriptions on mossy tombstones. Realizing that the family can come alive only if the people in it are viewed in historical perspective, I have attempted to picture what was going on in the world and in South Carolina and Georgia at crucial times in their lives, and to interpret their reactions to events in light of what they say about themselves in their own letters and memoirs and diaries, or of what is said about them in official records and histories of the times. In so doing, I have been fortunate in finding a plethora of previously untapped diaries, memoirs, and letters, as well as officially recorded court and land records. The narrative is woven around those personal papers, from the time the first family member arrived in America in 1630, until one of the units of the family lived in Macon, Georgia, in the 1930s.

To avoid interrupting the narrative by including genealogical material in each chapter, I have placed vital statistics and other genealogical data in the Appendix, which is referenced as seems appropriate. The List of Abbreviations in the Appendix serves also as a list of primary sources.

If you wish to place a person in his relationship to other family members, you will find his name in the Appendix in several places. For example, Richard Furman (1755-1825) may be found listed with his Furman forebears, as well as with one line of descendants in "The Furman Line." He may also be found on "Ancestor Charts A and D," which show his relationship to members of the Lawton-Willingham-Nottingham-Guttenberger family. Also, as a "Head of Family," he is shown in the "Family Group Records," where his children are listed, as well as the children of his son, Samuel Furman, who are pertinent to the narrative.

In the personal papers of family members and in official records, there often appeared evidence of an individual's political leanings, religious beliefs, or other personal characteristics. These primary sources are referenced

---

[2]Both Annie Miller and Robert Peeples are descendants of *Pasteur* Pierre Robert and other mutual ancestors.

in the footnotes, and I accept sole responsibility for conclusions drawn from them, or for errors in interpreting them. Always, I have tried to avoid what the historian Barbara Tuchman calls "spontaneous attribution."

The cooperation, patience, and understanding of dozens of genealogists, archivists, librarians and their staffs, as well as family members and friends, has been one of the most rewarding experiences of my life. A number of colleges and universities permitted me access to their archives, special collections, or manuscript divisions, for which I am most grateful. Dr. E. L. Inabinett, director of the South Caroliniana Library, Columbia, encouraged me to believe that the true story I was preparing could have wider interest than I first thought. The more than 1,300 manuscripts in the Lawton Family Papers and the Furman Letters there, together with the Lawton Files in the Southern Historical Collection of the University of North Carolina, Chapel Hill, formed the basis of the Lawton and Furman chapters. I am grateful to Dr. Richard A. Shrader, reference archivist, Southern Collection, for his invaluable assistance.

For the Nottingham source material, I am grateful to Jean Mihalyka, Cheriton, Virginia, as well as for her delightful letters in adding local color to the Nottingham family narrative. For the Guttenberger story, as a base of reference I have used "A Family History," written by Francesca Guttenberger Link (1835-1911) and family memorabilia made available by Loulie Forrester Burns, Macon. A copy of Francesca's unpublished manuscript is in my files. The Willingham narrative was developed from material made available by Nancy Watson and Willard Rocker, Genealogy Room, Washington Memorial Library, Macon; by Joseph Constance and Peer Ravnan, archivists, Middle Georgia Historical Society; and by Calder Willingham Payne, Macon, through his recent compilation, "Descendants of Benjamin Lawton Willingham."

For specific help in various areas, I must single out the libraries of Wesleyan College and Mercer University, Macon, and Furman University, Greenville, as well as the libraries of the Universities of North and South Carolina, and of the United States Military Academy. Especially helpful were the staffs of the Huntsville, Alabama, Public Library and of the Clayton Library for Genealogical Research, Houston, Texas. Others that were helpful were the Library of the Church of Christ of Latter Day Saints, Oakland, California; the Georgia Historical Society Library, Savannah; the Library of the Huguenot Society of South Carolina, Charleston; and the

Charleston Public Library. The State Archives of Georgia, South Carolina, and Virginia merit my appreciation and thanks.

Chapters of this book were read in draft by Thomas O. Lawton, Jr., Allendale, South Carolina; Robert E. H. Peeples, Hilton Head Island, South Carolina; Calder Willingham Payne, Macon, Georgia; and by Helen Crutchfield Johnson and Ruth Cole Weber, Huntsville, Alabama.

I owe a large debt of gratitude to Hayes B. Jacobs, wise mentor and kind friend. He guided me with warm encouragement through every phase of development, from the initial idea through numerous rough drafts. My husband gave unswerving support through the years: assisted with research, made a determined effort to "keep me honest" by checking sources and references. From a quiet room in which to work, to fine sets of encyclopedias right at hand, to a new typewriter when the old one expired in the middle of the last chapter, he provided them all.

To Susan Carini, my Mercer University Press editor, I am especially grateful. She applied her highly professional skills with a steady hand, a quiet patience, and a delightfully sunny spirit.

# INTRODUCTION

No one factor can explain the flow of forces that impelled all our American forebears to leave their native lands to settle in the New World. The English came, and later French and German and Dutch peoples, who were succeeded by scores of others. There were some with retinue, in linen and broadcloth; more came in homespun and haircloth; some were brought chained, in loincloths. That all learned to unite their talents, their muscles, their ingenuity, their heterogeneous endowments and longings in the creation of a United States of America speaks for the awesome triumph of the human spirit.

Historians have recorded at length the lives of the leaders and the events contributing to the advance of civilization in America. These mighty men, these administrative geniuses, these leaders in war and peace of whom they write, as well as earth-shattering revolutions of which they tell, are surely the stuff of which recorded history is made. Most men and women made few marks on the pages of history, but it is the unproclaimed masses of the new country whose struggles and aspirations in the long view are the substance of the land's spirit and the history of the nation. They are America.

This is the narrative of an American family, a Southern family. It is an ongoing story, as indelible and timeless as the story of America itself, of which every family is a quickening microcosm.

The Southern family whose portrait this book presents was in no way unique in its many branches and manifestations: there were English, Irish, German, Dutch, French, to name but a few; there were land-grubbers and men with vast landholdings, who acquired both new lands and slaves at a great rate; there were itinerant preachers and ministers of fine churches; there were lawyers, doctors, tradesmen, factors, surveyors, indentured servants, government workers under contract to the English proprietors; there were men who signed their name with an X; there was one who sent his nine sons to college; there were various large units of many children—one man had four children by one wife, and after her death had fifteen by a second wife; two groups of three brothers married two groups of three sisters from neighboring families. There were roots entangled in roots and branches sprouting from branches.

As cotton was dethroned in the South and the devastating Civil War became a thing of the past, there were those in this family who came to live in the cities and towns of Carolina and Georgia, establishing businesses and rebuilding their lives after the war had decimated them. In the towns of South Carolina, and later in the town of Macon, Georgia, lineal descendants of those first settlers—Lawtons, Willinghams, Nottinghams, Guttenbergers—made places for themselves. They became tradesmen in the town: teachers, clerks, agents, cotton factors, cotton and lumber mill owners, bankers, preachers, musicians, salesmen. There were others who clung tenaciously to their South Carolina and Georgia lands, violated though they were by the war. Rather than forsaking them, they tilled them as best they could.

That direct descendants of these diverse spirits melded into one small family is wondrous in the extreme. This is their story.

## Chapter One

# RICHARD FURMAN
## (1755-1825)

*. . . a close working agreement with God . . .*[1]

I n the spring of 1629 the hamlets and villages of Suffolk County on England's east coast were humming with the news that John Winthrop—a fine Puritan gentleman, a Suffolk native, Cambridge-educated—had determined to leave England and settle in the New World. He had, the newsmongers said, formed a company with Sir Richard Saltonstall, John Endicott, and others that was being incorporated to provide passage and grants of land in America to those who were approved to buy stock in the company.

---

[1]"The people who captured my imagination when I was growing up were of the Deep South—emotional, changeable, touched with charisma and given to histrionic flourishes. They were courageous under tension and unexpectedly tough beneath their wild eccentricities, for they had a close working agreement with God. They also had an unusually high quota in bull\*\*\*\*." (Morris, *North Toward Home*, 9.)

John Firman,[2] of a family of shopkeepers and craftsmen in the village of Stokes-by-England (family members changed the spelling of the surname "Firman" to "Furman" only after their arrival in America), listened to reports of Winthrop's plan with particular interest. Firman was galled by oppressive taxes and the mundane life of the village. For many years since he had reached maturity, he had longed to cast his lot in the New World. Upon inquiry, John learned that a self-governing commonwealth was to be formed in America for the express purpose of trade and profit. He became a staunch supporter of Winthrop and his Massachusetts Bay Company, as the new enterprise was called. Needing only to be a good, hardworking Puritan, and financially able to buy stock, John joined the company and set sail with Endicott on one of the eleven ships chartered by Winthrop and the Bay Company to transport settlers to new lives in America. The first of the ships landed at Salem, Massachusetts, on June 12, 1630. By the end of the year, a thousand emigrants had been brought over.

John Firman, his wife Mary,[3] and their two young sons, John and Josiah, were with him on the voyage. When they landed, John received his parcel of land and voting rights as a "freeman"—his due as a Puritan stockholder in the company. The family was soon settled in Watertown, Massachusetts, where John plied his craft as a tanner and Mary set about her duties. These were defined by John Winthrop—who was shortly elected governor of the colony—when he said: "Women [are] expected to stick to household matters and refrain from meddling in such things as are proper for men whose minds are stronger."[4] Regardless of whether Mary performed her household duties well and refrained from meddling in matters best left to her stronger-minded husband, many of the Furman men were said to have married extraordinarily fine wives who "had a profound impact and many times [a] controlling part in the destiny of the Furman progeny."[5]

---

[2]The name "Firman" or "Firmin" has been traced by genealogists to England, France, and Italy. The Firmans were said to be mainly craftsmen and shopkeepers. About 1660 the Firmin family in America changed the spelling to "Furman" without changing the pronounciation.

[3]See Appendix: Furman Lineal Chart, Ancestor Charts A and D, and Family Group Records.

[4]Beard and Beard, *Rise of American Civilization*, 1:182.

[5]Furman, *Furman Legend*, 18ff.

John continued to ply his trade in Watertown, but his two sons, when they reached adulthood, moved to Long Island, near what is today Hempstead. They farmed, as did their sons and grandsons, finding a ready market for their produce in populous New York City.

The Furmans continued to increase in number, to prosper as substantial tradesmen, merchants, and farmers. Second- and third-generation Furmans left their verdant country setting for other homes in various settlements in New York, Pennsylvania, New Jersey, and later in South Carolina. The family strove always to better their lot, and if that meant moving, they moved. Upon maturity, Josiah, who had come to America as a boy, moved to Long Island, where he became a merchant. It was Josiah's line that attained a degree of prominence in the remarkable person of Richard Furman (1755-1825).[6]

On April 20, 1742, a great-grandson of Josiah [I], Wood Furman, married Rachel Brodhead, apparently another of those "extraordinarily fine wives" the Furmans tended to marry. Rachel was Dutch, tinged with the blood of the English conquerors of her forebears. Perhaps at Rachel's urgings and possibly in the hope of securing better business connections, Wood moved his family from the farmlands to Esopus (now Kingston), New York. Their four children, including Richard, born October 9, 1755, were all born in Esopus. Later on, Wood again felt impelled to move. This time the move was exceptionally difficult and daring.

The colony of South Carolina, bordered by the Spanish-controlled Florida peninsula and the French-controlled Louisiana Territory, was a tempting plum to both Spain and France. White South Carolinians lived in a maturing society that had a thriving economy based on a variety of products. Charles Town was fast becoming a major seaport, which drew the planters to it for business as well as social and cultural events.[7] The British Parliament, fearful of an invasion of its prize colony, voted to make available substantial grants of land in South Carolina to colonists who could prove they had an English background. These newly granted lands, Parliament felt, would act as a deterrent to would-be invaders. The Wood Furman family made the move to South Carolina, and lived briefly in Charles Town until the first of Wood's land grants could be approved and arrangements made

---

[6]Cook, *Biography of Furman*, 1-35.

[7]Sirmans, *Colonial South Carolina*, 225.

to occupy the land. One of the land grants was dated August 13, 1756, another May 10, 1768.[8] Altogether, Wood Furman eventually gained possession of 2,000 acres.

When Furman received his first land grant in Carolina in 1756, the colony had been under Crown rule for a quarter of a century. The Carolina coastal plain encompassed roughly two-thirds of the colony's area, extending 150 miles or more to the Piedmont. Throughout the years before Furman took up life in the Piedmont, Charles Town had become the center of the colony's agricultural and commercial economy. Furman could expect to join the other Charles Town settlers in finding healthy trade with whatever pelts, rice, and indigo he could produce. Through the ages, rivers had cut valleys in the Piedmont, leaving a rolling surface and flat, broad plateaus above the hills and ridges of the Piedmont.

Wood Furman's new land bordered one of those rivers, and included rich farmland along the banks of the Santee River, as well as sloping and flatlands high above the river. His land included both sides of Beech Creek, which flows into the Santee River, then east to the Atlantic Ocean. The hamlet of Stateburg nestles in the valley. Wood Furman was granted the land and claimed it from the wilds; later generations of Furmans nurtured it. The Reverend Doctor Richard Furman, the little boy who was brought to the land as a baby, turned to it all his life as he managed his slaves and supervised the reaping of harvests. Additionally, the land provided a source of solace and a "renewal of spirit" for him.

Wood Furman became a surveyor, and although he found some demand for his services in the High Hills of Santee, the struggle for survival in the isolated land occupied almost every moment of the pioneer family's day. He had few, if any, slaves, and wresting the land from the wilderness was endlessly bone-wearying. There was no time for the intellectual pursuits he enjoyed, nor were there schools for the education of his children. Moreover, there was danger from Indian attack. Wood Furman found such conditions at least uncivilized for his tastes, if not unbearable. When he was offered a position to teach at a school maintained by a fund called Bereford's Bounty on the coast of South Carolina in the parishes of St. Thomas and St. Denis in Berkley County, he accepted the offer. The fund for the operation of the school was established through the Episcopal church, of

---

[8]Plot Book 6, 102; Plot Book 10, 168.

which Wood was a devout member. Wood taught for five years, then up-rooted his family again, this time to Daniel's Island, within sight of Charles Town. The Furmans remained on Daniel's Island long enough for Wood to make a few crops and for young Richard to enjoy an active boyhood on the land. He went along with his father on surveying excursions. Wood taught him languages. He learned to ride horseback; he tramped through the woods; and he read every book he could find.

When Richard was fifteen, there was still another move in his life. By May 1770, Wood, having proved his ability as a planter, moved his family back to his lands on the Santee. It was here he pursued the occupations of planter, surveyor, and Judge of the Ordinary in Camden District. He be-came a vestryman of the Episcopal church, and continued an active, busy life. He served on juries, and was a member of the first legislative assembly of South Carolina. He was a signer of South Carolina's Declaration of Rights to oppose trade and consumption of British goods through nonim-portation and nonconsumption agreements.[9] In sum, Wood Furman was a considerable man, and his considerable talent was used in teaching his son.

So Richard grew up in an ever-changing, active household; and his father both challenged and nourished his son's growing intellect. Richard grew to be six feet tall and became an excellent marksman. He read and reread the Bible, as well as books in Latin and French. An early biographer says Richard became "proficient in mathematics, physics, Latin, Greek, Hebrew, French, German, philosophy, logic, history, English grammar, and classical literature"—a remarkable achievement, if true, since he had only a few days of formal schooling in his life.

During the years the Furman family had lived away from the Santee area, many changes had occurred. The population increased, roads were built, and plantations had replaced the forest clearing of the pioneers. There were several churches, including a Baptist church. The Baptists in Carolina had been steadily gaining in numbers, in spite of the fact that, by law, their taxes went to pay the minister of and provide support for the An-glican church. Political factors favored a large membership for that church; but as long as dissenters—including Baptists—abided by the laws and paid their taxes, they were allowed freedom of worship.

[9]DAC, *Lineage Book*, 7:5, 15, 32.

By the 1770s, there were a fairly large number of Baptists in Carolina, many of whom were associated with the First Baptist Church of Charles Town.[10]

The Furman family was Episcopalian, associated with the Church of England, and Richard dutifully attended services with the family. A Baptist preacher from Charles Town came to the High Hills the summer Richard was sixteen, and Richard, together with practically everybody else for miles around, gathered at the Particular Baptist Church to hear him preach. Joseph Reese exhorted and cajoled, threatened doom and destruction, expounded and explained and, finally, promised eternal life to sinners who acknowledged their sins and prayed for forgiveness.

As he listened, Richard became excited and distressed; he was filled with dread and apprehension. These feelings were followed by a sudden sense of acceptance and release. In short, he was converted. He joined the church of Particular Baptists and expressed his intention to become a minister. Wood was clearly appalled, and with a firm *no* to Richard, he let it be known he would hear no more about it. Now the time that Richard had formerly spent reading and studying was often spent in composing sermons. Occasionally, he spoke in the pulpit of the High Hills Baptist Church. Before long, the congregation petitioned him to become their minister, and he forthwith accepted. Richard Furman was seventeen at the time.

In December 1773—Richard was then eighteen—a great Baptist camp meeting took place. Several ministers had been invited to preach, among them the Reverend Oliver Hart of the First Baptist Church of Charles Town. Richard joined in the preaching duties at this meeting. A friendship developed between the two, and on May 16, 1774, Hart ordained Richard as a Minister of the Gospel. Richard was now officially pastor of the Baptist Church of the High Hills. On a hot Sunday afternoon shortly thereafter, Richard led his only sister, Sarah, into the shallow waters of the Wateree, spoke the proper words, closed her mouth and nostrils with his hand over them, and while the faithful raised their voices in song on the banks of the river, he gently lowered her head beneath the water for a moment. She was the first of many whom the Reverend Richard Furman was to baptize in the faith during his long years of ministry.

---

[10]Townsend, *South Carolina Baptists*, 4-9.

Richard's mother became a Baptist with her son, yet Richard's father remained loyal to the Church of England. Shortly after his nineteenth birthday, Richard married Elizabeth Haynsworth, a member of the Church of England. Richard remained pastor of the High Hills Church for thirteen years, but he never converted Elizabeth.[11]

No one knows who fired first—the British or the Americans—on that morning of April 19, 1775, on the green at Lexington, Massachusetts. But by the time the colonies and Great Britain were irreversibly at war, conflict had been brewing for a long time. The idea of breaking with the mother country was slow in taking shape and slow in winning its way among the people. Months after that first shot was fired, many colonists still felt and expressed their affection for England and grieved over the inevitable bloodshed. Sermons were preached on the theme that "our interest lies in a perpetual connection with our Mother Country."[12]

There were many influential leaders and members of the plantation gentry in the South who believed there was a middle ground in the conflict that could be found. These American spokesmen did not want independence, and they opposed it with all their strength. At the same time, however, they refused to yield to the demand for the absolute subjection of American will to Parliament.[13]

Some South Carolina planters remained loyal to the Crown. They had received crop subsidies and continued protection against the Indians, Spaniards, and French. They could see no advantage in severing such a beneficial relationship. It took courage, however, for those who opposed freedom from England to remain steadfast in the face of growing support to make a complete break from the mother country even if it meant war. Many Loyalists were ostracized, discriminated against, ridiculed, or even subjected to harm of person or property. As the year 1776 began, men on both sides of the Atlantic were in the grip of illusions that were hurtling England and America "down a collision course to a military and political convulsion that would shake the civilized world."[14]

---

[11]Cook, *Biography of Furman*, 1-35. Haynsworth, *Furman and Allied Families*, 118-33.

[12]Beard and Beard, *Rise of American Civilization*, 1:236ff.

[13]Jensen, *Founding of a Nation*, 568-72.

[14]Fleming, *1776: Year of Illusions*.

Richard Furman carefully avoided discussing political matters in the pulpit of his church in the High Hills, but as war approached, he could not ignore the activities around him. Eventually, he threw himself into the fight with all his energy and began preaching the cause of the Revolution. One of his contemporaries said, "He took an early and decided stand in favor of liberty and the measures of Congress." A number of his sermons have been preserved, all composed after the Revolution, several on patriotic themes. Two were preached before the Society of the Cincinnati, an association of Revolutionary army officers. In the first one, Richard said: "There is great reason to believe the American Revolution was effected by the special agency of God."[15]

Richard joined a company of militia that had been created by his brother, Captain Josiah Furman, at the beginning of the war. In addition, Richard served briefly as chaplain, but was requested by Governor John Rutledge to return home to South Carolina where his influence would serve the cause better than if he remained in the army. Richard's sermons and agitation did not go unnoticed. Lord Cornwallis, made aware of Richard's influence and daring as an advocate of rebellion, offered a thousand pounds for his head. Cornwallis declared that he "feared the prayers of that Godly youth more than the armies of Sumter and Marion."

In the beginning of 1780, American prospects were at their lowest point, with Georgia virtually under British control and South Carolina seriously threatened. In early April, British frigates opened an attack on Charles Town by running past the guns of Fort Moultrie at the entrance to Charles Town harbor. By May, Charles Town was in the hands of the British. Richard, safe until now in the High Hills of Santee, took his family and fled across the Virginia border, where except for occasional secret visits back to Santee, he remained until danger had passed. Almost two years elapsed before the Furmans moved back home. When they returned to Stateburg, Richard found his parents safe and well. He resumed his pastorate. Wood Furman had taken an active part in political affairs while his son was gone, and had been elected representative to the Jacksonboro Assembly, which reestablished self-government in South Carolina. But in Feb-

---

[15]Preached on July 4, 1802, at the First Baptist Church, Charleston.

ruary 1783, Wood Furman died, and with sadness Richard preached his father's funeral.

*Richard Furman (1755-1825), dynamic minister and energetic crusader in the cause of freedom and higher education, caused Lord Cornwallis to delcare during the War of Independence, "I fear the prayers of that Godly youth more than the armies of Sumter and Marion."*

[Historical Collection, Furman University]

The land that Richard Furman inherited from his father at Stateburg on the Wateree, his beloved "hills of home," drew him back continually as long as he lived. In 1783, shortly after his father's death, Richard, together with General Thomas Sumter and several other gentlemen of the neighborhood, organized the Claremont Society, and opened a school and library that operated as a boarding school. General Sumter, the "gamecock of the Revolution," for whom Fort Sumter in Charles Town harbor was named, had settled in the High Hills after the hostilities were over. In later years he served as a senator as well as the minister to Brazil.

During the years following the war, Richard received repeated invitations to become pastor of the First Baptist Church of the city now called Charleston. Evidently he had trouble persuading "this unworthy soul," as he often called himself, to take up the challenge as minister of the first and largest Baptist church in South Carolina. Finally, in 1787, he accepted, and he held the post for the rest of his life.

Shortly before he went to Charleston,[16] Elizabeth died, as had one of their children. So Richard went to Charleston as a widower with two young children, Rachael and Wood [II]. Almost immediately Richard entered the cultural and religious life of the Charleston community. In 1788 he formed the Society for Promoting Christian Knowledge and Practice. Governing rules included:

> *Rule 2nd*: Each of the members shall be careful to behave in [a] Christian-like manner at every meeting. Angry disputes, laffing [*sic*], and indecent behavior are to be avoided.
> *Rule 10th*: No person whose life is seriously immoral shall be admitted or continued in the society.

There is no explanation of what comprised an immoral life, and no record of how long the society existed. During the course of his years in Charleston, there were many other organizations that Richard had a hand in promoting, for he was an inveterate organizer and joiner.

Dorothea Marie Burn, daughter of Scottish émigré Samuel Burn and his Charleston-born wife, caught the eye and won the heart of the widowed minister. Dorothea, a budding fifteen, the minister's junior by twenty years, was completely swept away by his attentions. Devoutly believing it was God's will, she became his bride on May 5, 1789. Henceforth she conscientiously fulfilled her obligations as his wife and mother to the children of the eminent minister, whom she addressed as "Mr. Furman" throughout their married life. Richard Furman's "dear Dolly" assumed the role of mother to his two children, and she later bore thirteen more—ten sons and three daughters.[17]

As the mother of many children, Dorothea fit the image of the early nineteenth-century wife who, even though assisted by a corps of black mammies, housemaids, cooks, and nurses, was completely occupied (if not overwhelmed) by the role of wife and mother. Most of the year the family lived in the manse, next door to the First Baptist Church. They seldom undertook the trek to the High Hills for summer visits, primarily because the

---

[16]Charles Town was renamed Charleston in 1783.

[17]See Appendix: Furman Family Group Record.

logistics were almost insurmountable. One early biographer said of Dorothea: "Her mental and personal endowments adorned the domestic circle, which her retiring virtues chose as their proper sphere." Richard noted in one of his letters to her from Philadelphia that she was "prudent in managing the multiplicity of domestic matters" he left to her when he was away from Charleston on his many trips. These included Baptist association meetings, missionary endeavors, and management affairs at the Stateburg plantation.

During the years that Richard was pastor at Charleston, he demonstrated that he was "fond of missionary endeavors" in the South Carolina hills as well as on nearby islands. As an outgrowth of this interest, a church was established at Georgetown in 1794; and with the aid of a wealthy parishioner of his Charleston church, Mrs. Hepsebah Jenkins Townsend, Furman built a church on Edisto Island. Mrs. Townsend, herself fired with missionary zeal, established the Wadmalaw and Edisto Female Mite Society, whose members contributed to the Edisto church endeavor. Churches at Goose Creek and Mt. Olivet also received Richard's missionary devotion. Frequently, when he made the trips for meetings with outlying congregations, he was accompanied by his young son, Samuel, who himself "answered the call" and in his adult years became a minister. Almost always, Richard combined missionary work and business, visiting his several plantations, conferring with his overseers, and struggling with the manifold problems of slave ownership and plantation management.

Richard was faithful in his correspondence with Dorothea on those occasions when he was absent from Charleston and the family. He wrote from his plantation at Stateburg that "the people at the plantation are Generally Well. . . ." He had sold "10 bags of cotton which averaged more than 300 lbs. apiece," and "unless urgent business requires a longer stay here, I hope to be in town by the 4th Sunday. . . ." From Society Hill, Peedee, he wrote that "Samuel and myself arrived safely here Saturday," and "there has been worship at the Church every evening since I arrived by Candlelight, & I suppose there has not been less than 300 people at each service. . . . Col. Edwards, a Lady & several Negroes were Baptized here yesterday & a considerable degree of seriousness appears to be excited among the Peoples at large. . . . Sammy writes with me in Love to you. . . ."

Richard sent similar letters reporting work on the plantations and preaching, as well as news from relatives and associational meetings, to Dorothea throughout the years from the High Hills of Santee, Stateburg on the Wateree, Society Hill, and Peedee. Always he reported on the weather, together with discussing the health of relatives and friends. He wanted her to give "remembrances for enquiring friends," and "tell the Negroes I wish them well." He sent his Dolly "tender affections."

So life continued: Dorothea with her duties in the parsonage, managing the house slaves, and rearing their children. Often she was in "a delicate way." Furman continued his duties apace in the church, in the town of Charleston, on the mission field, and at the plantations.

America and Great Britain had been in armed conflict since 1812, following a period of great stress between the two nations as a result of the treatment of neutral countries by both France and England during the French Revolution and Napoleonic wars, in which France and England had been antagonists. During this conflict American shippers took advantage of the hostilities in Europe to absorb much of the trade, evading seizure under a British rule that forbade neutral nations any trade during wartime that was not allowed in peacetime. The British seized American ships, and there was widespread warfare between the two countries in Canada, as well as in the United States.

The war had been well underway when President James Madison discovered how woefully inadequate American preparations for war had been. The first months of 1814 held gloomy prospects for the Americans. Although the finances of the American government had been somewhat restored by the end of 1813, the source of future supplies was in doubt, and England was devoting increasing time and effort to the war in America. The crowning indignity to the American people came in August 1814, when a British expedition took Washington, burning the Capitol and the White House. Through early 1814, South Carolina and the South had not been the scene of conflict, and Richard Furman earnestly prayed that the South would continue to be spared.

Many South Carolinians, and citizens of surrounding states whose lives had not been directly touched by the war, went about their daily lives as usual. In the spring of 1814, with the country still at war, the large and loyal congregation of the First Baptist Church of Charleston, South Carolina, urged their pastor to make a journey to Philadelphia to a meeting, the first of its kind, of American Baptists. Furman himself had worked long on this project, drafting the purpose of the meeting and setting up the agenda. The meeting would turn out to be a momentous one in the life of Richard Furman and of the Baptist church itself. By fervent prayer and exhortation, he had asked to be led in the way of the Lord; and now that plans were firm to make the journey, he turned his petitions to God to protect and keep safe until his return his dear Dolly and their children,[18] as well as his flock at the First Baptist Church, and the black souls God had entrusted to his care.

The journey by coach from Charleston to Philadelphia in 1814 was not easy. The road was either rutted and rock-hard or muddy and almost impassable when the spring rains came, but Furman was hardly aware of the discomfort. He was on his way to Philadelphia for spiritual fulfillment, and a holy excitement filled his being.

Furman's destination was the First Baptist Triennial Convention in the United States, which he himself had labored to bring about. At long last, his prayers were being answered and his hopes for his church were about to be realized. Through the convention he was to see a mission board formed and functioning, higher education furthered, and the influence of the Baptist denomination spread throughout the States. In 1787—almost twenty-seven years before—he had left the pastorate of the little church in the High Hills of Santee at Stateburg, and had become the pastor of the First Baptist Church of Charleston. In those years, Richard had served as an elected member of the body to form a new constitution for the state of South Carolina. Shortly thereafter, he advocated the "abolition of certain exclusive parochial distinctions, a remnant of the former ecclesiastical establishment." In brief, Furman loosened the grip of the Church of England on South Carolina's governmental affairs, one result of which was that *all* religious bodies were granted the right of incorporation. Legally, Baptists could now form a national association, and Richard was now on his way to establish that organization.

On the day before he set out on his journey, Dorothea directed the house slaves in preparing and packing the trunks for his departure. One who knew Furman described him as a man whose personal appearance befitted his character:

> He was six feet tall, and stout without obesity. His hair and eyes were dark, the latter full of expression. His voice was clear and strong,

---

[18]There were eleven children by 1814: Richard [II], Samuel, Josiah, Charles Manning, Dorothea Marie, Henry Hart, Sarah Susanna, John Gano, Thomas Fuller, James Clement, Anne Eliza. A twelfth child, William, died in infancy in 1818.

and his articulation was very distinct. His dress, to the last like that of men of Charleston of that day, was the costume of the Revolutionary times—coat with pockets in the skirts opening outwardly under the lapel, waistcoat reaching the hips, knee-breeches and long stockings, the latter protected in foul weather or on a journey by high-topped boots.[19]

Dorothea saw that his greatcoat and boots were packed in an easily accessible spot, for although the South Carolina April was mild, bad weather could be expected on the month-long trip north.

By the time Richard set out on the journey, he had become the most influential Baptist minister in America. Already he had organized the church on district and state bases, forming as early as 1785 the Charleston Baptist Association. Now, at the first session of the national association, he was to be unanimously elected president. He looked forward with pleasure to delivering his acceptance speech and getting the work of the new association underway.

The trip began from the plantation of one of Furman's parishioners, Dr. Irvine, at Goose Creek, not many miles from Charleston. The journey was to begin on April 15, 1814. Woody[20] had taken his father and his baggage in the family surrey to Dr. Irvine's the day before, so that he would be ready to set out with the others early the next day. Dr. Irvine supplied at least one well-appointed coach and coachman for the journey. From Furman's church, several elected delegates completed the company for the pilgrimage to Philadelphia. Woody loaded his father's trunks on Dr. Irvine's coach, bade his father good-bye, and returned to Charleston. On April 16, the second night that the group spent at the plantation, Richard wrote one in the series of letters he sent Dorothea throughout the years. He addressed the letter to Mrs. Dorothea M. Furman at the parsonage at No. 06 Church Street, Charleston.[21]

---

[19]Tupper, *First Baptist Church of Charleston*, 125ff.

[20]Woody was Richard Furman's oldest son by his first wife, Elizabeth Haynsworth. Woody was Wood Furman [II], named for his grandfather. He was thirty-five at the time he took his father to Dr. Irvine's plantation. Woody graduated from Brown University, and married Hannah Bowers of Somerset MA.

[21]All letters in this chapter are from the Letters of Richard Furman (1755-1825) videotape SCL R112.

Goose Creek, S.C.

16 April 1814

My dear wife,

You will probably be surprised to learn I am still at Dr. Irvine's Plantation. I was detained yesterday very much against my intention, in one Respect, in compliance with the wishes of Judge Talmadge, who on Thursday had some discharges of Blood from his Throat, and was afraid of the Weather in the morning. However, he seems visably [sic] better since we left Towne. Mrs. Talmadge appears to be fully well. I have not seen them yet this morning, as it is quite early. But we are by agreement to set out this morning, and the Servants are getting things ready for the journey. As the Day is Fine, I hope we shall meet with no Interruption.

We had a very heavy Rain on Wednesday, before we got to Dr. Irvine's, and I got much Wet, but I find no undesirable Effect from it, being pretty well through Divine Goodness. . . . The Judge and his Lady, being in a closed Carriage, kept dry.

Dr. Irvine, Mr. Keith & Miss Taylor are in their usual health; and appear to be much gratified in the Company of the Judge and his Lady. If they knew I was writing, they no doubt would wish to be remembered to you. I am afraid tomorrow will be a Silent Sabbath to us. However, the Event must be left to God, infinitely Good.

Give my love to all our children, as by Name . . . and to all inquiring friends. I hope the Lord will mercifully preserve and keep you. I remain, my dear wife, your affec' Richard Furman.

The next letter Dorothea received was written from Richmond, which the travelers reached on May 4, 1814:

We arrived at the Capital of Virginia last Evening, having rode 30 miles on that Day and 40 on the Day before. The Judge's Coachman being unwell, we stopped this Day to give him Medicine. The morning also is a little rainy, and we are in general fatigued, which Circumstances unite with the first mentioned to induce us to delay traveling until tomorrow. We are now about 260 miles from Philadelphia by the usual Rout; but we hope to go a nearer and better Road according to the Account we have received of it. We have encountered some bad Road lately, though not as bad as Report had represented it. The country here and for some distance back is hilly; I had almost said Mountainous; for many of the Hills are very high.

Richmond is a considerable place, in which there are a Number of good Buildings, and I suppose from appearances a considerable Trade. It is said to contain 10,000 inhabitants, including all descriptions.

I last Tuesday saw a Passenger on the Stage to the Northward, who had left Charleston not many days before. He knew me and mentioned a few things of an indifferent Nature. But to a Gentleman travelling with us, Mr. Finn, he mentioned the death of Mr. Gradick & his wife; and also that I had also lost another of my congregation, a Lady who lives on Kings Street; and Mr. Finn says he thinks he said it was Mrs. Goode and that she had died with a Sore Throat. I did not hear this till the Stage had gone on, so I could not make further inquiry. . . .

I hope, my dear Dolly, that the Lord will preserve and Bless you and all our dear Children. These repeated accounts of Death in the short time since I left and in the circle of our particular connection, do not only lead to impress on my mind a sense of the General Mortality, and the uncertainty of Earthly Enjoyments, but to produce particular anxiety, affecting you, our Children, and surviving Friends. . . . Oh, that God, for the Redeemer's sake, may deliver us Grace to serve Him, in Faithfulness and redeem our souls with his Heavenly Love—and then all will be well.

I anticipate receiving a letter from you at Baltimore, should I arrive there safely. Do remember me to all . . . to Woody and his family, to Samuel, Maria, Josiah, Sarah, and to all of the younger Children. Tell Susan that I hope she goes on well in her Grammar & Henry, John and Thomas that I shall hope to find that they attend well to their Books; and tell my little James and Anna that I long to have them on my knee.
The Lord bless you, my dear Dolly. I remain

> Your affectionate husband,
> Richard Furman

P. S. The Judge gets better; Mr. Talmadge is pretty well, and through Mercy, my own Health is not to be complained of. The Lord has been Good to an Unworthy Creature. Tell the Negroes I wish them well & shall be glad to hear a good account of them for their Own Sakes.

The travelers arrived in Philadelphia in time for rest before the convention was called to order. Richard was lodged at the home of friends, and his traveling companions also found accommodation with Baptist hosts. On May 18, 1814, Richard presented the convention's opening address, which began:

> The General Convention of the Baptist delegates for Missionary purposes, assembled in the meeting house of the First Baptist Church of Philadelphia, Wednesday, the 18th of May 1814; to constituents, the churches of Jesus Christ, the ministers of the Gospel and friends of religion in general, present Christian love and cordial views.
>
> Beloved Brethren and Friends, a convention has been assembled in Philadelphia, consisting of delegates from parts of our union nearby and remote, to devise a plan and enter into measures for combining the efforts of our whole denomination in behalf of the millions upon whom the light of evangelical truth has never shone.

As the business of the convention got underway, it seemed certain that the Reverend Doctor Furman would be elected president, as indeed he was, unanimously, as the first order of business. He presided over the remaining days of meeting, during which time his long-dreamed-of plans for the church began to be accomplished. Chief among those plans was the establishing of foreign missions within the church. Also, a plan for founding a college for training ministers had been underway since 1789. In the first triennial convention in Philadelphia, a mission board was appointed and the work to establish higher education progressed, as did many general activities of the denomination. At the second general meeting in 1817, Furman was reelected president and the activities that he had so zealously proposed and supported—especially in the areas of missions and higher education—continued apace. His address at the second convention inspired the creation of Columbian College, which later became George Washington University. It was not until after Furman's death, however, that the university that bears his name, Furman University, opened its doors in 1825.

Dorothea's letter of May 13, 1814, to Richard has not survived, but by early June Richard was able to reply to her letter by saying, "My own particular part [in the convention] is nearly performed." Still, he had first to "digest and prepare the minutes of their transactions and of the Board of Missions which they have established for the publication" and to "draw up an address to their constituents and the publick [sic] on the subject of their meeting." He went on to say that he was being urged to come to New York, but that he would be "detained here a week or more to complete the business of printing, etc."

Once he had made up his mind to make the trip to Philadelphia and leave his family and church even with the war still posing possible danger, Richard seems not to have been especially concerned. He was completely engrossed in the business of the association. However, in his letter to Dorothea of June 8, 1814, he wrote:

> We yesterday received the momentous news of the deposition of Bonaparte and of the restoration of the Bourbons, and of general peace in Europe on such authority as admits of no doubt of its truth. But this will reach you before my letter can. It will create very strong emotions in the minds of the American public. In some it will occasion powerful disappointment and mortification. I hope, however, these events are directed by Providence in the way of Mercy, and that we shall be partakers in that Merciful design and its results. However, if peace is not soon made, I

think we might expect War in reality in England and will have a large force at her command for its prosecution. In this view of the subject, I see strong reason for my returning home. Though I came to [a] decision to remain in these parts during the summer . . . it now seems prudent to wait for the direction of Providence respecting my future conduct in these respects. Perhaps Divine Goodness may so direct that Peace with America may enter into the general pacification among the European powers.

Richard did remain in "these parts" through the summer, receiving and dispatching letters from New York to Charleston to his "dear Dolly." In a letter of July 11, he does not mention the war, but expresses concern that Mr. Hand, who was supply preacher at the First Baptist Church during his absence, was a man who had "some oddities attending his manner of preaching, and behaviorisms." However, he hoped "that he is a good man, and that his preaching is owned of God." Richard commended Dolly in this letter, saying: "I have no doubt, my dear Dolly, of your prudence and economy in managing domestic matters. The accounts you transmit are perfectly agreeable. I hope you will be supported under this multiplicity of cares and trials to which you are exposed and have the necessary temporal supplies from the sources from which they may be acquired. It is to be regretted that the cotton is so bad as to command no better price."

Then, as usual, Furman ended the letter with his love to the children and all friends, not forgetting the Negroes who desired to be remembered.

When Richard returned to South Carolina in late summer of 1814, a British bombardment of Fort McHenry had failed and an assault against Baltimore had been abandoned. Francis Scott Key, detained aboard one of the British ships, recorded the British failure in verse, providing the lyrics for "The Star Spangled Banner." By the end of 1814, negotiators met and reached an agreement that is embodied in the Treaty of Ghent. It settled none of the issues that brought on the war, but by the spring of 1815, following the Battle of New Orleans, Richard Furman was able to reassure his family and parishioners that he believed peace had been restored. In any event he planned no more long journeys away from home—only short ones to his missions and to the High Hills.

Perhaps no undertaking in his entire life was dearer to Richard Furman's heart than building a new church. Robert Mills, the first American-born architect, who later designed the Washington Monument, was commissioned to design the church edifice. The First Baptist Church building was completed in 1822, replacing the rough wooden structure to which Richard, as a young man, had been called as pastor. Greek in style, columned and stately, the building boasted steeple and cupola and three entrance doors that could be thrown open to catch the cooling breeze on a sultry Sunday morning. A marble tablet was set in the outside wall of the edifice, showing that the church building was dedicated while Richard Furman was pastor. Robert Mills himself immodestly pronounced: "The Baptist Church of Charleston exhibits the best specimen of correct taste in architecture in the city. It is purely Greek in style, simply grand . . . and beautiful in detail."[22]

Among the furnishings was a solid mahogany pulpit, the material for which had been ordered by Furman from the West Indies for the sum of one thousand dollars. He paid for it out of his own pocket, from the considerable proceeds he continued to receive from his cotton plantation operations. Church records show that he received his salary as pastor by checks, that he endorsed them back to the church, and regularly contributed large sums to the building fund.

*The First Baptist Church, Charleston, built about 1822, was the pride of the Reverend Doctor Richard Furman's long ministry there. Designed by Robert Mills, who later designed the Washington Monument, Mills immodestly declared, "The church exhibits the best specimen of correct taste in architecture in the city. It is purely Greek in style [and] simply grand. . . ."*

[Georgia Historical Society]

---

[22]First Baptist Church, "Historical Sketch."

Richard's dear Dolly did not live to worship in the new church. Her son, William D. Furman, was born in March 1817, when Dorothea was forty-three years old. He was a sickly baby, and he died the following July. Dorothea followed him in death in 1819.

On a warm and gentle Sunday morning in 1823, the Reverend Doctor Richard Furman mounted the pulpit of the First Baptist Church of Charleston. In his sixty-eighth year, he was still a physical giant. His hair, iron-grey now, was sparse, his dark eyes still full of expression. He wore gown and bands, made fresh by Dorothea's house slave, who since Dorothea's death continued to perform household chores for the minister and his three unmarried daughters: Anne, Sarah, and Marie Dorothea.

On such pleasant Sunday mornings, the large congregations of affluent Charlestonians were likely to be seated in their accustomed pews, their surreys and carriages having first been secured along Church Street. Furman's three daughters could be seen sitting in the first pew on the left, leaving a vacant place by the aisle, out of respect for their dead mother. In the gallery, more often than not, his own house servants, in clean cotton, hands folded, would be sitting among the other slaves.

It was the minister's custom to ask the Lord's blessing on the congregation, lead them in reciting the Lord's Prayer, then place his hands upon the gleaming mahogany pulpit, and read from the Bible open before him such passages as:

> Servants, be obedient to them that are your masters, according to the flesh with fear and trembling in singleness of your heart and unto Christ; . . . knowing that whatsoever good thing any man doeth the same shall he receive of the Lord, whether he be bond or free. . . . All that have believing masters, let them not despise them, because they are brethren, and beloved, partaking of the benefit.[23]

Richard Furman often preached on the duties of masters to their slaves, and likewise on the duties of slaves to their masters. He admonished the slaves to obey and be faithful servants, and urged the masters not only to be just to slaves, but to treat them with kindness, saying that their souls were in sacred trust to their masters, who were commanded by God to guide

---

[23]Eph. 6:5-8; 1 Tim. 6:2.

them like children to the saving grace of Almighty God. He chose his phrases well; his words were erudite and his delivery confident.

At length he completed his sermon. It was an exhaustive compendium of religious and ethical arguments in support of slavery, a system that was ordained by God. It was an intricate body of logic, suffused with the glow of righteous sincerity and, in the end, with the glow of hope for eternal life to all—slave and master—who believed in the saving grace of Almighty God. After the sermon, the organist struck a chord and the congregation raised its collective voice in praise. They sang a hymn composed by their pastor.

On weekdays it was Furman's custom to put aside his gown and bands and don his usual costume of coat, waistcoat, and knee breeches. For trips to Edisto Island, where the trail might be rough or wet, he pulled on heavy boots.

When Furman preached at the Edisto mission and at associational, camp, and revival services throughout coastal Carolina, his theme was evangelical, with emphasis on sin and salvation. He waged a war on drunkenness, dancing, and frivolity in general, specifically exalting the virtues of industry and sobriety. As a master of the Bible, he drew its images from memory and utilized figures and arguments that stirred the emotions. He would hold a small Bible aloft, and quote verse after verse from memory, emphasizing points by long pauses after an especially moving passage. He would paint lurid pictures of eternal hell for the unbelievers. Then he would preach hope, forgiveness, and salvation by saying, in effect, "confess your sins, believe, and be saved."

After such meetings, Richard, exhausted, would return to his daughters in Charleston and report joyfully of the large assemblages and the many whose souls were saved.

In Richard Furman there was a commingling of several religious traditions; indeed, such was often the case in both the South and the North.[24] As was true of other mighty men of God in the Church of England and other Southern Protestant churches, Furman was an orator in the pulpits of the city, a hell-fire-and-damnation preacher in the mission field. He was a slaveowning, paternalistic man-of-property, and a profound patriot. He

[24]Eaton, *Mind of the Old South*, 218ff.

was a doer both in his church and in his state.[25] In manner and appearance he was cultured. He had only a modicum of schooling, yet he founded colleges and established educational funds and scholarships. The boy-evangelist[26] came to be known by the end of his life as mentally brilliant, closely approaching genius, of spotless character—a man who "had a close working agreement with God," and the recipient of grateful honors from both church and state.[27]

When Richard realized that he would soon die, he prepared a quite thoughtful will, so that all his children shared in his estate. He was especially foresighted in providing for his three youngest daughters. He wrote his will in early summer, 1825:

> I, Richard Furman, Pastor of the Baptist Church in Charleston, being of sound mind tho weak in body, do make this my Last Will and Testament, revoking all others heretofore by me made. . . . It is my will and desire that all my Estate, except such part thereof as my Executors shall find it necessary to dispose of for the payment of my debts, shall be kept together and the income applied to the support of my family and also the education of my younger children if it will suffice therefor until my daughter Ann shall receive the sum of fifteen hundred dollars above the others. . . . It is further my will . . . that my Executors as shall qualify upon this my will with the concurrence of a majority of such of my children as have arrived at the age of twenty-one years, to sell any part or all of my estate and the directions herein contained respecting the income and division of my present property . . . apply to such property as may be purchased by my Executors. It is my intention that my Executors shall use the greatest care and deliberation in making sale of any part of it, but especially of that body of about two thousand acres which lies near Stateburg on the Wateree River.[28]

Richard's sons—Richard [II], thirty-five at the time of his father's death, Josiah, thirty, and Charles, twenty-eight—qualified as executors of their father's estate when the will was recorded on September 19, 1825. They did, indeed, use care and deliberation in disposing of the beloved land

---

[25]Furman, *Furman Legend*, 56ff.

[26]King, *History of South Carolina Baptists*, 20-25.

[27]McClothlin, *Baptist Beginnings in Education*.

[28]Will of Richard Furman, 670-71.

in the High Hills of Santee. The land was not sold, but remained in the family for several generations to come.

On a sultry day in August, Richard was eulogized and laid to rest. As reported by a contemporary who attended the funeral:

> A solemn procession wound through the cobblestone streets of Charleston. In ranks six abreast, behind Richard Furman's horse-drawn hearse, marched the civic and social leaders of the city—the aristocratic, the powerful. Behind them, still six abreast, the humbler folk came in a line that stretched nearly three city blocks. When the procession reached St. Michael's Church, it halted momentarily, then proceeded again, and the bells in the tower began to toll—an honor reserved for very few.[29]

Thirteen children survived Richard—two by Elizabeth, eleven by Dorothea. Of Richard and Dorothea's children, Richard [II] was the oldest. After his graduation from the University of Maryland, he moved to family lands on Daniel's Island, and began practice as a physician, a vocation he continued for the rest of his life. The second son was Samuel, who like his father became a minister and educator.

A third child, John Gano, died in infancy in 1793. Josiah, trained to become a merchant, followed that pursuit awhile. Later, he too became a preacher. Several of Josiah's letters that were preserved along with his father's more prolific writings show that he felt a responsibility to advise and admonish his brothers and sisters on morals, along with family and business matters. The mantle of family head fell on Josiah's shoulders after his father's death.

Charles Manning, fifth child of Richard and Dorothea, became a lawyer, and served as treasurer of the state of South Carolina and Master of Equity. Josiah, in a letter to Charles dated June 18, 1839, advised his brother in another endeavor: "I am of the opinion your friends ought to propose you for the Presidency of the Bank in the publick [sic] print. An outsider should not be brought from Columbia for this job." Regardless of whether Charles followed Josiah's advice, he became president of the Bank of South Carolina. Charles also served as a member of the Board of Directors of the Blue Ridge Railroad.

---

[29]Haynsworth, *Furman and Allied Families*, 31-37.

Marie Dorothea, the first daughter and sixth child, never married. She lived in Charleston until her death on July 11, 1870, acting as a medium for family news and a go-between in family arguments. She and her younger sister, Sarah Susanna, apparently lived together in Charleston. Maria and Susanna and their youngest sister, Anne Eliza, all lived to ripe old ages. None ever married.

Between Maria and Susanna came Henry Hart. Henry left his South Carolina family and home early, becoming a cotton factor in New Orleans. In the person of Henry, still another Furman child was active in church affairs. While attending a church meeting in Clinton, South Carolina, he became ill and died in 1841.

After Susanna came another son, to whom his parents gave the name John Gano, the same name as that of his older brother who had died in infancy. A West Point graduate of the class of 1827, John died in Illinois on August 29, 1830, while serving in the infantry of the U. S. Army. Then there was Thomas Fuller, a physician, who lived on the family lands in the High Hills of Santee, helping in their management. James Clement, the next child, became a professor at Furman University. Child number twelve was Anne Eliza.

Samuel Furman was the "Sammy" who accompanied his father on many trips from Charleston to the plantation at Stateburg, and on field trips to the missions. Although he eventually held the prestigious job of head of Furman Institute to train Baptist ministers, Samuel was not always in the good graces of his brothers and sisters. He managed his inheritance poorly; he didn't rear his children properly, which caused "mortification and distress"—at least to Josiah, the self-appointed head of the Furman clan after Richard Furman's death.

To begin with, Samuel had married Eliza Ann Scrimzeour, a descendant of the earls of Scrimzeour of Scotland—standard-bearers for eight hundred years—who had titles "all the way from knight to earl." A Scrimzeour has borne a standard, it is said, at every British coronation and at every funeral of British kings. There was more than a bit of jealousy among Henrietta, Josiah Furman's wife, and the three maiden Furman sisters, as well as among the wives of the Furman brothers. Eliza Ann—they called her Ann—was the object of their envy.

Eliza Ann was the posthumous child of Alexander, the prospective head of the House of Scrimzeour. Along with whatever title the family held at the time of his birth, Ann's father was heir to a large estate. He was a man with a mind of his own, for without his father's sanction, young Scrimzeour married and forthwith set sail for America with his bride. He died on his way to America or shortly thereafter, leaving his widow alone to bear and rear their child. Who cared for the widow and child is unclear, but when Ann reached maturity, she married Richard Furman's son Samuel on May 5, 1814.[30]

Samuel and Ann moved to Furman lands at Coosehatchie, Beaufort County, South Carolina, where Samuel served as clergyman, managed the property, and taught at Furman Institute, the first of the institutions to bear his father's name. Beginning in 1815 with the birth of her daughter, Mary, Ann had a child almost yearly until there were nine in all.[31] Throughout the years Ann and Samuel never forgot that there might be a title for her eldest son, Richard [III], and an estate in Scotland that through her, he might be entitled to receive. (The Reverend Doctor Richard Furman had named one of his sons Richard [II], so that by the time Samuel's son was born, he was considered Richard [III].) By 1836 Richard [III] was twenty years old, his older sister, Mary Scrimzeour Furman, was twenty-one, and Samuel [II] was nineteen. Very soon Richard [III] would be reaching his majority. If ever Ann and Samuel were to claim the inheritance for him, the time was upon them.

All was not going smoothly at Furman Institute. Samuel was struggling with his conscience and his teaching duties. The principles upon which the institute had been founded and the purposes for which it had been established were undergoing change. Organized for the express purpose of training "pious young men" for the Baptist ministry, but admitting "other youth to the benefit of instruction," the school was being pressured to accept unqualified students who required excessive tutoring in the basic subjects of reading and writing. The changes at the school distressed and saddened Samuel. Finally, Samuel could bear the indignities and frustrations of teaching under such circumstances no longer, and he resigned, as did at least one other "professor," Mr. Marshall.

Samuel's brother Josiah, as was his usual custom, took his brothers' and sisters' concerns upon himself, advising and counseling them as he saw fit. So, late in the year, Josiah wrote a letter to his sister Susan:

---

[30]Clemens, *North and South Carolina Marriage*, 98.

[31]See Appendix: Family Group Record for Samuel Furman and Eliza Ann Scrimzeour.

> You have no doubt heard that both Samuel and Mr. Marshall have
> resigned their professorships. Sam[l] leaving it will be the wrench, for all
> or nearly all the students doing the same . . . . The character of the In-
> stitute has changed. The dissenters wanted it made into a manual labor
> Grammar School for their especial benefit. [Now it] *must not be done*!. . .
> I do not know what Sam[l]'s course will be. I find that he stands very
> high with the students, who are attached to him both as a man and as a
> preceptor. He was decidedly the favourite.

After Samuel resigned his professorship at the institute, he continued
in other pursuits until the spring of 1836. At that time, he and Ann took
their brood of children—all but Samuel [II]—and sailed to Scotland. They
left Samuel [II], only nineteen, in charge of the plantation and slaves. They
took up residence there and settled down for the two-year stay that was required under Scottish law for Ann to have the right to sue in behalf of her
son. Sons Richard [III], John, and William studied at the University of
Edinburgh. The two years soon passed, but the stay in Scotland was to no
avail. Ann was unsuccessful in capturing the title of Earl of Scrimzeour for
her eldest son, Richard [III]. She was successful, however, in returning to
South Carolina with a sizable sum of money after she sold the Scottish estate that she had received by entitlement.

Of all the children who went to Scotland with Samuel and Ann, it
was Mary who anticipated the visit with the greatest excitement. Already,
at the time the family set sail, it had begun to look as if she might suffer the
fate of her three maiden aunts. Young gentlemen who lived in Charleston
or on neighboring South Carolina plantations had chosen wives elsewhere.
Perhaps, just *perhaps*, she might meet an English gentleman who . . . So
Mary dreamed and planned and shopped and packed her trunks with her
new finery.

Mary's Uncle Josiah in Longtown, South Carolina, on June 10, 1836,
the eve of the sailing, felt impelled to take his pen in hand. He wrote to his
maiden sister Marie in Charleston, expressing the hope that, as the channel
for family news and advice, she would pass the contents of his letter to other
family members as well. He said he hoped her "anxiety regarding [their
brother] Charles has been removed by news of his safe arrival" on a trip he
was making beyond South Carolina borders. And then Josiah gets to the
real purpose of his letter:

> I should like to have seen Samuel and Richard before their depar-
> ture for Europe. I was surprised to find that Samuel took so large a part

of his family with him. If he should fail in his lawsuit the expenses of this excursion will put a finishing stroke on his property. Should [it] be reassessed and proven small in value, his circumstances will be very embarrassing. And even if it should be considerable, the disposition for extravagance in a *certain quarter* may perhaps render no blessing. I have been informed that Mary's fashionable and expensive dressing is a theme for conversation over the country. I refer particularly to her extravagance during the past winter in Charleston. I felt very much mortified and distressed at it, for I know that objections had been made much to Sam'l on that account while he was in the [Furman] Institution before and that it would be regarded as an insurmountable objection to his appointment again. Besides, it is painful and humiliating to hear the vanity of one's family (of the lowest kind, too, that of dress) made the subject of comment over the whole country. In the letter which I sent to you by Mr. Harrison, I made allusion to this subject.

Samuel perhaps saw it. If he did, he or his wife & Mary may have been offended. But if he knew how much disappointment in his respectability & welfare & usefulness . . . affected my mind, he would know that all I felt and said sprang solely from this cause & was far from being dictated by unfriendliness or indifference. I hope and pray that God may bring Mary to a right view of things, and to sobriety of conduct and dress, the invaluable accompaniments of a well-regulated mind.

From some conversation which Henrietta had with her sometime since, I had indulged the hope that a happy change had taken place in her feelings and opinions, but if what is reported of her extravagance last winter be true, I shall be constrained to abandon all the hope I had entertained for her amendment. I fear that this disposition will lead to a still more dazzling display in Great Britain & feel mortified at the sort of introduction it will afford the Publick [sic] here of an American clergyman's family. . . .

Y<sup>r</sup> affectionate Brother
Josiah B. Furman

In her Uncle Josiah's eyes, Mary Scrimzeour Furman, with her foibles and finery, may never have come to a "right view of things," but she found her gentleman in England and married him, thus avoiding the fate of her three aunts. John Miller, in a position granted by the Crown, was sent to Barbados from Scotland. Mary Furman accompanied him there as Lady Mary Scrimzeour Furman Miller.

Mary's youngest sister was Dorothea Furman [II], named for her grandmother. Dorothea found her gentleman close at hand, in the person of her neighbor, William Seabrook Lawton, one of the sons of Benjamin Themistocles Dion Lawton of Lawtonville, whose family lived on a neighboring plantation in the High Hills of Santee.

William Seabrook Lawton was well established, landed, and wealthy in his own right by the time he married Dorothea. His business dealings were not always astute, however. His indulgent father-in-law, Samuel Furman, pledged a substantial sum of money as security on one of William's ventures, in which William lost most of his own and many thousands of dollars from the estate of his mother-in-law. The eventual outcome of these dealings is lost to posterity. When Dorothea Furman married William Seabrook Lawton and later moved to Macon, Georgia, she joined a family of people, many of whom were "unexpectedly tough beneath their wild eccentricities."[32]

---

[32]Morris, North Toward Home, 9.

*Chapter Two*

# PAUL GRIMBALL
(1645?-1696)

*Keeper of the Great Seal*

T hroughout the sixteenth century, Carolina coastlands had been
the object of much attention among Spain, France, and England.
At one point, French Huguenots attempted to settle at Charlesfort,
but after only four years there, the French colony was pillaged and destroyed
by Spanish troops in 1566.

By 1663 Charles II firmly claimed the lands and parceled them out to
eight court favorites who came to be known as the lords proprietor. Through
this body Charles believed the colony could be securely held and equitably
governed by England. Indeed, the favored eight became almost absolute
masters of the land. The governing scheme was set in motion, but the Carolina settlers refused to ratify the plan, and the actual government consisted
of a powerful council, half of whose members were appointed by the lords
proprietor in England. Almost immediately, the colonists and the lords'
proprietor representatives were at odds with one another. Through the years
of the proprietary government (1663-1719), up until the time that Carolina

passed from proprietary government to direct government by the English Crown (1719), dissent and anti-British activities continued.

The lords proprietor of Carolina issued a plan and their first instructions for granting land in 1669, before the first fleet left England for the new province.[1] It was a plan in which Paul Grimball, sent to America expressly for the purpose, was to have a large part for a period of many years.

When the scheme was initiated, the regulations provided that a settler should first appear before the governor and members of his council to ask for land. The governor then issued a warrant, and the secretary of the province recorded it in his big book. The secretary delivered a copy to the settler. The surveyor general, under the terms of the warrant, was then ordered to make a plot of the land and to prepare a "return of survey." After several more passes of papers, an official grant was made, bearing the signatures of the governor and members of his council, as well as the secretary of the province, after which a registrar recorded the date of the transaction's completion in his book. Usually between the time a settler appeared before the governor to request a land grant, and the time the would-be settler clutched his copy of the grant, officially signed and sealed, many months may have passed.[2]

For at least the next forty years, instructions for granting land were continually revised and reformed. For twenty-five of those years, Paul Grimball—first as lords' proprietor deputy, later as secretary of the province of Carolina, member of the Governor's Council, or receiver general and escheater—was involved in phases of the land-granting process and in the ever-changing instructions and revisions of those regulations.[3]

Changes, revisions, and arguments over the regulations governing land grants were the least of the anxieties imposed by the lords proprietor, their governors and councils, on the colonists. Long-standing differences concerning trade and taxation continued throughout the proprietary government period.

Joseph West, appointed by the lords proprietor, was in the last months of his term of office as governor when Paul Grimball arrived with his family

---

[1] Salley, *Grand Council of South Carolina*, 20, 62.

[2] Salley, *Lands in South Carolina*, ix.

[3] McCrady, *History of South Carolina*, 210-17.

in Carolina in February 1682, to take over duties assigned to him in the Carolina colonial government.

Paul Grimball, twenty-seven, stepped ashore with firm and purposeful stride when he landed on Carolina shores. Confident and well organized, with official papers in hand, he presented himself straightaway at the offices of the governor and council in Charles Town. In his packet of papers was a letter dated April 10, 1681, from three of the lords proprietor, one of whom was Lord Shaftesbury. Shaftesbury's orders directed that "Mr. Paul Grimball, Merchant bound for Ashley River to settle there, be granted 3,000 acres of land."[4] Other official papers gave orders that Grimball was to serve as a deputy of the lords proprietor. Those orders were to govern Grimball's well-being and activities for the rest of his life.[5]

Paul plunged into preparing his land for habitation by his family, which consisted of his wife Mary and those of his five children who had been born in England—Mary, Ann, and possibly Providence. John and Thomas, the youngest children,[6] were born in Carolina after Paul and Mary had settled on Edisto Island.

By 1683, only a year after he arrived, Grimball had acquired land on the Cooper River, as well as six hundred acres "for him for arrival of self and servants." He also had established a house on his land on Edisto Island "forty miles by water" from Charles Town.[7] John directed his slaves in building a dwelling house and outbuildings, and in planting crops of tobacco and peas. Grimball carried on a brisk trade with the Indians; and with his plantation running smoothly and his wife and children cared for, he could turn his attention more steadily to discharging his obligations to the proprietary government, work for which he had been commissioned before leaving England. He became secretary of the province, and one of his official duties was to approve or disapprove the awarding of lands to would-be settlers. He

---

[4]Webber, "Grimball of Edisto Island," 1-3.

[5]McCrady, *History of South Carolina*, 210.

[6]See Appendix: Grimball Family Group Records, Ancestral Charts, and Grimball Lineal Chart.

[7]Salley and Oldsberg, *Lands in South Carolina*, 198.

affixed the official seal to land grants, warrants, deeds, and court records, and he kept the great seal and records in his possession.[8]

Grimball's home and plantation life proceeded smoothly, but in his work as secretary and "keeper of the seal," he was beset with problems. He became embroiled in the colonists' spirited opposition to the authority of the British Parliament, in which they were not represented.[9]

Joseph West's several terms as governor of Carolina had passed, and Joseph Morton had been confirmed as governor by the lords proprietor in September 1685. Paul Grimball was one of eight deputies of the lords proprietor and twenty commoners who convened in November 1685, for the purpose of subscribing to the Fundamental Constitution of 1682 and supporting its enactment. Immediately, all but seven council members refused to support the constitution as proposed by the proprietary body, and those seven—of whom Paul Grimball, as secretary of the province, may be presumed to be numbered—enacted all the laws passed at that session. Colonists grumbled at the ineptness of Governor Morton and the ill-judgment and impracticability of most of the proposed schemes. But one act was passed that found favor: an act to provide for better security of the province against threatened Spanish invasion. In actual fact, however, nothing was done to avert an impending attack.[10] The Spanish did eventually invade the Scottish colony at Port Royal, and Governor Morton and his few loyal councilmen and deputies also suffered in the assault.

On a hot summer day in 1686, Paul Grimball was in Charles Town, attending to his duties with the governor. Three galleys beached on Edisto Island. Bands of Spaniards with Indian and Negro recruits dropped on the beaches of Edisto, fanned across the island, and descended upon the houses of Governor Morton and Paul Grimball. Ruthlessly, they plundered and despoiled several island estates, including Grimball's house and the slave houses at Point of Pines. An indentured maid, Kitts Oats, was ab-

---

[8]Ibid. There are numerous documents throughout the official provincial papers that bear the seal and signature of Paul Grimball, including petitions (618-31); grants (421, 427); and warrants (313, 319, 493, 494). Some documents Grimball signed as a member of the Grand Council (373, 374, 376, 388, 393-98, 400-405, 408, 410); as secretary of the province (628-31); and as receiver general (433-36, 439, 443, 447, 450, 454).

[9]McCrady, *History of South Carolina*, 210-12.

[10]Ibid., 213.

ducted from the Grimball property and never found. Money, silver, and thirteen of the governor's slaves disappeared. The governor's brother-in-law was found murdered. The Spaniards then wiped out the Scottish colony at Port Royal, and the few settlers who remained alive fled to Charles Town for refuge.[11]

In the excitement, strife between the lords' proprietor men and the colonists was forgotten. Paul calmed his frightened family and restored the buildings that had been plundered or burned. In due time the community on Edisto Island became relatively peaceful again, and Paul and his family continued to live there. Morton was shortly removed from office by the lords proprietor, and James Colleton took up duties as governor of Carolina in 1686. Colleton, in spite of the colonists' bitter complaints that he was acting contrary to the honor of the English nation, accepted "a little filthy lucre" from the Spanish government to compensate for the atrocities perpetrated by the Spanish on Edisto and Port Royal.[12]

In spite of the troubles of the colony, its business increased, and in spite of his apparent displeasure with the governing abilities and policies of Colleton, Paul Grimball continued to discharge his duties faithfully. His official responsibilities were increased. In October 1688, he was appointed receiver general and escheator;[13] but before he assumed those duties, in July 1687, Grimball became a member of a committee to consider modification of the Fundamental Constitution in order to make it acceptable both to the lords proprietor and to the people. The committee consisted of Governor Colleton, Paul Grimball, and William Dunlap for the lords proprietor, and four commoners: Thomas Smith, John Farr, Joseph Blake, and Bernard Schenkingh. As could be expected, and as reported by the historian Edward McCrady, in spite of much labor, voluminous paperwork, numerous meetings, and discussions, a complete stalemate resulted. The lords proprietor ordered that no more meetings be held without orders from them. The committee dissolved. Colleton proceeded to govern as he saw fit, without benefit of any law. Chaos resulted. Every man acted as he thought proper, with contempt for the governor and deputies. Colleton's former sup-

---

[11]Ibid., 216-17.

[12]Ibid., 221.

[13]Webber, "Grimball of Edisto Island," 1-30.

porters deserted him, and "he quailed and shrank from the exercise of power he had assumed."[14]

When Seth Sothell claimed the government and overthrew Colleton's government, he removed the deputies of the lords proprietor who were opposed to him. Sothell dispossessed Paul Grimball of the records and the seal used for granting lands,[15] and threw him into jail.[16] To seize the seal and records, Sothell sent a constable and men to Edisto Island. They sacked and disrupted Paul's house, and terrorized his family. It was the second time his family had been paralyzed with fear by invaders—the first time by the Spaniards, this time by fellow colonists. Presumably while Paul was still in jail, he pleaded his cause in eloquent language to the governor and council. He described how Constable William Chapman at Charles Town took seven men on February 2, 1691, "forty miles by water to Edistoh Island Colleton County and entered his house with clubs, frightening his wife and family, pretending to hunt for papers and records . . . [going from there to] Mr. John Hamilton's house, your Petr's sonn in Law, a mile distant, and searched his house under the same pretence."[17]

Paul did not have long to wait for retribution. In May 1691, the lords proprietor reinstated him, overruling self-appointed Governor Sothell in this regard. The records and seal were restored to Paul Grimball's trust and, in the words of the order, he received concessions to "make the duties of the office as little irksome as possible." Under the new order, "Mr. Grimball [was to have] the power to appoint and remove Judges and Sheriffs of the counties at pleasure."[18] One of the delightful duties of Paul's new office was the prompt removal from office of Constable Chapman of Charles Town. Another happy result of Paul's reinstatement was that he was granted permission to stay in Charles Town "no longer than is needful." He could spend more time at his plantation on Edisto Island.

So, from all accounts, Paul's family life on the island and business life in Charles Town fared well for a number of years. Proprietary Governors

---

[14]McCrady, *History of South Carolina*, 226-28.

[15]Salley, *Lands in South Carolina*, 198.

[16]Murray, "Edisto Island," in Nueffer, *Names in South Carolina*, 7:4:73.

[17]Salley, *Lands in South Carolina*, 200.

[18]South Carolina Historical Society, *Collections*, 1:126.

Ludwell, Smith, and Blake followed Sothell in rather rapid succession. Paul continued in the good graces of the appointed governors, at least to the extent that his "hand and seal" appear on numerous official documents of the colony throughout those years.

Existing records support the view that Paul Grimball and his wife Mary brought their children safely through the frightening times of their childhood to become responsible adults. Two of their daughters, Mary and Ann, married men who followed in their father-in-law's footsteps. Mary married John Hamilton, who became deputy secretary of the province, evidently while Paul was secretary. Ann's first husband was Christopher Linkly. Her second husband, Charles Odingsell, also served as deputy secretary of the province before they were married. John became a hatter, leaving the family lands and following his trade in Charles Town. Thomas Grimball, the second son and youngest child, to whom Paul willed his plantation on Edisto, became the progenitor of subsequent Grimballs in South Carolina. By his first wife, Elizabeth Adams, whom he married before 1707, Thomas had four children, of whom Paul Grimball [II], named for his grandfather, was the oldest.[19]

By the time Governor John Archdale commenced his duties as governor on August 27, 1695, Paul Grimball was nearing the end of his career in the service of the lords proprietor. He had remained loyal to them through the terms of many governors. Governor Archdale spent the first months of his office endeavoring to "allay the heats of the people" and select his council. Archdale brought blank deputations from the lords proprietor. They admonished Archdale to fill the vacancies with care, and to assign them to persons who had been of greatest benefit to the colony. Archdale set up his council accordingly, priding himself on preserving the government "peacable and quiet in my Time" by appointing a "mixed body" of six councilmen, among whom Paul Grimball was numbered.[20] Upon opening the first meeting of the assembly, Archdale admonished, "I hope this Meeting with you will wholly extinguish [the heats of dissension] so that a solid settlement of this hopeful Colony will ensue."[21]

[19]Miller, Family Circle, 391-96.

[20]McCrady, History of South Carolina, 279-80.

[21]Archdale, Description of Carolina (1798) in McCrady, History of South Carolina, 280.

New settlers continued to venture to Carolina. They were generally tradesmen, merchants, farmers, and artisans. The French Huguenot colony on the Santee, of which Pierre Robert was *Pasteur*, was thriving, and the neck of land between the Cooper and the Ashley rivers, about six miles long, was well settled. Paul Grimball and his deputies were kept busy at the government offices in Charles Town, although Paul found it was less and less needful for him to spend extended periods of time performing the more irksome duties of his office.

Paul Grimball was near death when he had his own will recorded and the seal affixed on December 13, 1695. It was proved after Paul's death before Thomas Cory, Paul's successor in the office of secretary of the province, on February 20, 1696. In his will Paul gave his wife Mary his plantation on Edisto Island, including sixteen hundred acres of land and all the buildings on it. At her death, the inheritance was to go to his youngest son, Thomas. Thomas was directed to pay, within one year after his mother's death, certain monies to each of his three sisters: Mary (Hamilton) Odingsells, Ann Linkley, and Providence, who was unmarried at the time of her father's death. There was a special award of Paul's portion of land that he and his son-in-law, Christopher Linkley, had purchased together while Christopher was serving as Paul's deputy secretary. At his death, Paul gave Christopher his portion of the land they had owned jointly. Perhaps Paul was rewarding him for his loyal assistance through the years in the tedious duties of secretary of the province.

With his most valuable possessions allocated, Paul Grimball then designated that his wife was to receive "her choice of feather beds, one bolster, two pillows, two pairs of sheets, a blanket, curtains, a ring, a negro girl, Ginny, and one-third part of the remainder of the estate . . . and legacies to the value of £40 . . . and severall things yt. I gave her ye benefitt of & yt. shee shall not bee accountable for the same."[22]

One more item was recorded in the books at the end of Paul Grimball's will. On page 352 of the big record book, Deputy Secretary Odingsells wrote on February 22, 1696, that four witnesses were present "when Mr. Grimball gave ye Honble ye Governr. Archdale a good ring to be pd. by his executor as a token of respect."[23] Perhaps Paul and the governor had

[22]Will Book, SC, 1696, 350-52.

[23]Salley, "Court of Ordinary," 54-55.

become friends in the closing days of Paul's life and he could at last discharge his duties in relative peace and harmony, with the support of the governor. It remained for Paul Grimball's descendants to take up the cause of freedom from proprietary rule. John Barnwell, whose daughter Mary married Paul Grimball's grandson, Paul Grimball [II], was one of those deeply involved in the transition from proprietary government to royal government. The tottering powers of the lords proprietor were sustained only until 1717. In the reign of King George II, the full legal title to all of South Carolina reverted to and became vested in the king of England.

## Chapter Three

# JOHN BARNWELL
## (1671-1724)

### Tuscarora Jack

W hen John Barnwell left Dublin in 1701 and set sail for America, he came without family or other responsibility. In contrast to Paul Grimball, who preceded John to Carolina by nineteen years, he had no commitments, nor the promise of a job with the lords proprietor. In fact, Barnwell seems to have fit the pattern of many early adventurers who set out to explore and conquer the New World. He had no job of any kind and considering the records about him that remain, he seems to have been fleeing from responsibilities in Ireland that one his age—he was thirty at the time—might be expected to have assumed. John Barnwell did eventually become a responsible and "upstanding citizen" of Carolina. When his daughter Mary married Paul Grimball [II], the grandson of his neighbor, Paul Grimball [I] of Edisto Island, family bloodlines merged. Descendants of that merger in the persons of Richard Furman Lawton

(1841-1892) and Caroline (Carrie) Willingham (1853-1921) found their way to Macon, Georgia, and set up life there after the Civil War.[1]

Seven years after John Barnwell came to Carolina, on December 1, 1708, John Page, a family friend of the Barnwells, wrote from Ireland to John Harleston in Carolina:

> Cosson, pray in yo$^r$ next let me know whither there be any such man living near Charles towne which they call Mr. John Barnwell he went from hence about seven yearere agon; out of a humor to travel but for no other Reasson, he is the son of a verry good gentleman and Gentlewoeman, and hath Extraordinary friends and Relations in this Kingdom. And therefore let me know how he lives and in what condition.[2]

John did indeed have "extraordinary friends and Relations in the Kingdom." The Barnwells,[3] it was said, had flourished in Ireland and England for five hundred years before, and had been loyal subjects of the Crown, receiving just recognition for their allegiance by being dubbed barons and receiving other ennobling titles and lands. Through many centuries the Barnwells supported the English Crown; but in the last decades of the seventeenth century the family, including John's father Matthew, had joined the ongoing struggle for Ireland's freedom from the Crown. Matthew Barnwell, alderman of his native Dublin in 1688, was killed in the siege of Derry in 1690 while serving as captain in the Irish army. Family lands, including Archerstown estate, were lost when the Barnwells joined the revolution. Some Barnwell heirs attempted to regain their holdings at war's end; some took flight to the Continent. John set out for America.[4]

From John Page's letter to Harleston in South Carolina, one could conclude that John Barnwell had heartlessly deserted his widowed mother, friends, and siblings, since he apparently had not communicated with any-

---

[1] See Appendix: Barnwell and Grimball Lineal Charts, Ancestor Charts, and Family Group Records.

[2] Postscript to a letter from John Page—alderman of Dublin, subsequently lord mayor of Dublin—to John Harleston, December 1, 1708, as quoted in Salley, "Barnwell of South Carolina," 46.

[3] The Barnwell name, in Ireland and America through the years, has been variously spelled de Bernewall, Barnewell, Barnwall, and Barnewall. The spelling "Barnwell" is here used throughout.

[4] Barnwell, *American Family*, 1-20, 15, 26.

one back in Ireland during the seven years since his departure. Perhaps it was not wanton neglect on John's part, but rather preoccupation with his new, exciting life in Carolina—a life that was beginning to be filled with positions of diverse responsibility for him, and with problems of his own making. But John Barnwell was of a nature to slough off problems, or in at least one instance, to meet them head-on, "flying in the face of Governmt." His hot-headedness caused him not to be admitted to "live in Charles towne" for a time. In answering Page's letter of inquiry about John Barnwell, Harleston replied heatedly and in detail in March 1709:

> [John Barnwell] was one that flew in the face of Governmt & headed a Mobb against the Chief Justice Mr. Nicholas Trott, who is my Perticular Friend in Carolina; this Barnwell was Deputy Secretary & Clark of the Councill which was pretty considerable in Carolina, & threw this misdemeaner he was Turned out of all; I suppose his comeing in at present would not admitt him to live in Charles towne, which has made him settle a Plant[ation] at Port Royall near a 100 miles from towne, and thare he lives on what he has Cot by the government hom he soe Grossly abused. . . . This Barnwell had this Designe in his head some before but would not vent it till the Man of Warr sail'd lest they should stop his Proceedings. Barnwell would not have had so many Rioters to assist him but by reason of this, which was that the Judge then have the Church of England Established by Act of Assembly & sent home for ministers & Devided Parrishes & paid them out of the publick [funds] which has made the Decenters his Enemies Ever since. . . .[5]

There was no question that John Barnwell was well known in the colony of Carolina, certainly by Harleston, who was incensed by the young upstart who "headed a Mobb" against his "Perticular Friend," the chief justice of the colony, although the exact time and reasons for John's indiscretion have never become completely clear. John eventually vindicated himself, and approbation and a measure of fame came his way later when he earned the colonists' thanks and praise. Descendants gave him the sobriquet "Tuscarora Jack,"[6] in recognition of his leadership in the Indian wars.

---

[5]Ibid., 2.

[6]Salley, "John Barnwell, Tuscarora Jack," 46ff. Johnson, *Dictionary of American Biography*, 639-40.

Although John's intention when he came to America was "to travel but for no other Reasson," he evidently made an early decision to end his wide-ranging travels and take up life in Carolina, for he immediately made friends in high places; and by February 1703, he had been appointed clerk of the Governor's Council. At about this time he met and married in Charles Town Anne Berners, a "good English Lady" whose family was described as "perhaps more noble than the Barnwells." She traced her ancestry through Sir John Bourchier, first Baron Berners, who was a great-grandson of King Edward III. John Barnwell's marriage to Anne added another impetus for him to remain in Carolina. The couple settled on Port Royal Island on lands Barnwell had been granted. Their first child, Margaret, was born in Charles Town in 1704, and they had another almost every year, until there were eight in all.[7] A daughter, Mary, born June 25, 1709, on Port Royal Island, married Paul Grimball [II], son of Thomas Grimball and grandson of the late Paul Grimball [I], of neighboring Edisto Island.

After Barnwell's appointment as clerk of the Governor's Council, he was assigned the task of preparing a map of Port Royal Sound. This assignment increased his interest in and knowledge of the islands of Carolina—an interest that developed through the years into a deep love of the coastal lands and the acquisition of several thousand acres in the area. In surveying the land to draw the map, he became familiar with its natural beauty as well as its potential for profitable cultivation and development. He selected choice portions for himself. During the years 1704-1709, after he had completed his map of the Sound, John acquired lands on several other Carolina islands as well as on the mainland.[8] In addition to 2,150 acres in Granville County, John also made acquisitions that amounted in 1709 to the grand total of 3,414 choice virgin acres.

Throughout the years from 1703, in one capacity or another—as surveyor, official mapmaker, or simply because he liked nothing better than to document his wanderings over the land—John continued to make maps of whatever areas he explored. His official title at this time was deputy surveyor general. Notable among his works was a map of the Southeastern sec-

---

[7]See Appendix: John Barnwell Family Group Record.

[8]Salley, *Lands in South Carolina*, 226-27, 639, 643, 645. For a description of John Barnwell's land, see the Appendix.

tion of North America. This map became the basis for subsequent maps of the colonial Southeast.[9] John had taken sides with the Dissenters in the Church Acts troubles of 1704-1709. This was when he "flew in the face of Governmt & headed a Mobb" against the chief justice, as a consequence of which he was discharged from his various offices. He then moved to Beaufort on Port Royal Island in 1706. The Dissenters gained control of the assembly early in 1707 and Barnwell was reinstated, being made comptroller of the colony. In November of that year, he asked to be relieved of his duties. Beginning in 1710, John was a member of the Common House of Assembly, representing St. Helena's Parish, and he continued to live in "the Castle," his huge home on Bay Street in Beaufort. He journeyed to Charles Town only for business and to attend sessions of the assembly.

For many years Carolinians and the Indians had lived in relative peace, with only occasional dissension and minor skirmishes. To their mutual advantage, the Indians traded furs and deerskins to the colonists, in return for certain foodstuffs and supplies. Many colonists concurred with one settler's view of the arrangement: "We were Charfully received by these poore people into whose Country wee came [and we were] cherished and supplyed when wee were weake." But in return, the Indians were often cheated, beaten, and embroiled in conflicts, having their goods stolen by the traders and their women molested and raped.[10] As abuses by the traders increased, the Indians struck back, first in the Tuscarora War of 1711, later in the Yamassee War of 1715. The Tuscaroras, alarmed by the establishment of a Swiss colony in New Berne, North Carolina, had massacred as many as four hundred whites early in 1711. When John Barnwell was called to aid in the defense of the colony, he served admirably in that first Indian conflict in the history of the Carolinas: the Tuscarora War.

Upon Barnwell's appointment as commander of expeditionary forces, he mustered a small force of militia and several hundred Yamassee Indians to rout the Tuscaroras from the Carolinas. John and his forces left Charles Town in midwinter, and he led them in a skillful forest march to the Neuse River, where the Tuscaroras were waiting in ambush. The march ended

---

[9]Mills, *Mills's Atlas of South Carolina*, i-xii. Also see maps: Barnwell, Beaufort, Colleton, and Orangeburg Districts. Cumming, *Southeast in Early Maps*. See John Barnwell's map of Southeastern North America (1722).

[10]Hudson, *Southeastern Indians*, 438.

well, but John had mighty trials on the way. In his report to "Your Hon$^r$," the governor of North Carolina, dated "Feb$^y$ 4, 1711," John reported: "We were two days passing the river on bark logs and rafts, and when I drew up my forces on this other side, I soon perceived a great desertion of the [Yamassee] Indians [and] the desertion continued. . . ." By April 1, Barnwell had at last received word from Governor Hyde that Colonel Boyd "was coming to join [him] w$^{th}$ 70 men [and that] there was 2 sloops sailed with provisions." All this "rejoiced" John so that he ordered the newly arrived provision of corn to be brought to his fort, and that same night he also had brought up "10 gallons of rum, 2 casks of cider and a cask of wine." Immediately, "the fame of this liquor encouraged my white men in a few days to 152."

The problem was far from solved: John had plenty of spirits for the new troops, but in his words, "I could not furnish them with more than 7 bullets a man [and] all the corn I got with ye hazard of my life they devoured. . . . All ye Field officers came without a dram, a bit of meese bisket or any kind of meat but hungry stomachs to devour my parcht cornflour, & they began to grumble for better victuals w$^{ch}$ put me in such a passion, I ordered one of their majors to be tyed neck & heels & kep him so. . . ." And later John wrote, "May South Carolina flourish while I bleed and suffer!"

In spite of all John Barnwell's histrionics and impassioned pronouncements, the campaign was successful, as were others in North Carolina throughout 1712.[11] The remnants of the Tuscarora tribe fled northward, where eventually they became part of the Six Nations of the Iroquois League. For his service in routing the Tuscaroras, North Carolina authorities thanked Colonel Barnwell, as he was now known, although some months later the allegation was made that Barnwell allowed a treaty with the Indians to be broken. The validity of the accusation against Barnwell is still in doubt. However, he apparently continued to be highly esteemed throughout the Carolinas for many years. In 1715 he fought the Yamassees in his own colony of South Carolina. The war came to a close in 1717, but hostilities continued for another decade.[12]

John Barnwell was appointed to serve as one of five members of a board created by an act of the assembly to control trade with the Indians. Meeting

---

[11]Barnwell, "Tuscarora Expedition," 28-54.

[12]Hudson, *Southeastern Indians*, 439.

more than one hundred times during the first year of the board's existence, the salaried commissioners were able to prevent another uprising, setting up regulations by which trade with the Indians could be governed and abuses eliminated. Colonel Barnwell served as a member of the assembly until 1719, being assigned the task of directing operations of a Port Royal garrison to retrieve runaway slaves, patrol for Spaniards and Indians, and prepare the maps. It was during these years that the colonists, through the assembly, declared their rejection of the proprietary government and an end to proprietary rule by the English Crown.[13] The last proprietary governor resigned and in March 1720, John Barnwell sailed for England.

In London, Barnwell joined Joseph Boone. The two served as agents of a temporary government set up in the interim between proprietary government and royal government. Their mission was to persuade the Crown to take the colony under its immediate protection. Barnwell and Boone eloquently presented the deplorable condition of affairs in Carolina caused by the Indians and Spanish pirates. The king listened to their appeals, and by August 1720, an order was drafted whereby a governor of Carolina was commissioned to inaugurate the new government for His Majesty. Colonel Barnwell was especially consulted in regard to setting up proposed posts to protect Carolina against Indians, as well as Spanish and French on the south and west coasts of Carolina. In 1729 the proprietary government was permanently eliminated and South Carolina became a royal colony.[14]

While Barnwell was in London in 1720 to fulfill his task as agent of the temporary government of Carolina, he initiated one or more of the many "Designe[s] in his head" that Harleston had complained of to John Page when he responded to Page's inquiry about "any such man" named John Barnwell. While in London, Barnwell conferred with Sir Robert Montgomery and composed a letter for publication, in which he included a "Designe" by which the Golden Islands of coastal Carolina and Georgia were to be settled as a colony to be called Azilia.[15] Early in 1717 a small booklet was printed bearing the flowery title: *A Discourse Concerning the*

---

[13]Green, *Provincial America.*

[14]McCrady, *History of South Carolina,* 16-25, 35-38.

[15]Montgomery and Barnwell, *Golden Islands.* Montgomery, *Establishment of a New Colony.*

*Designed Establishment of a New Colony to the South of Carolina, in the Most Delightful Country of the Universe.* After Barnwell's visit to England and to Sir Robert, another booklet followed in 1720 with the published title, *Description of the Golden Islands.* Sir Robert Montgomery, baronet, was author of the first book, and the second one, containing John's neat drawing of his plan for the margravate of Azilia, was attributed to Colonel John Barnwell. Together the booklets comprised an unabashedly flagrant promotional bid for the settlement of the Golden Islands by interested persons, especially English gentlemen of means. Actual settlement of the islands would determine national control and ownership of the lands, which had been in dispute between Spain and England since 1670. Montgomery and Barnwell were never able to obtain the Crown's permission to colonize the Golden Islands under the Azilia plan. Azilia never materialized, but the layout of the city of Savannah, Georgia, planned and executed by General James Oglethorpe in 1733, is so similar to John's plan for Azilia that there is reason to believe that Oglethorpe followed John's "worthy Designe of Planting Azilia" when Savannah was laid out.[16]

The Carolina islands of St. Symon [*sic*], Sapella [*sic*], St. Catarina, and Ogeche, which were included in the original plan for the development of Azilia, all became part of colonial Georgia. There were several other islands, which John describes as "above twenty-six thousand acres more, very good Soil, and full of close Thickets and Woods, very proper for Shipbuilding" and "it is easy to infer, how fit they are for your settlement." John Barnwell was in the prime of life, working to establish new settlements on the coastal islands of South Carolina in the period of 1717-1720 when he wrote, "I am generally once a day at the Carolina Coffee house in Birchinlane. . . . ," presumably to transact business in connection with establishing Azilia.

Another master plan emerged from John's fertile brain in the years 1720-1721, which resulted in the eventual establishment of a series of forts surrounded by settlements—a plan that could be made applicable to the entire colonial frontier. Although the plan for Azilia was rejected, as was the proposal for immediately putting into effect the fort project, John did receive approval for the Altamaha garrison; for the allotment of lands for a town on the Altamaha; and for the Indian trade conference. This confer-

---

[16]Montgomery and Barnwell, *Golden Islands,* i-v.

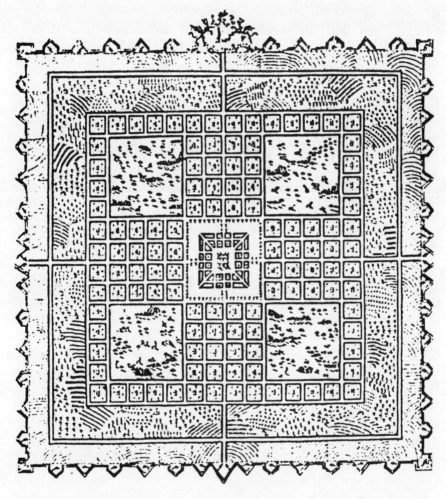

*John Barnwell (1671-1724) drew this plan for the colonization of Azilia on the Carolina coast. The colony never materialized, but the plan survived, and it is said to have been incorporated in the plans for the city of Savannah, Georgia, when it was founded in 1733 by James Oglethorpe.*

[Courtesy of Cherokee Publishing Company]

ence was to be held with Virginia officials, with whom a mutually agreeable solution to the Indian trade problem was to be worked out.

With the Crown's approval, by the summer of 1721, Colonel John Barnwell was on his way to the Altamaha with his garrison of men to carry out his scheme to build the fort. By October the fort was completed. Fort King George, surrounded by palisades and a moat, commanded a wide view of the river, marsh, old Indian fields, and St. Simons Island to the southwest. The first English fortification in what would become Georgia resulted when the Fort King George blockhouse, planned and executed by John Barnwell, rose above the marshes in 1721. The fort burned to the ground in January 1726; some say it was set fire to by disgruntled soldiers garrisoned there. It was never rebuilt.

As usual, John kept his mapmaking going. While the initial construction of Fort King George was underway—log by log—and afterward during the rest of July 1721, possibly longer, Colonel Barnwell undertook and completed the task of mapping the entire Sound.

Although John Barnwell was fully occupied with Carolina governmental and military matters in his various leadership capacities, he kept abreast of personal business, family, and social obligations. By 1709 his landholdings on Port Royal Island in Granville County exceeded 3,000 acres. By the end of 1717, John had been granted additional tracts as well. These lands were carefully selected and acquired—again based on his expert knowledge as a surveyor and his familiarity with the Carolina coastal islands and mainland. Certainly one of the choicest plots of land he owned, and one that became the most significant to succeeding generations of family members, was the acreage recorded in the Book of Royal Grants.[17] A

---

[17]Lands granted to John Barnwell on December 10, 1719, on Hilton Head Island, South Carolina, included:

"500 acres in Granville County bounding to the north on Port Royal Sound to the South on land not laid out, to the East on the Inlet and to the West on a Small Creek comeing out of the said Sound at one shilling p/hundred acres the said Grant is dated the tenth day of December 1717 and signed by Rob' Johnson, A. Skeene, Nicholas Trott, Sam' Wragg, Chas. I. Hart. . . ."

Another 500 acres of land granted were "bounded to the West on a Branch that leads to the River of May and to the East on a Creek and Marsh at one shilling p/hundred acres and the said Grant is Signed and dated as above."

third grant—for five hundred acres in Colleton County—is recorded on the same page for the same date.

From his ship, *Adventure*, Captain William Hilton first sighted Hilton Head Island in 1663. In 1698 Landgrave John Bayley was granted most of the island as a barony. Among the first grants for land in Granville County—this one in 1717, in whorling handwriting on yellowed pages—is a grant for 1,000 acres on Hilton Head to John Barnwell. Throughout the eighteenth century, many Barnwells, Grimballs, Lawtons, Mosses, Chaplins, Willinghams, Baynards, Ladsons—family members all—were granted or purchased properties on South Carolina's islands: Edisto, St. Helena, Port Royal, James and John, as well as Hilton Head. They were the lands that Sir Robert Montgomery and John Barnwell described as the "Most Delightful Country of the Universe." John and Anne Berners Barnwell chose to rear their family in Beaufort on Port Royal.

John was especially close to his sons, who accompanied him on map-making expeditions when they were in their early teens. Anne died before John, presumably in childbirth. Their daughter Mary, after her marriage to Paul Grimball [II] of Edisto Island, produced a daughter, Elizabeth Ann, whose lineal descendants by the beginning of the twentieth century were melded into the Lawton-Willingham-Guttenberger-Nottingham family of Macon, Georgia.

By the time of his death in 1724, John Barnwell was recognized as "the greatest planter of the Port Royal District," one of the "brightest young men of the Colony; a Colonial expert," and a member of a group that "originated every constructive development in South Carolina," or so it was reported in the *Minutes of the Vestry of St. Helena's Parish* several years later.[18]

Colonel John Barnwell was buried outside the east wall of St. Helena's Parish in Beaufort. His grave was covered by the present sanctuary when the church building was enlarged. On the site where John's "Castle" overlooked the Beaufort River, the Beaufort County Courthouse now stands.

And so he was: energetic, hot-headed, willful, in some instances certainly thoughtless, if not heartless. John Barnwell seemed to charge through life, executing his profusion of diverse duties for South Carolina, in the end receiving the plaudits of his contemporaries and winning for himself and the name "Tuscarora Jack" a few lines on the pages of history.

---

[18]Salley, *Minutes of St. Helena's Parish*.

*Chapter Four*

---

# PIERRE ROBERT
## (1656-1710)

### Pasteur on the Santee

T he Swiss city of Basel nestles in a picturesque valley between the
Jura mountains to the south and the meandering Rhine to the
north. In 1685, although the town seemed to be peaceful, the air
was tense with anxiety and irresolution. The streets were quiet, but many
of the citizens were in a state of incipient terror. As a member of a small
religious contingent called the Waldensian Church of Faithful Protestants,
Pierre Robert[1] was drawn into the vortex of their concerns.[2] Church members considered Robert to be prudent and wise, and they called upon him

---

[1]In early documents, the name "Robert" was spelled in various ways, including "Rhob-
ert," and the family is said to have retained the French pronounciation (Rho-bear) for many
years after the family became established in Carolina. For a comprehensive, thoroughly re-
searched study of the Robert family and their origins, as well as of Pierre Robert himself, see
Lawton, "A Tribute to Pasteur Pierre Robert," 1-13.

[2]Boardman, "French Huguenots," 69.

for aid in all areas of their troubled lives. Since his ordination in 1682 as Minister of the Gospel,[3] they had looked to Robert for spiritual guidance. Now in this fateful year of 1685, terrifying, unprecedented events occurred in France and to a lesser degree in Switzerland, forcing Protestants to make and act upon decisions that would affect the rest of their lives.

The first religious wars between Catholics and Protestants took place beginning in 1562, in the reign of Charles IX, and continued intermittently until 1598. During those years France experienced no less than six religious wars, and many of the French Protestants who lived near the frontier fled to England, Germany, and Switzerland. But in 1598, Henry of Navarre, a Protestant, brought peace to the kingdom by becoming a Catholic and issuing the Edict of Nantes. The Edict presumed to cancel past grievances and injuries, and it was heralded as a "star of Promise,"[4] the beginning of a new era of religious toleration that would be available to all Protestants, including the Huguenots, Waldensians, and Calvinists. The Edict eased more than eighty years of Protestant persecution.[5] Peace followed, but it was an uneasy peace: hundreds of Protestants continued to flee from France because of political harassments and restraints in trade, and because of niggling social inhibitions.

Finally, on October 18, 1685, the modicum of protection that the Edict had provided was withdrawn when Louis XIV signed the Revocation of the Edict of Nantes.[6] This was the final, official act that brought months of Protestant persecution and indecision to an abrupt end. Protestants would need to embrace Catholicism immediately and unconditionally, or be banished.

Pierre Robert, a young man of thirty when the Edict was signed, was deeply committed to his Protestant beliefs and to his flock of Waldensians. His Robert forebears had fled more than a century earlier from France to Switzerland, where Basel became a refuge for a little band of Protestants, including the Roberts. As Protestants, they could not hope ever to return to their lands in France; and now, in 1685, upon the Revocation of the

---

[3]Miller, *Family Circle*, 195.

[4]Hirsch, *Huguenots of South Carolina*, 3-4.

[5]DuBose and Porcher, *History of the Huguenots*, 16, 22.

[6]Cuttino, "Huguenots in History," 1-7.

Edict of Nantes, even Switzerland could no longer be considered a peaceful haven. The Swiss Protestants faced losing their church and their means of livelihood, if not their very lives. Momentous decisions must be made and acted upon forthwith.

Pierre Robert was the son of Marie Huguent and Daniel Robert, whose ancestors had migrated from France to Switzerland in the course of these religious wars. Protestantism had been established in hundreds of French towns, freedom of worship proclaimed, and substantial independence allowed to Protestant tradesmen and businessmen, among whom the Roberts were numbered. But the Roberts had lived in northeast France only partially free from abuse following the Edict of Nantes. Pierre's parents moved to St. Imier, near Basel, Switzerland, seeking a more friendly environment in which to work and worship their God, and Pierre was born there in 1656.[7] Throughout the years that the Roberts lived in Basel, French Protestants continued to be harassed, and thousands were forcibly converted to Catholicism.

By forcing the mass flight of Protestants from France, Louis XIV not only incurred the enmity of the entire Protestant world, he also lost to other countries many of the kingdom's most talented, industrious, and economically advanced members of French society. Entire provinces were depopulated. Countless people who refused to embrace Catholicism fled to England, the Netherlands, Germany, America. The Robert family and many Huguenots, Waldensians, and others of Calvinistic leanings, found haven in Switzerland. Emigrants to England were accorded entire freedom of religion, and many were offered every inducement to join the English colony being established in America. The British Crown had granted a patent for Carolina lands, and the lords proprietor were pushing colonization there.[8] French Protestants were known to be skilled in many trades, hardworking, used to privation, staunch in their religious beliefs, and expert in the cultivation of silk, and grapes for wine, as well as indigo and rice, as they later proved. They could be expected to work profitably for themselves and for their sponsors, the lords proprietor. Governor Seth Sothell, although governor of Carolina for only a short period in 1690, recognized the

[7]See Appendix: Robert Lineal Chart, Ancestor Charts, and Family Group Records. Miller, *Family Circle*, 187-90.

[8]Hirsch, *Huguenots of South Carolina*, 5ff.

usefulness and good character of the French and Swiss and he encouraged their settlement there.[9]

When word reached the little flock of displaced Frenchmen in Basel that they would be welcome to migrate to Carolina, Pierre Robert made the decision to take up life there. One standard (but as yet unverified) account of the migration to America is that Pierre Robert and his congregation of about 110 French Protestants gathered at LaRochelle on the west coast of France, joined Captain Phillip Gendron on an English ship, and set sail for America, disembarking at Beaufort in 1686. With Captain Gendron and Pierre Robert as their respective temporal and spiritual leaders, the new arrivals acquired cypress canoes and paddled up the Santee River, the waters of which are fed at their farthest reaches by brooks of the Blue Ridge Mountains. The waters of the Santee system flow a circuitous route of some 450 miles to cover a straightline distance of only 150 miles from the mountains to the Atlantic seacoast.

About sixty miles up the river from Charles Town, after many days of hard rowing on the twisting Santee, the settlers banked their canoes, climbed a bluff, and set about establishing there what one historian called "the most advanced settlement of Europeans toward the interior and Northern province" of Carolina.[10] Later, one young refugee seemed to speak for all of them when she wrote her brother back in Switzerland: "After our arrival in Carolina, we suffered every kind of evil . . . and every kind of affliction—disease, famine, pestilence, poverty, hard labor . . . [but] God has done great things for us, enabling us to bear up under so many trials . . . for which glory be unto him."[11]

The settlers had obtained an order from the earl of Craven and others, directed to Joseph West, Carolina governor (1684-1685), to assign "the first of the Swiss nation to settle in Carolina" 3,000 acres of land on the south side of the Santee River about fifty miles above the city of Charles Town.[12] Pierre Robert and his little band, who called themselves "Waldensians" in

---

[9]McCrady, *History of South Carolina*, 233.

[10]Howe, *History of the Presbyterian Church*, 114-15, 150-51.

[11]Savage, *The Santee*, 102: ". . .a letter written [translated from the French] to her brother by Judith Manigault, a twenty-year-old refugee."

[12]McCrady, *History of South Carolina*, 337.

Switzerland, now were called "French Huguenots" when they settled in Carolina. They were the same people with essentially the same beliefs; only the name was changed, or so tradition says. Robert now ministered to the Carolina parishioners who from their church's inception called it the "French Huguenot Church in the Parish of St. James, Santee," composed of the Protestant souls who sailed with Gendron from England.[13]

Pierre Robert was pastor to the settlers from the beginning—even before a church house could be built at James Town, the little town that later sprang up on the banks of the Santee. As itinerant pastor, Pierre "travelled much," and from the saddle of his horse Liberty, he "preached many an open air sermon." Several decades later, one of Robert's great-grandsons gave his fancy free rein in a letter to a cousin, where he wrote that "if old Liberty could have spoken, he might have sung some of those sweet songs of praise wh[ich] his master sang each day."[14]

In 1705 the lords proprietor ceded to the settlers a tract of land surrounding the completed church, to be used either for a common plantation or a town, as the people preferred. The site had the advantage of being near the river where a landing was located, and the church was erected only fifty yards from the river. Pierre Robert and several other settlers, including Captain Gendron, were elected commissioners for the settlers, and they decided to use the site for a town. The streets of James Town were laid out at right angles to each other, with the town common in the center. A church and cemetery flanked the common. Directly across the road from the church, side by side, were the homesites assigned to Gendron and Robert.[15]

Although the organization of the church conformed to the precepts set by the Carolina laws, the Huguenot Church of Santee retained distinct characteristics. With special permission, Pierre, as rector of St. James, Santee, read the service in French, according to a translation that was previously approved by the bishop of London. On Thursday, August 17, 1704, presumably in French, Robert performed the ceremony when Elias Horry and Margaret Hugar were married. In 1706 the church became the official

---

[13]Howe, *History of the Presbyterian Church*, 150, 155.

[14]W. H. Robert to A. R. Lawton, June 11, 1895.

[15]Hirsch, *Huguenots of South Carolina*, 48, 151, 166, 167.

64    Kith and Kin

Parish Church, and was Anglicized at its own request.[16] If Robert's great-grandson were correct when he wrote his cousin, *Pasteur* Robert led his congregation in "sweet songs of praise," first in French, later in English. He also received on more than one occasion not only regular tithes from his parishioners, but "the same allowance as ministers of other parishes," as provided by the proprietary government. There is further evidence that Robert received donations of several pounds from friends of the church, which may account for the church's later being described as prosperous.[17]

The records of the French Calvinistic Church in Basel show that Pierre's oldest child, Pierre [II], was baptized on May 9, 1675, before the family left Switzerland.[18] A second son Elias and a daughter Jeanne were said to have been born in Carolina.

By 1706, along the banks of the Santee—scattered through the wilderness surrounding the village inhabited by the first settlers of James Town, and extending even to the north edges of Hell Hole Swamp—French, Swiss, and later, English families settled. As they came, they cleared the bogs, grubbed the land, felled trees, built cabins, and eventually cultivated indigo, foodstuffs, and rice. They supported their church, were married by *Pasteur* Robert, and had their children baptized by him. Their resourcefulness and industry were rewarded, and through succeeding generations they became part of an autonomous, cultured society, one that in some instances fit the glamorized contemporary accounts of the Old South.[19]

For several decades after its settlement, James Town served as a center of trade with the Indians, and to a small degree served a similar function with Charles Town. Rice was first introduced into the St. James Parish area principally for home consumption; but as indigo declined, the rice acreage was increased year by year until it became not only one of the chief products of the Santee area, but of all Carolina lowlands as well. It was not until the early eighteenth century that cotton took the place of indigo and rice was abandoned.[20] The families who had dominated in the cultivation of rice

[16]McCrady, *History of South Carolina*, 447.

[17]Howe, *History of the Presbyterian Church*, 150, 155.

[18]Miller, *Family Circle*, 190.

[19]Savage, *The Santee*, 105-106.

[20]Doar, *Agricultural Society of St. James*, 13ff.

and indigo continued to dominate and prosper in the production of Sea Island cotton. John Lawson, in performing his duties as surveyor general for the English lords proprietor, and as one of the first travelers there, visited the wilderness settlement on the banks of the Santee. In 1701, the year of Lawson's visit, the Huguenot Church at James Town was newly completed, and the dwellings surrounding the church were yet to be built.[21] Lawson started his journey by passage through the marshes up the Santee River, setting out from Charles Town in a large canoe with nine others—six Englishmen and three Indians. Lawson's canoe, like those of the French settlers, was built of large, light-weight cypress trunks, which, when split down the middle and molded, were joined by planks and a keel. Lawson's crude boat carried two masts and Bermuda sails. Even when loaded with as many as sixty barrels of rice and provisions—if all went well—it would float in shallow water no deeper than four or five feet.

With hard rowing, Lawson's little band made steady progress toward "the first place we designed for"—the colony of French Protestants, of which Pierre Robert was spiritual leader. At the mouth of the river, where the strong current of fresh water mingled with the brackish waters of the marshes, the rowing was especially difficult. When night came the band made camp on swampy ground, and set out early next morning, rowing upstream into the Santee River. By the next night, they had rowed about fifteen miles to a house, being "the first Christian dwelling we met withall in that settlement." The group "lay all night at Monsieur Eugees [Huger]" and next morning they set out by land; all shared in carrying the canoes and provisions on their shoulders. By noon they had "come up with several French plantations, meeting with several creeks by the way."[22] Lawson was especially impressed by the French settlers he saw, who were "all very clean and decent in their apparel, their houses and plantations suitable in Neatness and Contrivance." A group of parishioners whom Lawson met coming from the little James Town church earned the thanks of the travelers when they assisted them to cross creeks and streams. By afternoon Lawson arrived at the home of Captain Gendron, where he and the others were provided with dinner. Later in the afternoon, Pierre Robert, whom Lawson wrote of

---

[21]Lawson, *Voyage to Carolina*, in Ravenel, "Huguenot Congregations of South Carolina," 31-33.

[22]Ibid., 34.

as "the French Doctor,"[23] sent a Negro slave to guide Lawson and his band over the head of a large swamp, so that the group was able to reach the "curious contrived house . . . built of brick and stone which is gotten near the place" of Monsieur Gaillard. From there they continued, Lawson reported, "through the marshes, turning and winding like a labarynth [sic] . . . the tide of Ebb and Flood [turned] twenty times in less than three leagues going . . . the French and Indians affirmed to me, they never knew such an extraordinary flood before." Surveyor Lawson reached the place he sought in the Carolina swampland where, he reported to the lords proprietor, the French inhabitants "wondered at our undertaking such a voyage through a country inhabited by none but savages, and them of so different Nations and Tongues."[24]

About the time that Lawson made the journey into the Carolina wilderness, Phillip Gendron was serving the colonists as chief commissioner and Pierre Robert as a commissioner. Gendron sometimes undertook a voyage to Charles Town to report to officials at the French settlement, to obtain supplies, and to discharge "friendly commission for many of his neighbors." On one occasion, Gendron made a trip by canoe to Charles Town

> for sales and supplies [where] he had undertaken friendly commission for many of his neighbors, but his return had been delayed. So long had the voyage been protracted that fears were felt that he had been lost. During this period of anxious suspense, on a Sunday whilst the Minister [Pierre Robert] was preaching, he suddenly paused and was observed to look intently forward as if to assure himself. He then lifted up his hands and said "*Voilà, Monsieur Gendron!*" The congregation rose in mass, and they and their minister went forth to meet and welcome Gendron as he ascended the slope.[25]

When Pierre Robert [II] was about to be married to Anne Marie Louise LeGrand,[26] his father arranged a marriage settlement for him. He

---

[23]Ibid., 35.

[24]Savage, *The Santee*, 58ff.

[25]Ravenel, "Huguenot Congregations of South Carolina," 36.

[26]See Appendix: Robert Lineal Chart, Ancestor Charts, and Robert Family Group Records.

caused it to be entered in the Records of the Secretary of the Province of Craven County, South Carolina:

> I, Pierre Robert, the elder, give to Pierre Robert, my son, half of all my possessions, present and future, both real and personal. Said estate will remain between my son and me that neither will be able to sell of his part but shall by mutual consent whenever we judge jointly, but to sell separately the fruits or revenue of the land.

Pierre [I] added further that "we shall live together in the same house, sharing expenses and income," and "if Pierre Robert, my son, shall happen to die before his wife or me, then one-half of everything shall belong to his wife and children of this marriage." Members of the two families gathered at the house of Isaac LeGrand, where they all signed the document on January 25, 1701.[27] So the families—Pierre [I], his wife Jeanne, and their younger children, as well as Pierre [II] with his bride Marie Louise—lived for several years together at James Town. One son, Pierre [III], who became known by his English name, Peter, was born to the younger couple, but the baby's mother died shortly thereafter, about 1704.

After Marie Louise's death, Pierre [II] married again. His second wife was Judith de Bourdeau, whose father, born in Grenoble, France, had also fled to Carolina after the Revocation of the Edict of Nantes.[28] Pierre continued as pastor of the French Santee church until 1710 when he resigned or retired, and was succeeded by the Reverend Philipe de Richbourg.[29] Apparently, Pierre [II] and Judith, Jacques [John], Elizabeth, and Madelaine continued to live in the family home after the elder Pierre's death in 1715.[30]

When Surveyor Lawson made his arduous journey through the Santee area in 1701, and wrote of the strong tides of "ebb and flood" and of an "extraordinary flood," he was reporting on conditions that proved not to be extraordinary: James Town and the surrounding area were constantly beset by freshets, if not raging floods, and the air was often miasmic and unhealthy.

---

[27]Moore, Records of the Secretary of the Province. Agreement between Pierre Robert [I] and Pierre Robert [II], January 25, 1701.

[28]Miller, *Family Circle*, 194.

[29]Ravenel, "Huguenot Congregations of South Carolina," 38. Lawton, *Saga of the South*, 32ff.

[30]Will Book, 1729-1731, 412-13 [recorded in French]. For the will of Pierre Robert, see Appendix.

The émigrés had chosen an unfortunate location. The constant flooding of the Santee River kept even the hardiest of the colonists in a state of apprehension, often accompanied by ill health. The spring plantings were often waterlogged and ruined, fresh foodstuffs were in short supply, and the colonists' pursuits interrupted and thwarted. For a number of years most kept struggling with the environment, adapting as best they could to hostile surroundings.

In the early decades of the eighteenth century, some of the settlers moved to higher ground on the north side of the river, including St. Stephens Parish and other sections that were safer from intermittent flooding. Others moved downstream to cultivate rice on the river's tidewater reaches; still others moved from the area entirely to more distant sections of Carolina. Eventually, James Town itself was completely abandoned. Much of the Santee reverted to undisturbed wilderness. Lands on the upper banks of the English Santee, as it was called, began to acquire settlers from England. They, together with the French colonists who moved to higher ground to avoid the floods, began to thrive as St. James Parish and James Town never had.

Descendants of *Pasteur* Pierre Robert continued to live in the Santee communities, some until a few years before the American Revolution. Pierre [II]'s grandchildren, Sarah Robert (1755-1774) and her brother John (1742-1826)—children of James Robert (1711-1774)—were born in Santee, as were Elias, Peter, Elizabeth, and others of James Robert's seven children.[31] All left the area eventually, Peter and Elizabeth migrating with their families to Mississippi and Louisiana.[32]

The popularly elected Assembly of South Carolina was in a state of impending revolt and constant war with, first, the English lords proprietor and, second, after the lords proprietor had been thrown out in 1719, with the English Crown. The latter turmoil led directly to the signing of the Declaration of Independence in 1776 and to the American Revolution. Until the recurring floods came, their heretofore happy condition and gratitude to England for providing a haven for them, free of religious oppression, made many of the Huguenot settlers reluctant to join the rebel forces. Even so, a number of outstanding rebel leaders emerged from the swamplands of

---

[31]See Appendix: Robert Lineal Chart, Ancestor Charts, and Family Group Records.

[32]Miller, *Family Circle*, 140, 188, 209, 238-39.

the Santee, most notable among them General Francis Marion, the "Swamp Fox," and his "Liberty or Death" boys, whom he organized in 1780. The latter years of the war were concentrated in the Carolinas, especially in the Santee and Cooper River valleys, which were turned into a bloody wasteland. Francis Marion and his men were at home from childhood in the gloom of the trackless swamps along the rivers and in the hills and valleys of the streams that fed those rivers.[33] From his hiding place in the swamps, Marion, with his tantalizing hit-and-run tactics, brought the enemy to such a state of confusion that his Liberty or Death boys, together with select brigades sent to Marion's assistance, completely intimidated and disrupted the British supply lines and outposts. The Swamp Fox and his guerillas contributed in large measure to bringing the war to an end.[34]

John Robert furnished food and supplies to the colonial army, and was detailed with others to find a safe hiding place for the slaves and horses of Generals Francis Marion and Thomas Sumter.[35] The search detail found an ideal spot in the lush lowlands along the Savannah River where earlier settlers had received headright grants.

In 1771 Elias Robert surveyed a 250-acre lowland tract in St. Peters Parish for Joseph Lawton. When he married Elias's sister Sarah in March 1773, Lawton came to live upon the land and establish his home and family there, in what became known as the Black Swamp-Robertville community. Still another of James Robert's children, Elizabeth, and her husband, John Grimball, were living in Robertville by 1775. By 1785 many of the Robert family from St. James Santee—together with Maners, Grimballs, Jaudons, Dixons, Hamiltons, Mosses, and other family, friends, and cohorts from the Santee—acquired lands along the Savannah River. There they transported their slaves, cleared and cultivated the land, acquired more slaves, built homes, begot children, built churches and academies and, on land known previously as Black Swamp, founded the town of Robertville.

During the years of its existence between the Revolutionary War and the Civil War, Robertville, for its size, spawned an inordinately large num-

---

[33]Savage, *The Santee,* 177ff.

[34]South Carolina Militia, "Revolutionary Records," 19.

[35]Salley, "Records Kept by Colonel Issac Hayne," 93.

ber of "fine, upstanding citizens," including several Robert men of upcoming generations.[36]

Sarah Robert and Joseph Lawton were progenitors of the Lawtons who became citizens of the town of Macon, Georgia, in the nineteenth century.[37]

---

[36]Details of the founding and naming of Robertville vary. The version given here is taken from Miller, *Family Circle*, 187ff.

[37]Munsell, *American Ancestry*, 9:207. Virkus, *American Genealogy*, 5:199. See Appendix: Robert Lineal Chart and Lawton Lines #1 and #2.

*Chapter Five*

# PHILLIP GUTTENBERGER
## (1799-1874)

*. . .in this dark world and wide. . .*[1]

D espite strong pressure on President George Washington to remain in office for a third term, he refused. His successor, John Adams, almost since the day of his inauguration in 1796, had been faced with evidence of deteriorating French-American relations. Commissioners that Adams sent to France had been brazenly insulted; both parties—the President's own Federalist party as well as the Democratic-Republican— were lining up behind the president to demand resistance to French aggressions. But when members of Adams's cabinet asked for a declaration of war, the president steadfastly refused. He realized, as did many of his followers, that war with France would have been catastrophic. What was essentially undeclared war with France continued into 1799. Secretly, by the turn of the century, a treaty between France and Spain had been signed ceding all

---

[1]Milton, "When I Consider How My Light Is Spent."

the Louisiana region to France. Navigation rights on the Mississippi River and related problems were now a French-American issue.

Disputes and wars between France and other civilized countries had been raging for years; our own war was but one example of these. As the French Revolution continued, a long series of French victories, beginning with Bonaparte's Italian Campaign in 1796-1797, and culminating in Germany in Marengo and Hohenlinden in 1800, pointed up the disunity of the German nation. In 1799 Germany was a patchwork of numerous small temporal and ecclesiastical principalities and free cities, one of which was Frankfurt am Main. Frankfurt, in central west Germany, was a thriving port city on the Main River, a tributary of the Rhine. The picturesque city of Heidelberg hugs the banks of the Neckar River, which also flows to join the Rhine.

Johann Martin Guttenberger, a native of Heidelberg, and Margarite Juliana Diehl of Frankfurt, had begun their married life in Heidelberg on November 6, 1784. Johann was said to have been a descendant of Johann Gutenberg, the master goldsmith who in the midfifteenth century invented the printing press. The surname was variously spelled Guttenberg, Gutenberg, Guttenburger, or Guttenberger. The family has retained the spelling "Guttenberger" since the seventeenth century. Johann Martin Guttenberger became a merchant in the town of Heidelberg in the mid-1700s, and enjoyed modest success in spite of turbulent times and constant threat of French invasion. By the fall of 1799, Johann became increasingly apprehensive that Heidelberg was in danger of invasion. With his pregnant wife, Margarite, he fled for safety to Frankfurt, the home of Margarite's parents. In a cellar there, with the rumble of battle in the distance, Margarite safely delivered a son on November 1, 1799: Phillip Gerhart Guttenberger.[2] The young family moved permanently from Heidelberg to Frankfurt in 1801, shortly after the free town came under the dominion of Frederick William III of Prussia. In Frankfurt, Johann reestablished a business, which grew and prospered into a large mercantile establishment. Young Phillip received

---

[2]Unless otherwise noted, quotations from the basic narrative of the life of Phillip Guttenberger, as well as dates and events in his life, were taken from the unpublished manuscript of his daughter Francesca (1835-1911), "Family History," a typed copy of which is in possession of the author. See Appendix: Guttenberger Lineal Chart, Family Group Record, and Ancestor Chart.

a fine education, including study, by his pleading, at a drawing school. Phillip's daughter, Francesca, years later in writing of her father's life, said:

> When father was eleven years of age he asked to be sent to the drawing school. After he had been there a year, a prize was offered for the best drawing. The pictures were exhibited before a large audience. His parents did not go to the exhibition, not knowing that their son had any special talent, but they regretted not going when they heard that he was called out on the stage to receive the prize.

The picture that won the prize for Phillip depicted a young English prince whose mother, Margaret of Anjou (1430-1482), had laid claim to the English throne for her son. In Phillip's drawing, the prince was being smothered to death, a historically accurate event, but an unusually morbid subject for an eleven-year-old boy.

After his early schooling in Frankfurt, Phillip was sent by his father to the University of Heidelberg where, from all accounts, he enjoyed not only the well-publicized romantic life of song and pleasure of the Heidelberg student, but also found time to paint charming scenes throughout the town and among the vineyards on the banks of the Neckar. After his graduation, during a short stay back home in Frankfurt, Phillip was notified that his application for entrance to the Academie Royale des Beaux Arts in Paris had been accepted. With a will, Phillip threw himself into his arduous, demanding studies in languages and in all phases of art. Early in his years of study in Paris, Phillip made the decision to spend his life as an architect. There were more than a hundred students at the school and, Francesca said, "Many of them would say that if father competed for a prize, it was not worth while for anybody else to try." During the five years that Phillip was a student at the Royal Academy, ten silver medals were offered, and he was awarded nine of these. One of the last medals he received before his graduation bore the inscription: *Academie Royale des Beaux Arts, P. G. Guttenberger, Janvier 1824, Franc et Nav Rex*, and a profile bas relief of the fat-cheeked emperor, Ludovicus XVIII.

Upon his graduation from the academy, both Phillip Guttenberger and a friend, Monsieur deLaprere, received coveted appointments by the French government to go to the South American colony of Guiana to assist in the development of the land that had been restored to French authority at the Congress of Vienna in 1815 after the Napoleonic wars. Madame Rosella Govain, deLaprere's widowed mother, upon her second marriage several years before, had emigrated from France to the state of Georgia with her new husband, who became a professor at the fledgling University of Georgia at Athens. The two friends decided to visit the United States before proceeding to South America to take up their posts, and to visit Madame Govain at her home in Athens to await an expected dispatch from the French government.

One of Phillip's large trunks that was borne to his room at Madame Govain's contained clothing suitable for the expected hot weather of South America. His guitar and violin were also in the trunk, despite Johann's scoffing at his son for taking musical instruments to the wilds of South America. Locked in a second compartment in a second trunk, beneath his artist's brushes and tubes of paints, were his nine silver medals, struck in the image of the French emperors, and bearing Phillip's name and various dates of the preceding four years.

*Phillip Gerhart Guttenberger (1799-1874) was a young honors graduate, fresh from the halls of Academie Royale des Beaux Arts in Paris when he set up a mirror and painted this miniature portrait of himself. He brought the miniature with him, together with a treasured violin and guitar when he came to America about 1825.*

[Collection of Loulie Forrester Burns]

While awaiting further orders from France, Phillip and deLaprere whiled away the spring days at Madame Govain's by exploring the town of Athens and the Georgia countryside. The streets of Athens were shaded by oaks and elms, and a stroll in their dappled shade and through the campus was vastly interesting to the young architects. Although the campus was often muddy and difficult to negotiate, Phillip and deLaprere discussed the attributes of one and another of the buildings as they made their way past them. One three-story, red-brick building, already two decades old in 1826, had been built from plans brought from New York by Josiah Meigs.[3] Meigs, formerly a professor at Yale, had been appointed president of the university in 1801.

The University of Georgia had a small beginning and a hard struggle for survival; but by the time Phillip and deLaprere wandered the streets of the town, Meigs had been president for almost three decades, and had brought the college that had languished "well nigh to despair" with a student body of seven, to a student body numbering one hundred, who attended classes in a fine new building called New College. The architects lingered in their walks to study the design of New College as well as the design of Demosthenean and Phi Kappa Halls, and the small building on campus that housed a grammar school.[4]

At the time that Phillip and deLaprere were visiting Madame Govain, a young girl, Emily Antoinette Muse, daughter of a north Georgia farmer, was living in Madame Govain's home and attending school at the academy in Athens. Emily's mother died shortly after Emily, the youngest of three children, had been born. In Emily's early childhood, her father found it difficult to care for his motherless children, and had sent Emily to live with her grandmother—Francesca called her Mrs. Hubbard—who, in later years, felt the burden of caring for her granddaughter. When Madame Govain asked for the child to come live with her and go to school in Athens, Emily's father and grandmother readily agreed. Through the years, Madame Govain "became very much attached to [Emily] and kept her as long as she could."

A day's horseback ride from Athens was the beautiful Tallulah Falls, nestled among the Smokie Mountains. In these mountains are many sparkling waters that fall from mountaintop to valley, where clear, calm lakes glisten in the sun. In early spring the mountain slopes are pink with laurel and rhododendron, after the sun dispels the blue haze of early morning. From the rim of Tallulah's great gorge the water plunges, cascades, and tum-

---

[3]Luckie, *Georgia Guide.*

[4]Brooks, *University of Georgia*, 18, 20-21.

bles to the depths of the narrow crevice. In the deep cut far below, the falls narrow to a churning rapid. As far as the eye can see, the waters flow, becoming calm and gliding silently as the streambed widens and forms a lake on the valley plain.

During the days of waiting at Madame Govain's, Phillip made several trips to Tallulah Falls, and painted two pictures in which he caught the grandeur of the falls. He spent long hours at his canvases. At other times he would make his violin sing, or strum his guitar on the piazza at Madame Govain's in early evening. Perhaps Emily listened as she studied in her room above the piazza.

One day letters from Germany as well as a dispatch from France arrived. The packet from France contained distressing and disappointing news for Phillip and deLaprere. Word had reached officials in France from the French colony in South America that a revolution was brewing there. It would be unwise for the men to proceed, they were told. Phillip was directed to "tarry in America and await further orders." DeLaprere received similar orders. He made a quick decision not to tarry, but to return directly to France.

The letter from Germany to Phillip was from his father and mother. They, too, had heard of the imminent danger in South America; they implored their son to return home immediately to Frankfurt. His father reported that the mayor had reconsidered an application Phillip had made before he left for the position of architect in the free town of Frankfurt am Main. That position might still be held open if Phillip returned, his father said. If that position were not available, his father wrote that his own large "mercantile establishment" was prospering, and with its prosperity it was becoming ever more burdensome for him to continue to manage. He would like to turn the business over to Phillip and his brother Carl. He implored Phillip to return home. Phillip made a difficult decision: He would remain in America and cast his lot in Georgia. He would never return to Germany.

Phillip completed his oil paintings of Tallulah Falls. Foolishly, he let a dealer have the two pictures on consignment. The dealer promised to sell the paintings in New York for large sums, but Phillip never heard from the dealer again. He continued to paint, however, making a miniature of himself, as well as many more scenes in and around Athens. He strummed his guitar and played his violin. Tallulah Falls drew him again and again. As his stock of paintings grew, his money dwindled. Phillip's work was appreciated among the university contingent, but only a few portraits brought any money at all. By now there were only a few crowns in his well-worn doublet. No further dispatches arrived from France. The order to proceed to South America never came.

With the use of steam as the motive power for vessels, the commerce of the city of Savannah, Georgia, expanded. Steamboat lines were established between Savannah and Augusta and later much of the commerce was handled by steamers plying between the city of Savannah and Northern or European ports. The first steamship to cross the Atlantic had, in fact, been named *Savannah*. She made the run from Savannah to Liverpool, and from Liverpool to St. Petersburg, Florida, thence to Savannah again. The year was 1818.[5]

When Phillip and deLaprere came to Georgia from France, they had come by ship through the port of Savannah, and Phillip thought of it now. By 1828, while Phillip remained at Madame Govain's in Athens, much trade and commerce with England and France was channeled through Savannah. Wealthy cotton planters and their factors plied their trade there. The theatre, the arts, and other leisure activities were rivaling those of the larger city of Charleston. The planters were importing fine furnishing for their homes from England and France. Some, Phillip had learned, were seeking artists to paint portraits of themselves and their families to grace the walls of their columned mansions. Surely, Phillip decided, he could "keep body and soul" together there with his art. He might find an opportunity to begin to practice his profession as an architect.

So Phillip left Madame Govain and her young charge, Emily, promising to return someday. Settling himself in a small hotel in Savannah, Phillip was allowed to exhibit examples of his work in the common room of the hotel. Those who came and went from the hotel soon passed the word of the "superior renderings in oil" by the young, Paris-educated, German-born artist. He entered a competition to design the Chatham County Courthouse, but he did not win. He painted the mural for the celebration of Washington's birthday in Savannah in 1831, and he received a few commissions for portraits. Wanting to impress his American patrons, he ordered the finest oil paints, camel-hair brushes, and canvases to be brought by steamer from Italy. In the same period he purchased a dashing new tai-

---

[5]Carse, *Great Colonial Seaports*, 295-96.

lored doublet for himself. He completed and displayed several additional portraits and paintings.

On more than one occasion, landowners visiting in Savannah for trade commissioned Phillip to bring his paints and brushes home to their plantations, where Phillip stayed for weeks at a time, painting portraits and miniatures of the master, of his wife, and often of his children. He was paid well for these commissioned works, and he made friends among the gentry.

Phillip was back in his room in Savannah one day after a particularly long and arduous midsummer stay at a Georgia plantation, where he had been urged by the owner to complete the family portraits as quickly as possible. There was to be a gala entertainment at the manor house in the fall. He wanted the portraits displayed on the walls by that time. Phillip had painted early and late until his eyes ached. Next morning he would pose his model again, and continue until each portrait was done. He saw to it that the pictures were properly framed in the gold-leaf frames he had ordered from Italy, and he directed the slaves as they hung the master's portrait over the first parlor mantel and the remaining portraits on the walls throughout the house. The work was finally done. Exhausted, Phillip returned to the somewhat cooler, high-ceilinged room in his hotel. As he lay back on his bed, unbearable pain suddenly pierced his eyes. Next morning he found his way to a physician.

Back in his room later that day, he lay on his bed again. There was no question about what the physician had said. He must quit work, and rest his eyes until they "should get right again."

As the time drew near for Emily Muse to receive her diploma from the academy, Madame Govain became more and more crestfallen. She had become attached to her through the years Emily had lived with her and gone to school. The thought of their parting was sad for them both. So it was agreed, with her father's consent, that Emily would stay through the winter with her second mother, Madame Govain.

Already leaves of the oaks lining the streets of Athens were turning to red-tipped gold and beginning to drift to the ground. They had formed a bright carpet on the ground when Phillip returned to Madame Govain's. In the restful atmosphere of her household and often in the company of Emily, Phillip recuperated until his eyes became free of pain. Occasionally, he would paint for short periods, until his eyes became painful again. More often he would pick up his violin, tuck it under his chin, and play for hours on end. When the German professor at the university asked him to instruct his children in violin and guitar, he set up a small studio where he gave lessons to the professor's children and to others who had heard him play. As winter progressed, Phillip's brushes were dry, and the paint tubes seldom opened. But his violin sang, his classes thrived, and his love for Emily was kindled and grew.

On a spring day in May 1834, Phillip Gerhart Guttenberger and Emily Antoinette Muse were married in the front parlor of Madame Govain's house. They went to board at a small hotel in Athens. One day in late summer after he had taught all day, he returned home to Emily. The evening was hot, but a breeze was stirring the curtains. He pushed his bed to the window and lay down with his head upon a pillow on the window sill. As a soft, cool rain began to blow across his face, he slept. Throughout the night he slept. Dawn came and as the sun's rays touched his eyes, the light seared into his brain. In his agony, he called for Emily. The pain subsided as she put cool cloths over his eyes and cradled his head in her lap. Eventually, he slept. When he awakened again, the pain was gone, but all was black. Phillip was blind.

Throughout the ensuing years, Emily Muse Guttenberger was her husband's "heart and eyes," as he often said. He continued to teach violin and guitar, and his classes grew. He found a piano, practiced diligently, became proficient at that instrument, and although self-taught, he added piano students to his class as well. When the offer came to become professor of music at a school in Monroe, Georgia, he accepted, and taught there awhile. From Monroe he went to Oxford, Georgia, where a college had recently been established. The move to Oxford was made in 1840, where Phillip taught music to students of all ages. Francesca, the oldest child, was five years old. A second daughter, Louisa, was three at the time, and Ferdinand, their oldest son, was a baby.

Many years later, Mrs. W. H. Felton, a former pupil of Phillip, wrote of her childhood in Oxford:

> I was a student at Oxford sixty years ago—a bit of a girl. I remember the campus. I played in a branch back of Mr. Guttenberger's house, and took my first music lessons from the blind professor. Do you recall his gifted child, Francesca? She was trained in music from her literal cradle. . . . What a heroic figure he was to make a living . . . perfectly blind with a large family of little ones to educate. Next year, he taught music one week in Oxford, and the alternate week in Decatur, and I can see him

yet in his carry-all wagon—negro boy driver, driving through heat and cold—storm and sunshine, to carry out his contract.

On December 9, 1822, the General Assembly of Georgia created Bibb County. One year later, on December 10, 1823, the Assembly signed the papers and affixed the seal of Georgia to incorporate the town of Macon, which they named for a North Carolina statesman.[6] As was true of other early towns in Georgia, Macon was laid out to be located on the banks of a navigable river, the Ocmulgee. By means of the rivers, the interior towns of the state could be reached by boat and barge, and the surrounding farmlands had access to other towns along the riverbanks and seacoast and to the Atlantic Ocean. By the 1830s regular steamer service was underway between Macon and the port town of Darien.[7]

First settlers of Macon built houses on the western banks of the Ocmulgee River. By 1826 cotton and produce passed toll-free over a new bridge, which also made possible access to the east bank of the river. Residential sections such as East Macon emerged, as did a residential area called "Vineville," which was north of the commercial district and west of the river. Wide streets were laid out. Neat, and in some instances imposing, residences were built. A county courthouse was erected. Commercial establishments—dry goods stores, banks, hotels, groceries—opened for business. Doctors and lawyers hung out shingles on streets bearing such names as Walnut and Cherry, Plum and Pine, Poplar and Mulberry. Mule-drawn wagons, loaded with bales of cotton or ears of corn for the grist mills, plodded along Wharf Street to deliver their loads to flat-bottom boats, which would journey down the Ocmulgee into the Altamaha and eventually to the seaport town of Darien.[8]

In 1839 "a splendid edifice" for the Georgia Female College (later named Wesleyan Female College, and still later Wesleyan College), designed by Macon architect Elam Alexander, rose as an eminence above the commercial district, facing College Street. Many of the surrounding hills were crowned with "private mansions of the most tasteful architecture,"[9]

---

[6]McKay, *Macon's Architectural Heritage*, 10.

[7]Sherwood, *Gazetteer of Georgia*, 30-33.

[8]Jenkins, "Antebellum Macon," 4ff.

[9]McKay, *Macon's Architectural Heritage*, 10.

some of which had been designed by Alexander. His houses and buildings brought national distinction to the town and to Alexander himself.

A charter for the college had been granted in 1836 as an institution of higher education exclusively for women. Wesleyan was founded on the premise, as one early advocate expressed it, that "the intellectual endowments" of females were equal to those of males and should be "fairly developed."[10]

The town of Macon had welcomed the opening of the college for young females, and the *Georgia Messenger* proclaimed upon the dedication in 1839 of the grand, new four-story building that "the prosperity of the college has passed our most sanguine expectations. . . . We feel that no school in our State affords equal advantages for the improvement of young ladies. . . . We are led to hope that it may be. . . . *A Pioneer in the System of Female Education.*" In part because of the presence of the college for young ladies, the town soon gained a reputation as being "a flourishing town," a "handsomely built town." It was inhabited by gentlefolk, by "men of liberality, taste, and talents," situated at the head of "the longest railroad in the world owned by one company," which in the 1840s had begun to make regular runs between Savannah and Macon.[11]

The college began operation after the first building—Elam Alexander's "splendid edifice"—was completed. One hundred sixty-eight students enrolled by the end of the first term in July 1839.[12] The first college catalogue listed John H. Uhink as professor of music, together with an assistant in music. Word had reached the trustees of the fledgling college concerning the "fine musicianship," fine character, and teaching abilities of Phillip Gerhart Guttenberger, the blind professor at Oxford. When Professor Uhink resigned, the position was offered to Guttenberger. In 1845 Phillip moved his young family to Macon.

The young college did manage to grow, but the period of 1839 to 1845 was one of hard times for Macon and Bibb County. The price of cotton, upon which the heretofore brisk commerce of Macon and central Georgia depended, seldom reached five cents per pound. Nationally, James K. Polk

---

[10]Akers, *Wesleyan College*, 2ff.

[11]McKay, *Macon's Architectural Heritage*, 10ff.

[12]Guttenberger Historical File.

had taken office as president, Texas had been annexed by a joint resolution of Congress, and the government of Mexico had broken off diplomatic relations with the United States. But the town of Macon seemed far removed from national concerns and the threats of war with Mexico. Life was circumscribed by the immediate concerns of making and selling the cotton crops. The banks were suffering and operating in confusion. With tuition and board at the college amounting to almost two hundred dollars per year, not including such extras as "firewood, washing, candles, and piano lessons," and with cotton still bringing only five cents per pound, many formerly prosperous Georgia planters were hard-pressed to keep their daughters in the college. Many made special sacrifices to have their daughters continue music lessons with their blind master.

*When this four-story building was constructed (ca. 1836) on a hill overlooking Macon, Georgia, it soon became the pride of the town as Wesleyan Female College, the first chartered college for women, who proved they were the "equal of strong-minded men" in mastering academic subjects.*

[Middle Georgia Historical Society]

By the time Phillip Guttenberger moved in 1844 to Vineville, only a mile or so from the Wesleyan campus on College Street, times were improving. Trade on Walnut and Poplar, Cherry and Pine was becoming brisk again, and the halls of the college were filled with young women who, under the guidance of "able and efficient instructors," were the equal of "strong-minded men" in mastering such subjects as Latin, Greek, French, Spanish, and Italian, as well as drawing, painting, and "Music on Piano."[13] As late as 1863 the college catalogue listed among the professors the name of an "instructor of Ornamental Needle-Work &c." Ten professors were listed, including Madame Schwartz, who taught the ornamental stitchery, and twenty-two members of the Board of Trustees, of whom twelve were "Reverend"—all ministers of the Methodist Episcopal Church and all seriously dedicated to seeing that the young females were well and properly taught.

*When Joseph Witman painted this oil portrait of Phillip Gerhart Guttenberger (ca. 1855), Phillip was at the height of his career as professor of music at Wesleyan College. Witman no doubt depicted acuity and expression in Guttenberger's eyes that in reality were not there. Guttenberger had become blind many years before.*

[Wesleyan College Historical Files]

Phillip Guttenberger, blind and thus dependent on his faithful Emily for so many of the mundane affairs of everyday life, took up his teaching at

---

[13]*Georgia Messenger*, December 13, 1838.

the college with enthusiasm. Although most often his black servant took Phillip by horse and buggy from his home in Vineville for the short distance to College Street, on a pleasant day he could be seen stepping briskly along, tapping his cane ahead as he walked. The lack of sight had the effect of sharpening Phillip's other senses. His acute awareness of gradations in tone and pitch, and his sensitive touch on the piano keys and violin strings earned him recognition as an accomplished musician of artistic skill.

In his studio on the first floor of the college building, he set up classes in violin, guitar, and piano. Together with scales and finger exercises that he taught by demonstration, he also taught the "scholars" to play from printed music scores. From memory he called out the musical notes; if wrong notes were struck, he stopped the pupil, patiently repeated the correct notes, and demonstrated the technique for troublesome passages. He had perfect pitch, it was said, and his students learned well. The professor taught them such compositions as Donizetti's "For Thy Love all Danger Braving," Mozart's "Landing of Columbus," Gottschalk's "The Banjo" and, for the senior students in voice, there were selections from Boieldieu's operas and Donizetti's "Lucia di Lammermoor."[14] Individual lessons were scheduled for each half hour of the day; when a pupil was late for a lesson, Professor Guttenberger made his way up the stairs to the student's room, rapped sharply with his cane on her door, and called out the time of day. There were seldom second offenders.

Examination days in July were the highlight of the year, anticipated with excitement and dread and preceded by months of special lessons and unending hours of practice. A specially appointed Visiting Committee examined the "scholars" in academic studies on one day; another day or two was taken up with a "Junior Exhibition" of original compositions, concerts, and commencement exercises. Always Professor Guttenberger's music scholars were presented in concert, and often he performed with them, playing duets with a talented student. On occasion, there were two-piano gavottes or polonaises for eight hands.

Phillip's oldest daughter, Francesca, had been her father's piano pupil since early childhood. The Visiting Committee for the year 1850, composed of six gentlemen from Georgia towns and chaired by Dr. C. Williams

---

[14]Wesleyan College Catalogues and Commencement Programs.

of Georgetown, South Carolina, presented a formal evaluation of the examinations, published on July 23 in the *Georgia Telegraph*:

> We take pleasure in expressing our high gratification at the very handsome manner in which different classes acquitted themselves in the various and thorough examinations to which they were subjected. We think we can safely assert that the classes generally would favorably compare without regard to sex, with those of any college in the land. Their thorough instruction in Geometry, Trigonometry, and Astronomy was demonstrated before a large audience without the shadow of a doubt. We were especially gratified with the ease and adroitness with which problems were solved, and explained upon the blackboard.

> We further remarked that the young ladies expressed themselves, very generally, in their own language, with great accuracy and promptness, . . . and in such forms as to elicit a thorough exposition of the principles involved in the subjects. The inference we drew is that there is on the part of the Faculty, not only sound scholarship in their respective departments, but likewise great tact in communicating instructions. They do not (as is too frequently the case) drill the memory at the expense of the judgment. . . .

> With respect to the music department, we are of the opinion that this institution is second to none in the Union. Professor Guttenberger and his accomplished daughter [Francesca] are, not only amateurs in this interesting branch of the fine arts, but they also attest by their performances the utmost artistic skill, besides the happy faculty of imparting to their pupils a thorough knowledge of the science. These facts were beautifully and happily demonstrated by frequent interludes of rich and varied music, both vocal and instrumental during the examination exercises. The concert on Tuesday night, amid so much beauty and enchanting music, beggars our humble powers of description. It was one of those scenes which could be felt, but not described. . . .

> [The graduates] will reflect the luster they have acquired upon the respective circles of society to which they may attach, and will also be the best possible recommendation of their *Alma Mater*.

Then, with an extra flourish, the report ends: "We can in all good conscience commend this 'nursery of science' to all who desire to furnish their daughters with a sound, thorough education, not forgetting the music department, and all that, too, in a place where attention to their morals is scrupulously given."

Phillip and Emily and their six children[15]—the youngest three, Charles H., Julia Helene, and Emily Jane (Emma) were born after they moved to Macon from Oxford—lived for more than thirty years in the white clapboard house set among grape arbors at the end of an oak- and elm-lined drive in Vineville. The arbors decayed and the grapevines died during passing years, but the name Vineville survived. Her father's "nice little property," as Francesca called it, was composed of a four-and- a-half-acre plot with a carriage way (later named Lamar Street) to Forsyth Road.[16] The name Forsyth Road was later changed to Vineville Avenue as Macon grew to include the little community of Vineville.

On his small acreage, Phillip kept a few horses and a cow, along with a few plum and fig trees, a small vegetable garden, and chickens. He owned no slaves, but he had at least one black servant, who drove his buggy for him and worked about the place. On at least one occasion, Phillip was troubled by his neighbor's wandering livestock. A notice appeared in the *Georgia Telegraph* (the name of Macon's newspaper changed through the years), printed by its new steam-powered press, on January 6, 1852:

> Came to my lot in Vineville, about two weeks hence, a Bay Horse, medium size, hind feet white, and a white spot on the top of his nose. The owner is requested to come forward, pay charges, and take him away. Phillip Guttenberger.

Phillip and Emily reared their children in the congenial atmosphere of Vineville. The four daughters and two sons studied piano, violin, and guitar with their father. Throughout the years, the house rang with the sound of music. The girls attended Vineville Academy and Gresham Academy. They were enrolled in Wesleyan College and, in due time, were graduated. Francesca became her father's assistant in music at the college, teaching piano and Italian harp before her marriage to Erastus H. Link (1850-1855) and afterward (1860-1861). Even as late as 1901 she taught Italian harp as a member of the faculty. Louisa also assisted in the music department (1859-1861). Julia (Jule) learned to play the piano, was graduated from Wesleyan in 1866, and later married Clark Davis. They settled in Eatonton, Georgia, where she taught piano for many years.

---

[15]See Appendix: Guttenberger Family Group Record.

[16]Deed Book M, 286-87.

Then there was Emily Jane (Emma), Phillip's youngest daughter, who graduated from the college in 1869. Musical education was especially significant in her life. She married John Jacob Nottingham in 1870, at the age of eighteen. She, John Jacob, and their children continued to live in the house on Vineville Avenue after her parents' death.[17] John Jacob, many years Emma's senior, left Emma a widow with small children. In the house in which she was born, Emma supported herself and her children by teaching piano until her own death in 1920.

Both of the sons of Phillip and Emily had careers as musicians. Charles, who lived most of his life in Barnesville, Georgia, was described upon his death as "a thorough musician, a man of lovable disposition and strict integrity."[18] Ferdinand was the son who exuberantly carried forward the musical proclivities and talents of the Guttenbergers. He learned to play all the instruments his father had mastered and added a few of his own, including mandolin, organ, and cornet. He also taught at the college, from 1896 to 1901. Ferdinand opened a "commercial establishment," F. A. Guttenberger and Co. at 452 Second Street, "Dealers in pianos, organs and Musical Merchandise." With verve and aplomb, he demonstrated all the instruments he offered for sale. Through the years he organized all sorts of musicals, enlisting his sisters to play duets, violin solos, organ and piano ensembles, two-piano, eight-handed compositions. He made up chamber orchestras and marching bands, and performed at everything from soirees in the college parlors and grand balls in the elegant Lanier House to band concerts in Central City Park for Fourth of July celebrations. On Sundays he would frequently play the organ for services at Mulberry Street Methodist Church. Solemnly he would play dirges for funerals and, backed by candelabra and arrangements of smilax and white roses, he would play "Love's Old Sweet Song" on his violin at wedding receptions. He composed a Grand March for commencement exercises at Wesleyan.

At the college the corridors of the piano practice rooms resounded with a cacophony of sound, and at Phillip's home the piano keys were seldom still. Phillip at the piano, and his children playing flute and violin, often filled the Vineville air with music on a summer's day. In rare moments

---

[17]See Appendix: Nottingham Lineal Chart, Family Group Record, and Ancestor Chart. Also see Nottingham chapter.

[18]*Georgia Telegraph*, May 8, 1887.

of quiet, Phillip picked up the treasured violin that he had brought with him from Germany years before. His daughter told that as he played, the sound of the rushing waters of Tallulah Falls filled his ears, and an image of the frothing cascade filled his blind eyes.

*From this little bandstand in Macon's Central City Park, Jefferson Davis reviewed Confederate troops in reunion after the Civil War (1887). Ferd Guttenberger led bands in Fourth of July concerts under its canopy, and Lawton family members received blue ribbons there at yearly agricultural fairs held in October during the early decades of the twentieth century.*

[John J. McKay, Middle Georgia Historical Society]

Phillip's little vegetable plot that the children helped him care for, together with the cow and the chickens, had enabled the Guttenbergers to enjoy a bountiful table during the depression years of the 1850s, in spite of Phillip's rather meager salary from the struggling college. But by 1860 Macon had never before shown more "go-aheadedness, more energy, faster men, or prettier women."[19]

Threats of secession and friction between the champions of states' rights and those who advocated the abolition of slavery swirled around the college. In early February 1860, Senator Jefferson Davis of Mississippi introduced a set of resolutions in the United States Senate on the political and constitutional aspects of slavery. Those resolutions defended the legality of the institution in the states and territories, as well as honoring the legal right to recover slaves. The next week, on February 8, 1860, on the front page of the *Macon Telegraph* (the name of the town's newspaper had been changed again), there appeared:

> Hoop skirts avaunt! Gone at last are these cumbrous and to us ungraceful appendages of female attire, and we presume the narrow skirts and wide headgear—and those graceful little caps are to give way to huge bonnets. . . .

Fashion was of first importance. The full impact of the possibility for the terrible war that was brewing had yet to penetrate beyond the walls of the college for young ladies. As the battle over slavery's extension reached its climax after the November election of Abraham Lincoln, and South Carolina became the first state to secede from the Union, the full import of the momentous decisions being made throughout the South began to permeate the towns of central Georgia. South Carolina seceded on December 20, 1860, and between January and early June 1861, ten slave states followed, Georgia on January 19. On January 12, 1861, the *Macon Telegraph* reported:

> We are looking forward to this patriotic portion of the state to arm and enroll itself into Volunteer companies as rapidly as possible. . . . It behooves us to be prepared to meet the fanatical legions, whenever they presume to pollute the soil of Georgia with their fanatical presence. [On

[19]Jenkins, "Antebellum Macon," 255.

January 14] . . . We are disappointed in our expectation of receiving news this morning. The town is full of rumors which are traceable to no authentic sources. It is confidently asserted and believed that Fort Sumter at Charleston will be assailed this week.

Fort Sumter was not assailed that week, but throughout the week Macon streets were filled with "a fine young company of Macon Guards on parade," while drays of knapsacks, kegs of powder, and other munitions of war passed to and fro as if they were the "most innocent things in the world."

When the news of Georgia's secession reached Macon on January 19, 1861, it was received with excitement and delight, and what was long to be remembered as "Illumination Night" resulted. On the evening of January 21:

> An immense crowd, at the firing of a single gun, moved from the courthouse and marched up Mulberry Street until they reached the Lanier House hotel where a patriotic ode was sung by a choir of thirty young ladies. After a pause for refreshments at the house of the Honorable James Nisbet, they proceeded to College Hill. Each dwelling was brilliantly illuminated along the whole route of the procession, past the College and Asylum for the Blind. Long, loud, hearty shouts went up in response to waving handkerchiefs from the College. . . . For the citizens, the imposing College building on the hill, with candles burning in all the windows was a thing of beauty. For the students, it was the night when rules were suspended because of the fateful event which had occurred.[20]

In the same week of Illumination Night on College Hill, Georgia volunteers, amidst much excitement and misplaced enthusiasm, managed to "capture" the Federal fort Pulaski, at the mouth of the Savannah River. Its garrison, one elderly United States sergeant, surrendered forthwith.[21] Next month, on February 18, Jefferson Davis was inaugurated president of the new Confederate States at the capitol in Montgomery, Alabama.

On June 12, 1861, the *Macon Telegraph* reported:

> We are authorized to announce that the Guttenberger family will give a vocal and instrumental concert for the benefit of the S[oldiers]

---

[20]Akers, *Wesleyan College*, in *Macon Telegraph*, January 21, 1861.

[21]Lane, *William T. Sherman*, xvi.

R[elief] F[und] at Concert Hall, next Friday evening June 14. The great musical talents of this musical family cannot fail to insure a most agreeable entertainment, and we are sure that the Macon public will respond with enthusiasm to the noble and patriotic motives which have prompted this tender. Recollect next Friday night!

Throughout the following three years the war raged in Virginia, Tennessee, and Mississippi, but there was no sustained military action in Georgia. In Macon, volunteers were mustered and a small cannon factory was put into operation. There were minor military episodes along the Georgia coast, and Macon's seaport outlet, Darien, was burned in the spring of 1863. Federal ships blockaded or captured South Carolina and Georgia seaports, including the port of Savannah.[22]

During these first years of the Civil War, Wesleyan College was one of the few institutions of higher education in the Confederacy to keep its doors open. Stringent economies, reduction in faculty and salaries, and difficulties in obtaining supplies to maintain operation, all contributed to the hardships of continuing the college's activities, but continue it did. The fertile lands of Georgia produced great crops of foodstuffs and livestock, and the prosperous farmers continued to send their daughters to Wesleyan, where they felt they would be as safe behind the walls of the college as they would be at home. Phillip Guttenberger nurtured his music department and an assistant in music was added. By the end of the war, the faculty had shrunk to only seven members, two of whom were Phillip and his assistant.[23] Phillip's double contribution as artist and performer as well as professor of music continued to be noted with appreciation in the Macon newspapers throughout those early war years.

General William Tecumseh Sherman and his army began their momentous march through Georgia in May 1864. For forty days under Sherman, the Union forces bombarded Atlanta and Confederate forces fled the city on September 1, 1864. From Atlanta the Union army marched in three parallel columns toward Savannah and the sea, leaving death and destruction in its wake. A cavalry column forged ahead toward Macon, and when

---

[22]Harden, *History of Savannah*, 435.

[23]*A Macon Directory*, 83.

word reached the town that Macon was in the enemy's path, terrified citizens braced themselves for the invasion. But the cavalry fell back to Gordon, bypassing Macon, and rejoining Sherman's forces in Milledgeville, Georgia's capitol. Sherman truthfully reported: "We have devoured the land. All the people retire before us and desolation is behind." Later he provided another account of the situation:

> We rode out of Atlanta by the Decatur road, filled by the marching troops and wagons of the Fourteenth Corps; and reaching the hill . . . we naturally paused to look back upon the scenes of our past battles. . . . Behind us lay Atlanta, smouldering and in ruins, the black smoke rising high in the air and hanging like a pall over the ruined city. . . . The day was extremely beautiful . . . and an unusual feeling of exhilaration seemed to pervade all minds. . . .[24]

Refugees, wounded soldiers, disabled and displaced persons fled before the invaders. Emergency hospitals were set up in Macon. Classes were temporarily suspended at the college. Trainloads of wounded soldiers received care at churches and other city buildings that had been set up as hospitals to receive them. Almost six thousand were cared for, a number equal to the white population of the city at the time. The Wesleyan Board of Trustees noted the college's contribution by saying that it "constitutes the homes of numerous permanent residents composed of the families and children of the Faculty . . . and numerous pupils cut off from their homes with no other shelter."[25] Phillip Guttenberger and his family probably were not among the faculty families who sought refuge at the college; yet if they did indeed live there during the emergency, they were shortly able to return to their home in Vineville. Sherman marched ahead through Georgia, passing through Milledgeville, Sandersville, Louisville, and Millen. By December 21, 1864, Sherman sent his famous communication to President Lincoln in which he said: "I beg to present you as a Christmas gift, the City of Savannah."

Macon's native son, the gifted poet Sidney Lanier, and his parents were among those who lived at Wesleyan College during 1865. In a brief two-decade span of production, Lanier earned an enduring place among America's dominant figures in literature. He had an intimate knowledge of music that enabled him to teach himself to play piano, violin, guitar, and

---

[24]Lane, *William T. Sherman*, 147-48.

[25]Akers, *Wesleyan College*, 84-85.

flute. Lanier enlisted in the Confederate army in July 1861. He was captured in November 1864 and imprisoned. When he became weak from illness, he was released and made his way from Federal prison camp to Macon. Throughout his imprisonment, Lanier kept his silver flute safely hidden. When he left the camp, Lanier rolled his carefully preserved flute in a tattered haversack. Back at Wesleyan, his health improved, Sidney Lanier put the flute to his lips and joined Phillip Guttenberger and his pupils in impromptu musicals. At Wesleyan, Lanier met and later married Mary Day, the girl for whom he wrote some of his most poignant and beautiful poetry, and whom he serenaded with his silver flute.[26]

Macon had indeed escaped the direct assault of Sherman's army as it marched to the sea in 1864, but in March 1865, Maconites were feverishly preparing to resist the advance of Major General James H. Wilson, who was gathering heavily armed cavalry in Tennessee. Wilson's "Raiders" left their camps along the Tennessee River and swiftly advanced through Selma, Alabama, and Columbus, Georgia, and along the Macon and Western Railroad to Macon. As they had done before Sherman's advance on Atlanta, citizens fled before Wilson's troops. Throughout the night of May 18, wagons, horses, and conveyances of all types could be heard as they hurried away from Macon, ahead of Wilson's advancing cavalry. A haggard Sidney Lanier was observed boarding a train that was hastily assembled and packed with refugees fleeing Macon.[27]

The war was over. Lee had already surrendered. The Confederacy was dead. One of Wilson's last acts as his Raiders swept through Georgia was the capture of Jefferson Davis, the Confederate president, who had been pursued to his camp near Irwinville on May 10, 1865. Wilson brought Davis and his family to Macon and housed them temporarily in the Lanier House, where he had a "sumptuous meal" served to them. Later Wilson sent Davis, in chains, to Fort Monroe, Virginia, where he remained a prisoner for more than two years. Finally, charges of treason against him were dropped, and he was released on December 25, 1868. In old age and despite ill health, the Confederate president nevertheless continued eloquently to urge reconciliation with the North until his death in 1889.

---

[26]Lanier, *Poems and Letters*, v, 15.

[27]Jones, *Yankee Blitzkrieg*, 165.

Macon had suffered relatively little damage at Wilson's hands, if by comparison one thinks of the burning of Atlanta by Sherman's army. Macon soon was restored to a semblance of normalcy, and the citizens returned to their usual occupations. Wilson had taken up headquarters at the Lanier House with the assigned task of "restoring order." Union soldiers assisted Macon authorities in "clearing the city of strange negroes." Wilson observed that Maconites, "perceiving that we were not barbarians . . . gradually softened in their behavior, and some even went so far as to speak of us as fellow countrymen."[28]

Phillip Guttenberger had resumed teaching. Classes at Wesleyan had been suspended for only two days when Macon was surrendered to General Wilson, and for only two weeks in November 1864 when Sherman's raid of Macon had been imminent. Captors and captives alike were ready for peace and restoration throughout the town. *Macbeth* was performed on schedule before a large audience in the theater house, and Cooke's restaurant on Mulberry Street did a brisk business in mint juleps and turtle soup. Commencement exercises, including the traditional instrumental and choral presentations, took place as usual during the course of a few blazingly hot July days.

It was not until three years later, during the period of Reconstruction, that Sidney Lanier was aroused "to authentic if brief lyricism" when he wrote "The Raven Days":[29]

Our hearths are gone out, and our hearts are broken
And but the ghosts of homes to us remain,
And ghostly eyes and hollow sighs give token
From friend to friend of an unspoken pain. . . .

Oh, Raven Days, dark Raven Days of sorrow,
Will ever any warm light come again?
Will ever the lit mountains of To-morrow
Begin to gleam across the mournful plain?[30]

Throughout those "dark Raven days of sorrow" about which Lanier wrote, Phillip Gerhart Guttenberger had brought some respite, some

---

[28]Ibid., 182-83.

[29]Parks, *Sidney Lanier*, 46.

[30]Cady, *American Poets*, 399.

"warm light" into the lives of others through his music and his teaching at Wesleyan. "Instrumental Music," taught by Professor Guttenberger and his assistants, still found a place in the college catalogues throughout the Reconstruction years, along with the notation that music "might be taken at the option of the parent or guardian in such a way as to impede as little as possible the progress of the pupil in her regular studies." It appears that Professor Guttenberger had changed both the types and technical difficulty of the music taught through the years. In response to this, one rather petulant reviewer wrote after attending a long commencement musical concert on a hot July day: "The programme was just one-third too long [and] there was too much scientific music in the programme, and not enough of that kind of music which pleases the popular taste."

The name of Emily Jane [Emma] Guttenberger of Vineville, Georgia, appeared on the July 14, 1868 Commencement Program when she read a composition, "Workers and Wishes."[31] The following year, again on a hot day, Emma received her degree from Wesleyan at the age of seventeen.

Phillip's will, dated October 21, 1872, and filed for record on July 9, 1874, in Bibb County, was a model of simplicity:

> I will and bequeath to my wife, Emily Guttenberger all my real estate consisting of my house and lot in Vineville . . . and at her death, all my property to be divided equally among my six children, and I . . . appoint E. H. Link as my executor.

Erastus Link guided the hand of his father-in-law as Phillip signed his will with an X.

Eleven years after the death of her father, Emma Guttenberger Nottingham purchased from her five brothers and sisters their portion of the willed property.[32] Thus Emma became the owner of the house in which, for a century and a quarter, Phillip Guttenberger and his descendants lived and made music. In later years, Emma and her husband, John Jacob Nottingham, moved the house at the end of the tree-lined carriage way, and had it rebuilt closer to Vineville Road, which by then was called Vineville Avenue. The carriage driveway became Lamar Street, along which lots were sold and houses built among the elm and oak and sweetgum trees that

---

[31]See Appendix: Guttenberger and Nottingham Lineal Charts. Also see Nottingham chapter.

[32]Deed Book 78, 523.

lined the block. For another half century the house of Phillip Guttenberger and his descendants stood among its own elms and wisteria-draped cedars at the corner of Lamar Street and Vineville Avenue.

In the August 30, 1964 edition of the *Macon Telegraph*, there appeared this commemorative to Phillip Guttenberger:

> When Wesleyan brought Phillip Guttenberger to Macon, that institution did as much for the mid-twentieth century city as it did for the little mid-nineteenth century town of Macon, and its new college for females. For Phillip Guttenberger started a musical dynasty that continues to the present and that has continuously furnished Macon with teachers and performers of music and composers, musicians to whose tunes generations of feet have danced or marched, musicians with whose accompaniments generations of voices have been raised in church hymns or have burst into quicker time in popular song.[33]

---

[33]*Macon Telegraph and News*, August 30, 1964.

*Chapter Six*

---

# Smith B. Nottingham
## (1799-?)

*. . .Squandered. . .his substance in debauchery. . .*[1]

D uring the years 1640-1650, many sturdy British farmers and their families remained loyal to the Stuart king, Charles I, in the king's disputes with Puritan leader Oliver Cromwell. By 1642 British subjects were faced with the troubling necessity of choosing sides, since the issues at stake—Cromwell's struggle for the rights of Parliament and the common law on the one hand, and the king's resistance on the other—were so fundamental to certain men of the landed gentry that compromise proved impossible. Men were torn by conflicting loyalties. Numbers of English families emigrated to the colony of Virginia, rather than remain in England during the ongoing contests between the Crown and Cromwell's army, which had dealt Charles's forces a resounding defeat at Naseby in 1645. Among those who fled England during the years of English Civil War were some members of the landed gentry known as Cavaliers. They became

---

[1]Chancery Causes Determined, 1831-1842. Divorce petition dated December 3, 1834.

the masters of vast lands in Virginia that they developed into plantations, the splendor and comfort of which had never before been seen in America. These gentlemen, relatively few in number, with their fine clothes, rare wines, elegant furniture, well-bred horses, and many servants, brought a distinctive taste of English country life to Virginia.[2] Those wealthy planters were almost unanimous in their allegiance to King Charles and the Anglican establishment.

The Richard Nottinghams of County Kent were one such family of landed gentry who, at the time, were fiercely loyal to the Crown, and who chose to cast their lot in America, preferring the uncertainties of settling on the unknown shores of Virginia to the known hazards of domestic war. Since the early sixteenth century, the Nottinghams had built upon, occupied, and nurtured lands in County Kent, which lies between the Thames estuary and the Strait of Dover in southeast England. Chalky North Downs crosses the county from east to west, and to the south lie the fertile Weald and Romney marshes.

Richard (born about 1621) was the scion of the County Kent branch of the Nottingham family that elected to migrate to America.[3] Richard's mother was of the Pett family, noted for distinguished sea service and credited with founding the English Navy many decades before. Elizabeth Hutton (in some sources called "Lady Elizabeth") became Richard's bride in her early teens. She was not concerned with political matters; yet she was attracted to the unknown, and as filled with a spirit of adventure as was Richard. She sailed with him to America, arriving on the Virginia shore in 1645. Well supplied with a fair measure of worldly goods, as well as with a contingent of manservants and maidservants, they left the perils of conflict in England behind them. Richard sailed with his family's blessing and, what is more important, with a fat purse of sovereigns on his person and more in his strongbox.[4]

Richard Nottingham and Elizabeth (the title "Lady," if she ever had it, was precipitously dropped when they disembarked on the Virginia shore) were well settled in Northampton County in what is now known as Wil-

---

[2]Craven, *Southern Colonies*, 224ff.

[3]Tyler and Lewis, *Virginia Biography*, 5:827.

[4]Ezell, *Family Encyclopedia of Southern History*, 191.

sonia Neck, on the Eastern Shore of Chesapeake Bay. They were thus the first Americans in a long line of descendants bearing the "ancient and honorable English name of Nottingham."[5] They had a family of five sons and one daughter, records of whose marriages survive, as well as several additional daughters about whom little is now known.

Unlike many earlier colonists who came in poverty, and through hardship and privation established lives in Massachusetts and Virginia, Richard and Elizabeth were almost immediately able to set up a life—if not of ease, surely of comfort and plenty, and not unlike the lives of the gentry from the English countryside. With his plentiful supply of gold sovereigns, Richard bought land located "between Hungar's Creek and Mattawones" in Northampton County. A tract of one thousand acres just north of Eastville was purchased from Captain William Stone, who in 1648 was appointed governor of Maryland by Lord Baltimore.[6] From the years 1651 through 1682 there are numerous records of land and livestock purchased by Richard Nottingham, including, on two occasions, purchase of a total of 450 acres of land in Northampton County from William Whittington.[7]

Richard served as a road surveyor, and there is a record that on December 29, 1687, he was "ordered to clear the way for the road from the Hornes to the Bridge at Hungars." This was a task that, although done under direction of Northampton officials, was sure to benefit Richard personally, as some of his property was located in the Hungars Bridge area. County records of Virginia during the seventeenth century—deed books, marriage records, court records, and other county documents—include an "extraordinary array of names, which . . . have been intimately associated with English social or political history." Among those is the name of "Nottingham, which, after 250 years association with the social and political life of the Eastern Shore, . . . continues to be one of the most prominent of all those seated in that part of Virginia."[8]

---

[5]Whitelaw, *Virginia's Eastern Shore*, 317ff.

[6]Nottingham, *History of Upson County*, 965.

[7]Deed Book for year 1657: purchase by "Richard Nottingham, Gent., of 1,000 acres from Capt. William Stone, on 13 May 1657." Whitelaw, *Virginia's Eastern Shore*, 318. Grantors and Grantees, 1632-1732: 4:33; 7:41; 9:115; 11:92; 14:58.

[8]Bruce, *Social Life of Virginia*, 58, 98f.

Richard planted his lands in tobacco, and turned profits year after year. He entered more and more into the social, political, and religious life of the Eastern Shore. Almost immediately upon becoming established, Richard was drawn into joining with his neighboring Northampton landowners in voicing their anger when Parliamentary commissioners imposed a tax upon them of forty-six pounds of tobacco per poll:

> We, the Inhabitants of Northampton Countie doe complayne that from tyme to tyme wee have been submitted & bine obedient unto the paymt of publeq taxacons. Butt after ye yeare 1647, since yt tyme wee Conceive & have found that ye taxes were very weightie. But in a more espetiall manner . . . the taxacon of forty sixe pounds of tobacco p. poll (this present yeare). And desire yt ye same bee taken off ye charge of ye Countie; furthermore wee alledge that after 1647, wee did understand & suppose or Countie or Northampton to be disioynted & sequestered from ye rest of Virginia. Therefore that Llawe wch requireth & inioyneth Taxacons from us to bee Arbitrarye & illegall; forasmuch as wee had neither summons for ellecon of Burgesses nor voyce in their Assemblye (during the time aforesd) but only the Singular Burgess in September, Ano., 1651. We conceive that wee may Lawfullie ptest agt the pceedings in the Act of the Assemblie for publeq Taxacons wch have relacon to Northmton Countie since ye year 1647.[9]

Richard enlarged his holdings in lands on which, under continuing protest, he paid his "publeq taxacons."

Along with most of the Anglican settlers who came to Virginia in the midseventeenth century to escape the civil strife in England, Richard was loyal to the Crown during the first few years he lived in Virginia. As with most Virginians, an ideal arrangement for Richard Nottingham would have been one in which he was on friendly terms with the English government, but was left free in his trade of the considerable produce—mainly tobacco—raised from his lands. Yet it was necessary to accommodate the authority of Cromwell's regime as a first condition for this arrangement.[10] By March 1651 Richard Nottingham was, to all intents and purposes, compelled to make such concessions. Oliver Cromwell sent out an expedition to force the colony of Virginia to adhere to the Puritan Commonwealth; the Articles of Surrender are dated March 12, 1651. But the day before, on March 11, an

[9]Wertenbaker, *Shaping of Colonial Virginia*, 139.

[10]Clerk's Office, "List of Tithables in Northampton," 195.

important paper was initiated to which the signature "Rich. Nottingham" was affixed, along with the signatures of 175 additional tax-paying, land-owning Northampton County citizens. "By the terms of the Engagement they do not exactly *surrender* to the British Parliament . . . but only agree to yield a peaceable and orderly obedience to it, as to the government *de facto*, if not *de jure*: a fair distinction, and, no doubt, a piece of sound discretion."[11]

> The Engagm't tendered to ye Inhabitants of Northampton County Eleaventh of March 1651. Ano. 1651. . . . . Wee whose Names are sub-scribed; doe hereby Engage and promise to bee true and faithful to tht Common-Wealth of England as it is Nowe Established without Kinge or House of Lords. . . .[12]

Following the "surrender" of the colony to the Commonwealth government, like other Virginia planters who had taken leave of England during the early years of Civil War there, Richard and Elizabeth Nottingham and their children[13] lived comfortably and expansively. Indeed, with the Commonwealth busy at home in England, Virginia was practically independent until 1680, engaging in free trade with foreigners, and enjoying the profits of an expanding tobacco trade. Richard gave personal attention to his slaves and plantation affairs, and was especially active in attending political meetings, church services, and vestry meetings at Hungars Episcopal Church. The first vestry had been appointed in 1635, and although the exact record of the date is unfortunately lost, an edifice to house the Hungars congregation was built near that time in the midst of a grove of sycamores, seven miles north of Eastville. Members of the Nottingham family served as vestrymen throughout the ensuing years, including Richard's son, Benjamin, his grandson, Joseph, and others of Richard's kin.

Richard [I] Nottingham was seventy-one when he died. He bequeathed his estate to his sons, including Richard [II], his eldest, born about 1652. In 1981 some of Richard [I]'s land was still owned by his descendants. His children were considered "an honor to their father." They participated in political affairs of the country and served as vestrymen in Hungars Church. One was county peace commissioner, and another became high sheriff of Northampton County, appointed by Queen Anne

---

[11]Craven, *Southern Colonies*, 248.

[12]Virginia Historical Register, 1-2:163-65; 1:263.

[13]See Appendix: Nottingham Lineal Chart and Family Group Record.

through a special patent for "conspicuous service."[14]

By astute management of his lands, Richard [I] increased his fortune in his life-time. His two sons, Richard [II] and Benjamin, between whom the bulk of Richard [I]'s properties were divided upon his death in 1692, became wealthy "gentlemen of property." Richard had continued in America a pattern of achievement and land man-agement that his forebears had established in County Kent in England. His sons and grandsons carried the tradition forward on the Eastern Shore of Virginia.

Richard [II] was married three times: first to Mary Clark (about 1672), who was the daughter of Elizabeth Clark Bundick, and the stepdaughter of Richard Bundick. [15] The fact that Mary Clark was the stepdaughter of Richard Bundick contributed to the ongoing good fortunes of the descendants of Richard [I] Nottingham; for Mary's mother gave her the estate she received from her second husband, Richard Bundick, as recorded in the Northampton County Deed Book on October 28, 1698. [16] Richard Bundick's considerable fortune thus succeeded to his stepdaughter, Mary Clark Not-tingham, and through her to her son Jacob [I] Nottingham. [17] Jacob [I]'s[18] lands and goods passed from son to son, going to Thomas [II] (1730-1797), to Jacob [III], who married Bridget Brickhouse on January 26, 1794, and from him to his son, Smith B. Nottingham, who was born in 1799.

Thomas Nottingham served his country during the Revolution, as shown on the muster rolls and payrolls of the 27th Regiment of the Virginia Militia of Nothampton County. In the Minute Book for the years 1777-1783 was recorded: "The Court doth recommend to his Excellency Patrick Henry Jun[r] Esq[r] Governor of Virginia—Thos Nottingham Jun[r] Ensign of Captain Glanville's Company." The notation is dated Sep-tember 9, 1777. [19] Another notation shows that "the Court doth appoint Thomas Not-tingham, Jun[r] Lieu[t]."

The poll of vote of Northampton County, Virginia, held in 1789 for president of the United States, includes in the list of voters the names of Thomas Nottingham and his good friend, John Brickhouse, Sr., whose children had married members of Nottingham's family. The 1789 election was the first election held for president of the

---

[14]Tyler and Lewis, *Virginia Biography*, 817.

[15]See Appendix: Nottingham Group Record.

[16]See Appendix: Nottingham Lineal Chart.

[17]Grantors and Grantees, Deed Index, 1632-1732, 7.

[18]Ibid., 20:196; 19:359, 120.

[19]Ibid., Will Book, 30:302.

United States. Henry Guy was the elector who was expected to vote for George Washington, and it was for Guy that Thomas and John cast their votes on January 7, 1789. George Washington was indeed elected, and was inaugurated later that same year.

The wills of men in the Nottingham family, many of which were carefully recorded in the Will Books of Northampton County, for the most part reflect astuteness, thoughtful planning, concern for their heirs, and special requests that their lands be well cared for and remain in family ownership. Often there were warnings not to sell the lands outside the family, as if the departing spirit might return to haunt offenders.

There was one especially sagacious Nottingham will, recorded in Northampton County on July 10, 1797,[20] when Thomas Nottingham gave

> the whole of my Estate to my loving wife SCARBURGH NOT-
> TINGHAM during her natral life & at her death . . . to my Gran Son
> William Nottingham two hundred & seven Acors of land liing in the
> north side of my plantation where I now live [and] to my Gran Daughter
> Sally Nottingham one negro Gail name Dinah and a Dressing Table . .
> . to my three Gran Sons Nary Samuel Williams and John Williams and
> William Williams Sons of John Williams and Edith Williams[21] twenty
> pounds each & for them to have no other part of my estate. . . .

As later recorded in his will, Thomas, seven years before his death in 1797, had already given his son Jacob [II] his just portion of land from the estate, which consisted of "all the land that I purchased of Rispus Liing on King's Creek." Jacob [II] was to "have no more of my estate but what [was] given in October 11, 1790." So Jacob [II] received his share of the estate from his father, and he inherited his portion of the estate of Richard Bundick,

---

[20]Ibid., 31:489.

[21]See Appendix: Thomas [I] Nottingham Family Group Record. Note that Edith Nottingham married John Williams and Mary Nottingham married John's brother, William Williams. Also note that Thomas [I]'s daughters Margaret, Sarah, and Susanna married three Brickhouse brothers. Several daughters of one family marrying several sons of a family from a neighboring plantation was not rare in Virginia and South Carolina in the seventeenth and early eighteenth centuries. With distances great and opportunities slim for meeting potential marriage partners, double and even triple ceremonies among neighboring families and among first and second cousins were frequent.

his mother's stepfather. Jacob [II] had received the gift of land from his father a few months after he married Bridget Brickhouse.[22]

Jacob started married life as a "man of wealth and position" and his children, Margaret (Peggy), Mary S., Smith B., and possibly others, were born into a family of affluence and prestige. Thomas, Jacob's father, seems especially to have benefited during his lifetime from improvements in transportation for his tobacco crops and the growth of scientific agricultural methods in the processing and curing of his tobacco crops. Whether Thomas participated in the growing business in Virginia of breeding slaves for profit is unclear, but he was a slaveowner, as were his forebears.

Thomas did his part in husbanding the family lands and monies, as did his son, Jacob [II]. The same was not so of Jacob's son, Smith B. Nottingham, born in Northampton County in 1799.

In a few short years, Smith B. Nottingham put an end to the portion of the family fortunes that he inherited from his father, Jacob [II]. "He squandered . . . his substance in debauchery,"[23] and money and property that through generations had been guarded, cherished, astutely managed and increased, vanished in an alcoholic breath. By 1830 Smith B. Nottingham had become "desperate and reckless in his conduct . . . wanton and cruel . . . intoxicated and menacing." These were harsh words for a man who seems to have meant no harm to his frail and gentle wife, Mary Elliott Nottingham (1805-1859), until "Demon Rum" reared its head. There can be no doubt that Smith was an irresponsible, ill-tempered, drunken rascal of the worst sort, who was prone to wife-beating. The likes of Smith the Nottinghams had never before seen among their kind.

Smith B. Nottingham, born September 20, 1799, was the oldest of the two sons of Jacob [II] and Bridget Brickhouse Nottingham. Smith's sisters were Margaret (Peggy), who married Obed Hunt, and Mary S., who remained single; both girls were older than Smith. Smith grew up in an affluent household, waited upon by the family slaves, pampered and spoiled, especially by his mother after his father died when Smith was nine years old. Smith grew to maturity apparently carefree and undisciplined by his doting

---

[22]Princess Anne County Records, 1:5:121.

[23]Chancery Causes Determined, 1831-1842. Divorce petition dated December 3, 1834.

mother. Smith's father had made his will in 1804, and it was proved on October 9, 1809.[24]

Bridget occupied the plantation her husband left her for a year after his death, managing it with the aid of the slaves, then selling the crop "for the benefit of my Estate" as Jacob had decreed. He also willed "to my loving wife Bridget Nottingham my plantation with my negroes until my Son Smith Nottingham arrives at the age of Twenty-one years, with her supporting and educating my children until that Period."

Unlike the sagacious wills made and executed by the Nottinghams throughout the decades—by which Nottingham "goods and chattels" had been passed from generation to generation—the will of Jacob Nottingham [II] brought about disastrous consequences.

When Smith became twenty-one years old in 1821, as specified in his father's will, his father's estate was sold, and the money "ensuing from such sale" was equally divided among his children. Until Smith reached his majority, all in accordance with the will, Bridget supported and educated the children "until that period." When Smith was twenty-three, on December 29, 1823, the slaves owned by Jacob [II] were equally divided among his five children.[25]

By 1824 Smith was in full possession of the lands, goods, and slaves willed him by his father. He reveled in his substance. With Henry B. Kendall, he bought a schooner he named *Delta*. In addition, he ran up bills of various kinds. There are numerous records of suits filed to satisfy his indebtedness. The poor management of his money cost him the *Delta*. Everything seemed to come easy for Smith, and just as easily slip from his hands. For a while there also seems to have been plenty of substance from which to draw; and it was in this period that he appeared to Mary H. Elliott as a fine, trustworthy gentleman of good family and character. She agreed to marry him.

Mary H. Elliott (1805-1859) was the daughter of John Elliott (1778-1816) and Polly Nolen. Mary (called "Polly" in her father's will) had an older sister named Nancy, who was married in 1820 to Daniel G. Smaw. John and Polly Elliott had other children: Grace, Rosey, and John Thomas. However,

---

[24]Grantors and Grantees, Will Book, NCV, 5:33, 128.

[25]Ended Causes, November 1823-February 1824. Bill of Complaint for Execution of Will of Jacob [II] Nottingham and division of slaves and property.

it was to her sister Nancy and her husband, Daniel Smaw, that Mary turned for understanding, love, and support in the difficult life she lived as the wife of Smith B. Nottingham. John Elliott made his will on November 30, 1815, and by May 13, 1816, he had died; the will was proved on that date.[26] Mary was a child of ten when her father died. Indeed, both Mary and her future husband were left fatherless as children. By the time that Mary was married at seventeen to Smith, she was recorded as the "Ward of Daniel G. Smaw," her sister's husband.

For some years after their marriage on April 4, 1826,[27] Mary H. Elliott and Smith B. Nottingham "lived together quite happily."[28] Two children were born and lived to maturity: John Jacob (1830-1887) and Martha Ann (1835-1897).[29] Shortly before John Jacob was born, Smith was licensed to keep a tavern at Scott's Branch. Perhaps increasing family responsibilities that he was ill prepared to accept, and the temptations of tavern ownership combined to bring about Smith's downfall, for his name became more and more evident in court records. He was sued for nonpayment of debts and charged with excessive drinking. Moreover, in drunken fits he mistreated his wife and children.

Having endured the humiliations and bodily harm inflicted by a habitually drunken husband, and after agonizing soul-searching, Mary Elliott Nottingham filed a divorce petition. That she brought herself to the point of petitioning for divorce was in itself an act of great courage, because she feared for her life and the lives of her children. In 1834 divorce was a most dreadful sin: it was whispered about behind handkerchiefs and never mentioned publicly. It was at risk of being completely ignored, or worse, being ostracized from her church and society, that on December 4, 1834, Mary made one of the few recorded petitions for divorce in Northampton County in the early nineteenth century. She filed through her brother, John T. Elliott, as her "next friend"[30]:

---

[26]Grantors and Grantees, Will Book, NCV, 34:296.

[27]Nottingham, *Marriage License Bonds of Northampton*, 67.

[28]Chancery Causes Determined, 1831-1842. Divorce petition dated December 3, 1834.

[29]See Appendix: Smith B. Nottingham Family Group Record.

[30]Chancery Causes Determined, 1831-1842. Divorce petition dated December 3, 1834.

To the Honorable Abel F. Upstien, Judge of the Circuit Court of Law and Chancery of the County of Northampton: . . . your oratrix MARY H. NOTTINGHAM, a *feme covert*, who sues by JOHN T. EL-LIOTT, her next friend [on the] 9th day of April 1825, intermarried with a certain SMITH B. NOTTINGHAM of the County of Northampton. [She shows] that for some years past, the said Smith B. Nottingham has been an habitual drunkard; and when intoxicated, is sometime desperate and reckless in his conduct, threatening to kill your oratrix and treating her in a most cruel and unusual manner; . . . [his treatment was] so wanton and cruel to [her] that she cannot live with him without the utmost danger to her personal safety. That the weapons of civility, kindness and conjugal affection have not been able to disarm his temper of its impetuosity, nor his conduct of its recklessness and cruelty that his words of menace, importing the danger of bodily harm, have been so frequently used and so often executed upon your oratrix that she verily believes, were she living under the same roof with him, she would be constantly liable to be grievously and cruelly treated, and her person in imminent danger. That she has frequently been compelled to get gentlemen to accompany her home (who were her acquaintances and relatives) and they have seen his open treatment to her to be such as has impressed them with the belief that her personal safety was in great danger. That he has frequently struck as well as otherwise illy treated your oratrix, threatening to kill her.

That the said Smith B. Nottingham no longer keeps house, but is going from place to place, spending his substance in debauchery. . . . That he turned your oratrix pretty much upon the charity of her friends.

In support of Mary Elliott Nottingham's petition for divorce, depositions were taken from several family friends who were her "acquaintences [*sic*] and relatives." These included one from John W. Beggs, a neighbor who swore under oath on January 9, 1835, that he frequently heard Smith threaten to "whip his wife and abuse her in a shameful manner." Beggs swore that in 1831 he had been at Smith's house and that "while the family was at supper [Smith] rose from the table, threatening to whip his wife," and he would have done so had not Beggs "interferred, and carried Mary away through the rain to the house of a neighbor."

The deponent, Victor A. Nottingham, Smith's cousin, swore that "in the year 1831 or 2 he lived with Smith B. Nottingham . . . he frequently knew the defendant to come home intoxicated during the night—to excite by menacing conduct, fears in the mind of his wife for her personal safety, so much so that she several times left her home with her child, at a late hour and remained from home for several days until the defendant got over his drunken frolic." Walter Luker swore that when Smith was having one of his "drunken frolics," he had seen Mary pass his store on the way to her sister's house; and Severn Wilkins testified he had "frequently heard Smith abuse and threaten his wife, and [he had] repeatedly heard him do so on public occasions."

The divorce petition was filed, with the case well buttressed by the most damning evidence ever brought against the ancient and heretofore honorable name of Nottingham. Smith failed to appear and answer to a subpoena, and the final decree was granted on November 13, 1825.[31]

One item of the decree stated that "in tender consideration of the premises, . . . the said Smith B. Nottingham" was restrained and enjoined from disposing of the three slaves that belonged to Mary and of the thirty acres of land that were lawfully hers, having been willed to her by her father. The court further ordered that "the plaintiff and the defendant be separated from bed and board forever." It was "the duty of each of them to live chastely during their Separation;" neither of them during the life of the other should "contract matrimony with any other person." Mary received the custody of the children and Smith was enjoined to pay Mary for their support. Significantly, Mary now had "possession and absolute control of the tract or parcel of land" and the slaves that were hers.

From that time on, Mary Elliott Nottingham and her children, John Jacob and Martha, were presumably left in peace in her house and on her land in the lower part of Northampton County, east of Capeville. At least Smith must have kept up his payments for support of the children, for the name of Smith B. Nottingham disappeared from the court records, indeed from all Northampton County records. No record of his date of death has been found.

Mary and her sister, Nancy Elliott Smaw, were close and supportive of each other throughout their lives. Nancy's husband, Daniel, who had served as guardian for Mary before her marriage to Smith, died before 1832 at an early age.[32] After Mary sold her land in 1837—the acreage left to her by her father—she took her children and slaves, including one named Rosie, and went to live with her sister Nancy. The two single women— Nancy by Daniel's death and Mary by one of the first recorded divorces in

[31]Ibid.

[32]Will Book for year 1832, 199.

Northampton County—combined their families and resources. Martha and John Jacob Nottingham were reared with the Smaw children. Martha never married, died in 1897, and was buried in a small, abandoned plot near Cheriton, Virginia. Her mother, Mary Elliot Nottingham, was also buried there after her death in 1859, at the age of fifty-four, from what the records show as "consumption."

Mary lived a joyless and difficult married life; but through her children, who were both quite young at the time of the divorce, she found purpose. She reared her children well, and left them a legacy of love for themselves and others that sustained them throughout their lives. When John Jacob married years later and had a daughter of his own, he named her Mary Elliott (May) Nottingham for his beloved mother; and when Martha died childless, she willed her small estate to her brother's children, whom she thought of as her own.

By 1850, when he was twenty-one years old, John Jacob had left the home of his mother and aunt and was maintaining a dwelling place of his own. In that year his residence is listed separately from his mother, and he is shown as a "Schoolmaster" in the census records of Northampton County. Of the many generations of Nottingham ancestors who had preceded him in America, John Jacob Nottingham may well have been the first—there have been many since—who made it through life without the benefit of at least a modicum of inherited wealth. His father had done a thorough job of disposing of his inherited substance as well as a good deal of his wife's inheritance. John Jacob Nottingham became a schoolmaster to make a living for himself.[33]

In the *New York Herald* of August 19, 1848, an article appeared announcing the discovery of gold in California around the hills east of Sutter's Fort. As did many impecunious, adventurous, and unattached young men of all breeds and intents, John Jacob Nottingham read the accounts and listened avidly to the stories that there was gold in those California hills for the taking. The next year, on February 28, 1849, the first shipload of gold seekers docked at San Francisco. John Jacob left his job as schoolmaster, bade his mother, aunt, and sister goodbye and set out for the Land of Gold. He left, not on the first shipload, but months thereafter, possibly joining one

---

[33]Virginia Census, 1850, Family 23.

of the wagon trains assembled on the banks of the Missouri for the trek westward on the heavily traveled California Trail.

There is a later account that claims John Jacob Nottingham prospered as a young man in California.[34] Just where he prospered and how long he stayed in California is not clear. Perhaps he returned to Virginia when he heard that his mother was ill; she died in 1859. There is no doubt that wherever he was, he knew of Virginia's desperate effort to maintain a moderate course in the rift over the future course of slavery. Not until April 25, 1861, when President Abraham Lincoln called up the Federal troops after the firing on Fort Sumter, did Virginia finally throw in her lot with the Confederacy.

John Jacob Nottingham let his beard grow long during the months he "prospered" in California. He kept it long the remainder of his life. When war broke out, he returned home to Virginia to enlist in the Confederate army, where he served in Mosby's Rangers. He was captured, and remained in a Union army prison until war's end. He came to Macon after his release to visit relatives, and remained there to take up life as a businessman and small dairy farmer.

[Archives, Middle Georgia Historical Society]

[34]*Macon Telegraph*, February 8, 1887.

John Jacob returned to Virginia to serve as a Partisan Ranger in Mosby's Regiment of the Confederate army.[35] On the receipt rolls for the fourth quarter of 1864, "J. J. Nottingham" signed a receipt for clothing. There is a certificate from Union Army Headquarters dated May 17, 1865, that John J. Nottingham signed as a prisoner of war, in which he swore: "I do hereby give my solemn Parole of Honor not to take part in hostilities against the Government of the United States until properly exchanged. . . ." So he served in the army, was captured, made prisoner, then released, and was back in Virginia as a civilian by mid-1865. John Jacob remained with his sister Martha and Aunt Nancy Smaw for awhile. Perhaps he visited his mother's grave at the small plot just south of Cheriton. The stone bore the inscription: "Mary Elliott Nottingham, born April 14, 1805, died October 14, 1859."

Several cousins of John Jacob Nottingham—all descendants of the Richard Nottingham [I] who had come to Virginia in the late seventeenth century—had migrated to Georgia in the mid-nineteenth century. One of those cousins was Dr. Custis Bell Nottingham, born in Northampton County, Virginia, in 1818. Custis married Rebecca Virginia Thompson and they had several children, among whom were sons Warren and Marshall. During the years before the Civil War, Dr. Nottingham, a graduate of the Jefferson Medical College in Philadelphia, had "attained marked prominence as a skillful practitioner" in Macon, Georgia. When war was imminent, he promptly volunteered his services and was assigned to a post in Louisiana. Upon his return to Macon on January 1, 1866, his former patients "rejoiced at his return, and soon he was again in a large and arduous practice."[36] Members of the Hunt family were also cousins of John Jacob who had earlier come to Georgia and made lives for themselves in Macon.

The war was over. Macon's share of the 174,233 ragged Southern veterans had struggled home.[37] Few could look to the future without misgivings, if not despair. But they were proud people, and they set about cleaning and patching up their clothes and their lives. Atlanta was energetically rising from its ashes and Macon, like other cities of Georgia, was finding the

---

[35]Confederate Roster Books, 13:331.

[36]Southern Historical Association, *Memoirs of Georgia*, 2:229.

[37]Ezell, *The South Since 1865*, 25.

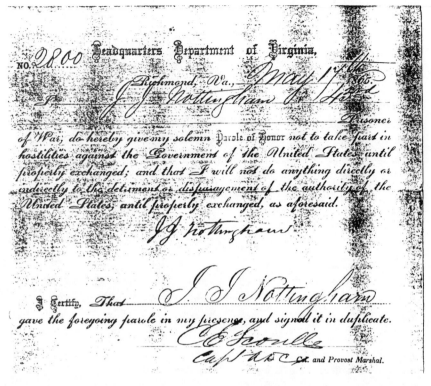

John Jacob Nottingham received this parole of honor, dated May 17, 1865, upon his release from Federal prison at the close of the Civil War.

[National Archives, Washington DC]

Reconstruction years to be a time of resurgence and economic growth. New commercial businesses were prospering in Macon. Old businesses—those that during the war dealt in the manufacture of war supplies—gave way to industries such as small cotton or lumber mills. New banks were opened, the railroads into and out of town were improved and extended. Displaced planters were moving to town, seeking and finding work in the mills, opening small stores for "hard goods and soft goods." Factors and lawyers, ministers and doctors were in demand, as well as grocers, hotel operators, accountants, mill hands and blacksmiths, buggy and wagon dealers, carpenters and bricklayers. The Brown Hotel and Lanier House were filled with traveling drummers ready to supply for a fee many of the goods and services unavailable in war years. The pages of the local press were filled with announcements for banks, dry goods stores, and forthcoming concerts and musicals; but the newspaper did not always provide the news on time: "Last night while the power press was in operation, a long screw driver was dropped into the machinery, and cogs flew like hail stone," read the article in the *Telegraph*. A late paper was delivered to subscribers with apologies.

For the most part Macon, as well as all of Georgia, was slowly recovering from its war wounds. Macon began to share in the good; the dark days were passing. Law and order was prevailing, and business was picking up. More often than not, Dr. Nottingham's bills were paid in cash, by checks that could be validly cashed at the bank. Less frequently were his fees paid now by produce from the land: a dozen eggs to treat an earache, or a couple of fat hens to set a broken arm.

When Dr. Custis Nottingham and the Hunts invited John Jacob to visit them in Macon, he readily accepted. He had no job that held him, no wife, no close ties beyond his sister and aunt in Virginia. So he came to Macon to look around and perhaps, if all he heard about the prosperity of the town were true, to find employment and take up life there. He visited awhile with the Hunts and the doctor's family, attended services with his hosts at the First Presbyterian Church on Mulberry Street, and fell in love with Emily Jane Guttenberger, the daughter of the Wesleyan College music professor, for she had looked particularly pretty singing in the choir that morning. John Jacob found a job as a bookkeeper for Jones and Cook, wholesale grocers with offices at the corner of Cotton Avenue and Cherry Street in downtown Macon. He found a place to live and for a few months his two young cousins, the sons of Dr. Nottingham, lived with him: Marshall, twenty-one, who was employed as a drug clerk, and Warren, nineteen; their names were listed with his in the 1870 Bibb County Census.

John Jacob paid court to Emily Jane at the Guttenberger home on Vineville Avenue. When the two were married, John Jacob slipped a wide gold wedding band on her finger bearing the inscription "JJN to EJN Dec. 6, 1870." Emily Jane—he called her Emma—was eighteen, John Jacob, forty. Whether the difference in age between the two gave John Jacob pause in marrying Emma is uncertain. Undoubtedly he would precede Emma in death, leaving her with small children. Still, for sixteen years they enjoyed a happy family life—something that John Jacob had never known as a child.

He continued to work at Jones and Cook, and later with E. Price's Sons. The couple boarded awhile, then went to live with Emma's parents in the Guttenberger home in Vineville. Emma's father died in 1874, after which management of the land devolved to John Jacob. He started a small dairy and continued work with a wholesale grocery firm. Julia Lee was born, followed by Stonewall Jackson—everybody called him "Gen"—so named because of his father's admiration for the Confederate general. When a second daughter was born in 1879, John Jacob named her for his mother. Mary Elliott Nottingham [II], known as "May" all her life, was only eight when her father died and the baby called "J.J." was eight months old.

*Emily Jane (Emma) Guttenberger was eighteen when she married John Jacob Nottingham, who was twenty-two years her senior. Left a widow in 1887 at thirty-four, Emma provided for her family by teaching music, following in the footsteps of her father, Professor Phillip Gerhart Guttenberger.*

[Archives, Middle Georgia Historical Society]

One summer evening after John Jacob had herded the dairy cows into the barn for the night, he returned to the darkened house. As he entered the door, an intruder hit him a blow on the head and bolted into the darkness. John Jacob never knew what felled him. He at first seemed to recover, but only a few months later he was dead:

The death of Mr. John J. Nottingham occurred at his residence in Vineville yesterday morning at 8:30 o'clock, after an illness of ten days with pneumonia.

Mr. Nottingham was 56 years old. He was born in Northampton County, Virginia, but most of his younger days were spent in California, where he prospered. When the war broke out he returned to Virginia and entered the army, through the whole of which he served with distinction. Some time after the war he came to Macon and married Miss Emma Guttenberger. For a number of years he was employed as a bookkeeper for George S. Jones and Company. He made a good citizen, loved and respected by all. The funeral notice appears elsewhere.

The day of the funeral, February 9, 1887, Emma put on mourning clothes. Her dress was black silk to the wrists and ankles. A narrow white ruff edged the neck and a long black veil flowed from her small black bonnet. Black gloves and purse and high-button black shoes completed her costume. From that day forward, whenever she stepped out of the house, she wore widow's weeds—all black in winter, white in summer.

Emma had grown up in a house filled with music. As the daughter of Phillip Guttenberger, she was taught to play the piano as a child. Throughout her days at Vineville Academy and later at Wesleyan, she continued her studies in piano and voice. Now that John Jacob had died, her love of music and her faithfulness in practicing became her salvation. With her father's grand piano set up in the parlor, she began teaching. Neighbors and friends sent their children to Miss Emma. Each half hour after school in the afternoons, the pupils came, carrying their Czerny exercise books and their sheet music—Chopin, Liszt, Bach, and Beethoven. On a fair day, an early arrival would sit in the porch swing by the open parlor window, swinging in time to the music and awaiting his turn at the piano. Some of Miss Emma's pupils became inspired to continue their study of music and their parents sent them from these in-home lessons to study at conservatories.

The fatherless family managed rather well on what Emma realized from her piano classes. Although the house was "free and clear," the family "had everything but money." Yet one important asset they had were close Guttenberger and Nottingham relatives who contributed to the well-being of the widow and her children. The children's maiden aunt, Aunt Martha, visited from Virginia. When she died, John Jacob's children became heirs of her small estate.[38]

---

[38]Court of Ordinary, November Term, 1896, 198.

Julia Lee, the oldest child, married Thomas Cook, shortly thereafter becoming the mother of another "Emily." Julia Lee died when the baby was only eighteen months old, and Emma, at Thomas's request, became the baby's guardian. Emily Cook was accepted in the household of her grandmother Nottingham, and spent much of her childhood with her. While May was a student at Wesleyan, on many occasions she cuddled the baby Emily in one arm, held a textbook in the other, and by lamplight studied as she rocked her baby niece to sleep.

By 1917 most Americans and virtually all Southerners were unified against Germany for the cause of the Allied nations; but it was not until it became known that Germany was planning to invade the United States through Mexico that the country was ready to enter combat in World War I.[39] Emma saw J. J.—who had been born only months before his father's death—off to the war in France, and she lived to celebrate his homecoming from "over there" after the Armistice was signed.

Emma became ill with what Dr. J. R. Moore called Bright's disease. To the best of his knowledge, there was not much he could do to cure her, so he ordered her to stay in bed. She asked that her bed be rolled into the front parlor, near the piano. From that bed, for many months until her death, she carried on her teaching. She gave her last lesson only a few days before she died. On the front page of the *Macon Telegraph* on Sunday, November 7, 1920, the story appeared:

> Mrs. Emma Nottingham Dies. Funeral will be Held Tomorrow from Vineville Presbyterian Church In the homestead in which she was born and reared, Mrs. Emma Nottingham, widow of J. J. Nottingham, died at 6:30 o'clock last night, at No. 417 Vineville Avenue.
>
> Mrs. Nottingham was one of Macon's best known women, a gifted musician and teacher and beloved by a wide circle of friends. Mrs. Nottingham was the daughter of Phillip Guttenberger, who was one of Wesleyan College's first Professors of Music.
>
> She is survived by two sons and one daughter, S. J. Nottingham and J. J. Nottingham, and Mrs. Furman D. Lawton, all of this city.
>
> The funeral will take place at the Vineville Presbyterian Church on Monday at noon, the service to be conducted by Rev. J. H. Owens, the pastor. Interment will be in Rose Hill Cemetery.

---

[39]Linton, *The Bicentennial Almanac*, 290.

Mary Elliott Nottingham Lawton (May) inherited the house on Vineville Avenue from her mother, and she and her husband Furman reared their children there. After Emma's death the formerly detached kitchen house was joined to the main house and everything was papered, painted, and renovated. A gas lighting system replaced the oil lamps; a monstrous gas Instantaneous Hot Water Heater was installed in the bathroom. The telephone operator responded promptly with "Number, please" when the crank was turned on the new phone in the back hall. Furman parked his new Model T in the driveway between the house and the Taylors' house next door.

On Vineville Avenue, tracks were installed and bright new trolley cars clanged up and down the entire four miles from Cherry Street to Crump's Park, where *Orphans of the Storm* was being shown at the moving-picture house.

## Chapter Seven

# BENJAMIN LAWTON
# WILLINGHAM
## (1829-1898)

*Patriarch and Provider*

A long the Southeastern coast between the mouths of the Santee River in Carolina and the St. James River in Florida, there is a low-lying chain of sea islands. The Spanish claimed and partly occupied them in 1568. Sir Robert Montgomery and John Barnwell[1] named them the Golden Islands in 1720 in a promotional brochure issued after the English made the islands part of the Carolina colony. Some of the islands were early looked upon as private little kingdoms. Rice and indigo and later cotton grew on lands granted by English kings to settlers who developed the region into plantations in many ways similar to English baronies.

As the islands were surveyed and settled, they were given such names as St. Helena, Hilton Head, Edisto, Hunting, Sullivans, Ladies, Fripp, St.

---

[1]See chapter on John Barnwell.

Simons, or simply, Sea Island. Boats and ferries, and in more recent years, bridges and causeways, link the islands to Charleston, Beaufort, Darien, Savannah, and the coastal plain, stretching inland for a hundred miles or more to the Carolina and Georgia Piedmont. There the land rises to terrain where short-staple cotton grows and where almost year-round, fruits of the land mature in plenty.

On the Golden Islands and in the Low Country coastal plain abound cypress and magnolias and oaks draped with Spanish moss. There are pines and gums, waterfowl and raccoons, reptiles and mosquitoes. There tall grasses of the marshy lowlands sway in the tidewaters. Rice and indigo and, later, silky Sea Island cotton became the foundation upon which fortunes were built on the Golden Islands and it in turn created need for the black man's labor.

In east England, on the Humbar estuary and the North Sea, lies Lincolnshire County over which—unlike the balmy breezes of the Golden Islands—blow cold winds and mists. Like the Sea Islands and coastal plain of Carolina, Lincolnshire is generally low and flat, with extensive marshes along its coast. Lincolnshire is crossed by many dikes and canals and, because of abundant water and soil nurtured through the ages, in the early eighteenth century was an important agricultural area.

In the early decades of that century, three Willingham brothers were born and reared in Lincolnshire on family lands in the area of Market-Rasen. America had become free of British rule only a few decades before and the Willingham brothers took their patrimony and sailed for the United States to seek new lands and warmer climes. Dr. Henry Woodward is often credited with introducing a crop that later would bring prosperity to those Willingham brothers and to other Carolina Low Country and Sea Island landowners. Potential treasure lay in a bag of Gold Seed Madagascar Rice that a sea captain had placed in Woodward's hands. He was told that "it grew well in open fields and even better in swampy lowland,"[2] as indeed it did. By 1696 so much rice was being produced that the planters were granted permission by the governing assembly to pay their quit-rents in the commodity.[3] The rice boom had begun, as had the boom in African slaves,

[2]Snell, *The Wild Shores, America's Beginning*, 156.

[3]Taylor, *Ante-Bellum South Carolina*, 1.

who under hard taskmasters were taking over the drudgery of rice production in the mosquito-infested, malaria-ridden swamplands.

The Willingham brothers decided to cultivate the tidal rice fields that were being developed at the time they received land grants. The method depended on banking the silt in wide beds of the rivers and fresh-water estuaries by a system of ditches, banks, and floodgates. The method required back-breaking labor often performed by working in shallow water for hours on end. It was labor that was performed by slaves. No fertilizer was required. Rewards were superlative. The fertile silt fed the growing plants year after year as it flowed over the fields. Gathering the ripe grains and especially husking were the most time-consuming aspects of making a crop; but after 1790, when Jonathan Lucas's successful method of pounding the husk from the grain was put into use, Low Country rice production became ever more profitable.

It was into a large, thriving community of well-fixed, industrious, slaveowning Carolina rice planters that the Willingham brothers settled. Two of the brothers—Joseph and Thomas—received six parcels of land between 1786 and 1788[4] as well as earlier grants in the Low Country. When the last grants were made to the brothers, America had been an independent nation for only a decade. George Washington was presiding over the Federal Constitutional Convention, and was yet to be sworn in as the first president of the newly united states.

By the time of his death, Joseph Willingham had a large number of rice fields under cultivation. He was living at his home, Myrtle Hill Plantation, St. James Parish, on the Santee River, when he died in 1789. The proceeds from the sale of his lands were left equally to his six sons, one of whom was Thomas Henry Willingham [I] (1772-1798).[5] Thomas [I], well endowed by his father's will, as well as by "the right to receive profits thereof" from his wife Sarah Chovin's marriage settlement,[6] took up what

---

[4]South Carolina Land Grants, 1786: 9:399; 11:458; 11:363. For 1788: 22:83; 24:303; 68:146.

[5]See Appendix: Willingham Lineal Chart, Ancestral Charts, and Family Group Records.

[6]South Carolina Marriage Records, 1796. Marriage settlement between Sarah Chovin and Thomas [I] Willingham. For the text of that settlement, see the Appendix.

promised to be the pleasant and affluent life of an island rice planter who would enjoy the rewards of his slaves' labors—slaves who year after year produced bumper crops of the staple.

Thomas [I] and Sarah Chovin (1780-1823) settled circa 1797 on Sullivan's Island at the lip of the Carolina harbor,[7] on which Fort Moultrie was located. During the American Revolution, British naval units had been repulsed and seriously damaged by Federal troops shooting cannonades from the battlements of Fort Moultrie only a month before the Declaration of Independence was signed on July 4, 1776. Now the red, white, and blue flag of the United States of America flew over Fort Moultrie almost within sight of Thomas's rice fields. The location of the plantation was ideal, for he could transport the harvest by flat-bottom boats to the counting houses of Charleston.[8] From Sarah's point of view, the charms of Charleston, where one might pass pleasant hours with friends, outweighed the appeal of the remote and lonely plantation.

Their son, Thomas Henry Willingham [II], was born on December 23, 1798. There was a double celebration that Christmas both through traditional Christmas merrymaking and rejoicing in the birth of a first-born son. But Thomas [I] sickened and at twenty-seven, when his heir was only three months old, he died. Sarah Chovin Willingham, a young widow of property, remarried within the year on November 14, 1799, to Elias Jaudon (1772-1826). The baby Thomas [II] was given to the care of a special black nanny, and he grew to manhood in the household with his ten Jaudon stepbrothers and stepsisters. When he reached maturity and married Phoebe Sarah Lawton in November 1823, he chose to take his new wife to Savannah, out of which he worked as a cotton factor and managed his plantations, which eventually stretched from the rice fields of South Carolina to the Sea Island cotton lands of south Georgia.

Evidently the many duties and responsibilities Thomas [II] assumed as heir took their toll, for his health "became impaired and on the advice of his physician he moved to the country."[9] When Thomas [II] left Savannah,

---

[7]Miller, *Family Circle*, 376, 551-52.

[8]Easterly, *The South Carolina Rice Plantation*, 11.

[9]Pound, *Memoirs of Jerome B. Pound*, 179, 198.

he returned to South Carolina, and in 1828 built a home on the site of the present town of Lena, near Lawtonville.

Unlike his father, whose life was cut short in his twenties, Thomas [II]'s health greatly improved after he moved, and he lived to the age of seventy-five. In mid-nineteenth century, he was considered one of the most astute, sagacious, and pious personages of South Carolina. "All of his plantations were well improved," a great-granddaughter wrote. "He provided hospitals for the sick, and everything [was] conducted in the most orderly and methodical manner."[10]

Thomas Henry Willingham [II] and his friend and neighbor, Benjamin T. D. Lawton—whose daughter, Phoebe Sarah, married Thomas[11]—were credited with being "deacons of historic service to Pipe Creek Baptist Church." After 1889 the church was known as Lawtonville Baptist Church, and Deacon Thomas served it for forty-seven years.[12] His obituary in the Christian Index for August 7, 1873,[13] and even the words chiseled on his tombstone in the Lawtonville Cemetery praise Deacon Willingham for having "died in happy expectation of a glorious immortality."[14] Thomas [II] and Phoebe Sarah had seven sons and five daughters. The second son was Benjamin Lawton Willingham, named for a grandfather with an imposing name: Benjamin Themistocles Dion Lawton.

---

[10]The great-granddaughter was Anne Willingham Willis (1888-1974), daughter of Thomas Henry Willingham [IV] and Frances Harper Wright. See Willingham Family Group Records in the Appendix.

[11]See chapter on the Lawton planters.

[12]Johnson, Two Centuries of Lawtonville Baptists, 134-35.

[13]Christian Index, August 7, 1873: "Mr. Thomas Willingham [II] . . . has been a consistent and active member of the Baptist Church for 50 years, and for forty years one of the most efficient deacons. . . . He was possessed of a good business education, discriminating mind, and remarkable clear and sound judgment; he seldom erred in the election of any enterprise he undertook; which, coupled with indomitable energy ensured success . . . and he became a man of fortune. [With his family he was] loving, confiding, and respectful as a husband; tender, affectionate and indulgent, but prudent and firm in discipline as a father."

[14]The gravestone of Thomas Henry Willingham [II] in the Lawtonville Pipe Creek Baptist Church Cemetery bears the inscription: "He was a tender and loving Parent, Husband, and Friend, and a wise counsellor, a good and useful citizen, a noble man. For a number of years he was a zealous member and faithful Deacon of the Baptist Church, and died in happy expectation of a glorious immortality."

Two years before Benjamin Lawton Willingham was born in 1829, President John Quincy Adams's men in Congress were putting together a new tariff law aimed at protecting New England's industries—a tax proposal hateful to the South, which was heavily dependent on imported products. In 1830 Vice-President John C. Calhoun, a native Carolinian, threw his considerable fiery eloquence and political strength into a declaration that a state had the right to bar enforcement within its borders of what it conceived to be an unconstitutional Federal act. Shortly thereafter Calhoun resigned the vice-presidency, was elected to the Senate, and became South Carolina's advocate of Southern interests. Already the most pressing issue—more than thirty years before the first gun was fired in the Civil War—was the irreconcilable differences in opinion and philosophy over slave ownership. Slavery, Calhoun maintained, was "a positive good, both for the slave and the white." As senator from South Carolina, Calhoun wore himself out in defense of his concept of the Union: a nation of sovereign states, open to slavery. It was in Carolina and into a family of staunch Calhoun supporters that Benjamin Lawton Willingham was born and grew to maturity. Benjamin lived through the Civil War, which finally erupted when he was thirty-seven. Furthermore, he was able to bring himself and his large family safely to a new life, remote from his beloved South Carolina Gravel Hill Plantation.[15]

The household into which Benjamin was born on April 21, 1829, and in which he grew to manhood was in Barnwell District—later called Barnwell County—South Carolina, on the Savannah River. The household and its environment were typical of Carolina plantations of the time: plantation life was stable and solid; the laborers were, apparently, perfectly subordinated in the production of cotton and rice; the family was situated among others of its kind, which together formed a community bound by close ties of mutual affection, kinship, and similar devout religious convictions. They were especially drawn together in their opposition to abominable tariffs that would in any way jeopardize free trade in cotton with England. John Calhoun was their champion and voice in fighting the tariff and in defending slavery. These matters were in Calhoun's capable hands, they felt, and the boy Benjamin grew up in a household where such things were discussed

---

[15]Davidson, *The Last Foray*, 264. Payne, *Descendants of Benjamin Lawton Willingham*, 1-55.

out of earshot of the children, perhaps on bright Sunday afternoons under the live oaks at the Pipe Creek Baptist Church.[16]

With the advent of Dr. William H. Brisbane's ministry at the Pipe Creek Church in 1833, a tremendous upheaval was caused among the membership that might well have resulted in the church's demise. (Dr. Brisbane had several years before married his first cousin, Anne, daughter of B. T. D. Lawton.) Articles that Brisbane wrote during 1834 supporting slavery were reprinted "with commendation" in the *Charleston Mercury*.[17] Later, though, as the result of prayerful reading and study, Brisbane began to question the divine sanction of slavery in his sermons. Such views were untenable to the slaveowning congregation of Pipe Creek Church. He forthwith resigned or, more likely, was evicted from the pulpit, eventually took twenty of his slaves to Ohio, freed them, and thus temporarily salved his conscience.

However, the members of Pipe Creek Church and his many slaveowning Lawton and Willingham kith and kin had not heard the last of William H. Brisbane. Although he left the state to follow his conscience, he was to return to South Carolina again and again. After the Civil War he was appointed chairman of the United States Tax Commission and in that capacity, some say gleefully and in a spirit of vindictiveness, authorized confiscations for nonpayment of property taxes on many of his relatives, incurring their everlasting enmity.[18]

Benjamin Lawton Willingham was born a big baby; he grew to be a big boy of boundless energy, given to racing around the plantation at top speed, breathlessly followed by his faithful little black playmate. In the Thomas [II] household, as well as in Benjamin's family when he later had children of his own, each child was assigned a black nurse at birth. As the child grew older, a boy-servant was provided for each boy, a girl-servant for each girl. Benjamin had six brothers and five sisters, and an academy was set up on the plantation, with a tutor hired to teach them.[19] Benjamin was big and buoyant, and though he cared little for books, he was intellectually

---

[16]Beard and Beard, *Rise of American Civilization*, 1:666, 680, 703.

[17]King, *History of South Carolina Baptists*, 209.

[18]Johnson, *Two Centuries of Lawtonville Baptists*, 134.

[19]See Appendix: Thomas Henry Willingham Family Group Record.

curious and skillful in getting to the heart of a problem.[20] He exasperated his parents and made life miserable for his brothers by taunting and teasing; but if anyone else bothered them, he came to their defense with fists and bluster. He fished, hunted, rode horseback, and endured the hours in the tutor's classroom. When he was in his early teens,[21] Benjamin was sent to the Citadel in Charleston, "where civic pride knows no boundaries [and the belief is widely held] that Southern manhood most closely approaches divine majesty among the . . . cadets at the Citadel, the Military College of South Carolina." So said a writer in 1980 concerning the Citadel, adding that "boys with spirit have been transformed into men of purpose for 139 years" at the school whose mission then as now "has always been to produce leaders."[22] While Benjamin Lawton Willingham did not stay at the Citadel for the full course, he did become a leader in South Carolina and Georgia. Later he sent his sons there, to be followed by the sons of his sons. After his studies at the Citadel, Benjamin attended Madison College, now Colgate University in New York. He left after only a year, returned to South Carolina, and at eighteen married Elizabeth Martha Baynard (1839-1887)[23] who was seventeen when they married on February 15, 1848. Elizabeth's parents, Archibald Calder Baynard and Martha Sarah Chaplin, had sent Elizabeth from their plantation on Ladies Island on the Broad River near Beaufort, to Miss Ball's Academy for Young Ladies in Charleston. It was there they met when Benjamin was a cadet at the Citadel. Elizabeth's sister, Cecelia, had already married Benjamin's brother, Thomas Henry [III], in 1846; and another of Elizabeth's sisters, Florence, was married in 1863 to another of Benjamin's brothers, Winborn. Three Baynard sisters married three Willingham brothers. Relationships, kinships, alliances, cognations, and tie-ins among the Lawton-Willingham-Baynard and other branches of the clan became ever more intertwined and complicated as time passed.

Elizabeth and Benjamin spent the early years of their married life in Beaufort, where he joined the traditional family business of plantation management. Thomas Henry [II] gave lands and worldly goods to his second eld-

---

[20]Willingham, *Life of Robert Josiah Willingham*, 13, 14.

[21]Pound, *Memoirs of Jerome B. Pound*, 299.

[22]Schneider, "The Citadel," 44-49, 54-55.

[23]See Appendix: Baynard Family Group Records.

est son, Benjamin, even before his legacy to him at death. This legacy included lands in Barnwell District and in the Allendale and Santee River areas of South Carolina. Benjamin also acquired a plantation near Albany, Georgia.

*Deadly serious, Elizabeth Martha Baynard and Benjamin Lawton Willingham pose stiffly on their wedding day, February 15, 1848. Their solemn demeanor portended a staunch and lasting relationship that carried them through war and desolation to a more rewarding life in Georgia, far removed from their South Carolina birthplace.*

[Collection of Virginia Marshall Flatau]

Benjamin's plantation, Gravel Hill, five miles west of Allendale, to which he and Elizabeth moved and where most of their large family of children were born and reared,[24] was in the Carolina upriver section of the Savannah River. During the course of the American Revolution in the late 1770s, the river valley and the big plantations near the city of Savannah had been desecrated by the armies marching up and down the river banks. But the Willinghams and other plantation owners had "set the land straight" again, as they said, by the time the states were free of British control. When Benjamin moved to Gravel Hill, the plantations were thriving, there was brisk trade in slaves, and new towns were springing up along the river and its tributaries as centers for the marketing of rice, tobacco, and later, short-staple, green-seed cotton.[25]

Benjamin channeled his considerable energies into developing his plantations to produce short-staple cotton. He aimed for his lands to be the finest, the highest producing, and he intended to maintain the good name of Willingham above reproach. His lands, his family, and his church were his life. No less impressive in her staunch endeavors to be his helpmate in all he desired was his wife, Elizabeth Martha Baynard. Together they made a stalwart couple. Benjamin took affectionate pride in his children, and a sense of humor was seen lurking in the corners of his mouth, which often twitched in his effort to suppress a booming guffaw, likely to burst forth at inopportune times. His slaves he ruled with firmness and studied patience; his children with prayer and whippings; his church he supported with time and money, giving generously of both. At home there were prayers in the morning and at night, and the children never forgot the oft-repeated petition at these times: "Grant that our children may be useful men and women in society."[26]

---

[24]See Appendix: Benjamin Lawton Willingham and Elizabeth Martha Baynard Family Group Record.

[25]Stokes, *The Savannah*, 190-91.

[26]Willingham, *Life of Robert Josiah Willingham*, 15ff.

*Early years of the married life of Martha and Benjamin Willingham were spent in this plantation house, Gravel Hill, near Allendale, South Carolina, which they built about 1855. They and their many children occupied it until Sherman's invasion was imminent, and then they fled to central Georgia in 1865.*

[Collection of Cecilia Willingham Grove]

By the time that Benjamin began serious development of his home plantation, a new element had been introduced into the planting system of the South. Eli Whitney's invention of the cotton gin had precipitated a burgeoning growth of cotton production that brought great wealth to Benjamin and to other South Carolina and Georgia planters. He rode the crest of the cotton boom at Gravel Hill Plantation and at his other plantations, a crest that remained high until the Civil War, when the cause for which John Calhoun spent his life was lost.

Before the invention of the cotton gin, in one day, by hand, one slave could detach only about one pound of cotton fibers from their green seeds: it was time-consuming, costly work. When a hand-cranked Whitney gin was used, as many as fifty pounds could be cleaned.[27] Under favorable

---

[27]Eaton, *The Growth of Southern Civilization*, 25ff.

weather conditions of at least two hundred frost-free days, free also of rain when the bolls were white, good soil produced a 500-pound bale per acre.[28] Because the bolls ripened unevenly, several pickings were required to pluck the fleece from the mature bolls, and in this operation all hands fell to— women and children as well as adult male slaves. After a picking had been ginned and pressed into bales, it was sent to the nearest cotton market town by wagon overland along the river road to Savannah or on flatboats to Savannah and Charleston. From the ports the bales were shipped in most instances to England, where the cotton was manufactured into cloth and twine and thread.

John C. Calhoun, still the symbol of the Old South, became in the latter part of his life an unwavering champion of states' rights as laid down in the Constitution and supported by the slaveowning cotton planter. He defended slavery to the end of his days, arousing anti-Southern feelings in states in which slaveowning was unlawful. His vehemence and loud-voiced pronouncements at every opportunity made enemies for him among abolitionists and may well have been a major contributing cause, not only to the ongoing disputes among the states on tariffs and slavery matters, but to the Civil War itself. Many of his longtime South Carolina friends stuck by him, but he never unified the South.

Calhoun's health and fortunes were declining rapidly by the late 1840s, and sympathetic friends—Benjamin Lawton Willingham is thought to be numbered among them—raised more than $27,000 for his use. Calhoun died before the money could be presented to him. As he lay minutes away from death on May 31, 1850, he was heard to whisper, "The South, the poor South."[29]

Under Benjamin's management, his holdings in lands and slaves expanded until by 1860, 104 slaves were quartered on his Barnwell District lands alone.[30] There were additional slaves under the supervision of overseers on other Carolina and Georgia plantations. In 1860 Benjamin contributed many thousands of bales of cotton to the Carolina planters' "greatest crop of over four and a half million bales." He was inevitably uni-

[28]Ibid., 28.

[29]Taylor, *Ante-Bellum South Carolina*, 48-49.

[30]Davidson, *The Last Foray*, 1, 2, 264.

fied with his plantation-owner cohorts, both economically and politically. There was some indication that they might be overproducing, but they fared well, certainly until the period of the 1860s.

The small house in which Benjamin and his family had been living since their move from Beaufort to Gravel Hill was fast becoming too small. About 1855 Benjamin decided that he wanted a grand house, one that befitted his station in life and one roomy enough to house his wife and six children, including the toddler Caroline, his "little Carrie."[31] For his new house, Benjamin selected a plot at a distance from the high road from Allendale,[32] in a grove of oaks. The approach led to spacious grounds that girdled the new residence and cook house. In the outer circle, farthest removed from the main house, were the stables and barns; farther still was the row of slave cabins for the house and yard servants. Out of sight of the Big House stood the Negro quarter and the overseer's house.

The tradition persists that Benjamin was his own architect for the Gravel Hill home. He probably did develop his own concept of a home large enough to accommodate a family that eventually included eighteen children. He probably employed a journeyman architect or a trained master workman to plan and execute details of the house and its outbuildings. His slaves were used to build the house of the choicest timbers from the hard woods on the plantation. Oak was used plentifully. Certainly his slaves made the rough brick for the foundation from Gravel Hill's own clay pits.

The imposing high-ceilinged, wide-halled house was well suited to the climate. There were huge fireplaces, wide-board oak floors, and a graceful stairway to the second floor. The parlor or drawing room had elaborate mantels, moldings, and medallions. The family room, adjoining the dining room, was divided by a wall composed of folding doors. The three rooms were often thrown together for banquets, weddings, and entertainment. The master bedroom and nursery were on the upper floor, as were additional bedrooms that sisters shared with sisters, and brothers with brothers. The children were often moved about to accommodate guests. It was a splendid house, lively, active, brimming over with children, nurses, house slaves, and more likely than not, with those guests who stayed for extended visits.

---

[31]See Appendix: Benjamin Lawton Willingham and Elizabeth Martha Baynard Family Group Record.

[32]Lawton and Wilson, *Allendale on the Savannah*, 56ff.

For a number of years, life at Gravel Hill proceeded in a relatively un-complicated manner, ruled amidst all the commotion and bustle by Ben-jamin and Elizabeth. Every weekday the smaller children received schooling from a private tutor at a little schoolhouse built on Gravel Hill Plantation by their father's slaves; the older children rode the two-and-a-half miles in a Jersey wagon to Allendale Academy. On Sunday everyone attended Sunday school. In the long summers the boys rode ponies, fished, set bird traps, hunted. The girls, including Carrie, played dolls and baked teacakes in basement rooms.

December 23rd was the birthday of Thomas [II], the children's grand-father. Each year the entire clan for miles around gathered at the family's Lena Plantation. Christmas really began on their grandfather's birthday, the children felt, and with his white beard and white hair he looked like Saint Nicholas himself.

The family gathered for the annual birthday-Christmas celebration as usual in 1864. By that year there were almost a hundred Willinghams among the three generations who lived in the Barnwell and Beaufort Dis-tricts—in Allendale, Robertville, and Lawtonville. Three of Benjamin's brothers had mounted their horses and galloped off to join the Confederate forces. But many family members managed to come to wish Grandfather Thomas a happy birthday and the best Christmas possible under the cir-cumstances. Benjamin and Elizabeth brought their newest baby, Josephine Mary, born the previous October, to put in her grandfather's arms for a mo-ment. Josephine Mary appeared puny, but Grandfather Thomas was quite well. He lived for almost ten years longer, but there would never again be the same gathering of the clan at his house.

Sherman had presented to President Lincoln the munificent Christ-mas gift of the city of Savannah. Atlanta lay in ruins; the miles-wide path of ashes through central Georgia to Savannah still smoldered. The presi-dent conveyed to Sherman his "high appreciation of the campaign just closed." The *Macon Telegraph* called Sherman "Judas Iscariot, a betrayer, a creature of depravity, a demon of a thousand fiends."[33] Had he not lived in the South, in Louisiana for a time? Sherman knew the South. Had he not left as a friend? These facts rankled the Southerners who were his victims. For a month he rested in Savannah, having taken over a mansion as head-

---

[33]Sandburg, *Storm Over the Land*, 327.

quarters in which to relax and plan his next tactical move. Neither the *Macon Telegraph* nor any other news-gatherer, Yankee or Rebel, knew for certain just how and where Sherman would strike next: Would it be first along the coast to Charleston? Or inland to Columbia? Sherman issued new orders based on a determination to make this offensive far more devastating than the march through Georgia, for he knew which state had first seceded to begin the conflict.[34] Sherman said the march through South Carolina would be many times more difficult, many times more important than the march from Atlanta to the sea. Able Confederate generals who knew the danger of the swampy Carolina lowlands reported it was "absolutely impossible for any army to march across lower portions of the State in winter."[35]

Dauntless, Sherman issued orders to his 60,000 troops. Streams had begun overflowing their banks from continuous winter rains. In two columns from the Savannah River toward Columbia, with forerunners and outriding cavalry, the men moved over the turgid soil. Sherman himself sailed from Savannah to Beaufort on January 21, 1865, to join General Howard's command on the opening drive into South Carolina. Sherman's course was northwestward into the Piedmont uplands to Columbia. He moved from column to column on each day's march.

At what point Benjamin Lawton Willingham made up his mind to flee Gravel Hill with his family is uncertain. Inevitably, Sherman would sweep through the South Carolina lowlands. Most certainly those days at Christmastime when the Willinghams gathered together at their grandfather's were filled with anxious discussions of plans and preparations for evacuating Gravel Hill and Lena plantations and the other homes of family members in Robertville, Allendale, and Lawtonville. Sherman was planning to concentrate his forces in South Carolina—of that the Willinghams were certain. When they would seek refuge must be decided. Flight was imminent.

Benjamin directed, and his slaves and children packed. By January 9, 1865, bedding had been loaded in the wagons as well as rugs, carpenter's tools, pots and pans, hams and bacon, barrels of apples and cornmeal, and

---

[34]Pierce, *Deep South States of America*, 386.

[35]Sandburg, *Storm Over the Land*, 361.

mounds of clothing. In Benjamin's own carriage, he placed his leather-bound Bible,[36] along with the chest of silver.

Elizabeth tied her rings in a handkerchief and bound them around her waist under her chemise. The slaves threw rough cotton tarpaulins over the loaded wagons, and the next morning their teams were backed up to the traces. Benjamin wrote in his Bible:

> I left my home in Barnwell District on the 10th of January, 1865 with my family[37] and about 50 negroes, all of my mules and wagons, with enough provisions to last me to my plantation in So. W. Georgia to get out of the way of Sherman's Army. I had twelve children at the time, and one infant Josie was very feeble, and we never gave a dose of medicine on the trip.

It was midwinter when the caravan set out: Benjamin, his wife, children, and fifty slaves, his father, and at least one of his brothers and his family. The days were sunny and at night the travelers gathered around a big campfire for a hot meal cooked over the coals by the slaves. Then they slept in the carriages and wagons, and in tents made by stretching carpets over poles. The women and girls rode, many of the boys walked most of the way. The journey was an exciting adventure for the children. Only the adults realized the gravity of the move. Progress was slow over the rutted roads and paths and the many creeks and streams. The trek from Allendale to Albany, Georgia, took almost twenty days. On Sunday they rested. When the procession reached Albany, several of the older boys ran ahead, calling out to the plantation overseer. Prayers of thanksgiving came first. Then everybody—children, slaves, masters—pitched in to set life going again in Georgia.

Food and shelter were now of main concern, and with seeds the family had brought from South Carolina, the slaves put in food crops. Except for the baby, Josie, the family was in good health and the south Georgia spring was mild and pleasant. News from South Carolina was sparse. Rumors persisted that the enemy was coming to south Georgia. Carrie and her brother

---

[36]Benjamin Lawton Willingham's family Bible, now in the possession of Francis Fries Willingham, a great-grandson.

[37]Benjamin's father, Thomas Henry Willingham [II], and Louisa Lawton, whom Thomas Henry married after the death of his first wife, Phoebe Sarah Lawton Willingham, were said to be with the caravan on the trek to Albany, as was the family of Benjamin's brother, Thomas Henry Willingham [III].

Bob buried some of the silver that had safely made the journey from Lena to Allendale. They rolled a log over the spot. Yet Sherman did not return to Georgia. Confederate General Robert E. Lee was forced to surrender to Grant on April 9, 1865, signaling the war's end. Food crops were harvested as they matured in the summer. Most of the slaves, knowing no other home, remained with the family and continued the work they had done all their lives. While the older children thrived, Josie languished. Before leaving Allendale, Benjamin had written in his big Bible: "Born—Josephine Mary, our sixth daughter and twelfth child, born 7th Oct, 1864—Allendale." In Georgia, Benjamin added: "Died—on 23rd Oct, 1865—Josephine Mary—1 year and 16 days old."

The older children needed to be in school; however, no teacher was obtainable for the plantation in south Georgia. Among family lands still available and left relatively unharmed was a plot near the small village of Forsyth, Georgia. Again the family gathered together its possessions. The silver was unearthed and packed. Another notation in Benjamin's Bible reports: "I moved from my So. W. Georgia plantation to Forsyth on the 15th day of Nov. 1865 by R.R. BLW" The trains in parts of Georgia were again in operation after the war. The trip from Albany to Forsyth was an easy one. Presumably the children received several months of schooling in Forsyth. Among Benjamin's first considerations, wherever the family lived, was the education of his children. But Forsyth was to be home for only a few short months.

Officially, Sherman's orders to his officers were against capricious violence and destruction on his army's sweep through South Carolina. But the true desires of their leader filtered back to Sherman's men as they slogged through the swamps under the dripping moss of the live oaks in South Carolina Low Country. Sherman issued few, if any, restraining orders to the troops. South Carolina was where treason began, and there, Sherman swore, was where it would end. And so, to Sherman's implied commands, the troops responded with a greater vengeance than they had in Georgia.[38] When it was over, Sherman declared that the march from Savannah to Columbia was one of the longest and most important marches ever made by an organized army in a civilized country.[39]

---

[38]Sandburg, *Abraham Lincoln*, 18, 19.

[39]Ibid., 138.

Benjamin and his family had fled Allendale only a week before Sherman's left wing, the Twentieth Corps, crossed the Savannah River by the Charleston and Savannah Railroad bridge into South Carolina on January 17, 1865. Sherman's forces moved northwestward through Beaufort and Barnwell districts. Three divisions of Colonel Hugh Judson Kilpatrick's cavalry crossed the river at Two Sisters' Ferry on January 30. Sherman himself, with General O. O. Howard, joined the invaders for the advance that fanned through the little towns and countryside of Beaufort and Barnwell Districts. Sherman's plan was to capture the state's capitol, Columbia, and press on, ending the campaign at Goldsborough, North Carolina. Villages in Sherman's path through the Low Country were virtually obliterated: Hardeeville, Purysburg, Robertville, Lawtonville, Allendale.[40] At least one brigade—often two or more a day—marched through, pillaging and flattening the towns and the lands between mid-January and early February 1865. The forces commanded by Lieutenant Colonel Edward S. Solomon of the 82nd Illinois Infantry of Operations seem to have been particularly efficient in razing the hometowns of the Willingham and Lawton families. The following are excerpts from Colonel Solomon's field reports written from Regimental Headquarters near Goldsborough on March 29, 1865:

> Of the part taken by my regiment in the campaign from Savannah, Georgia, to this place, I have the honor to submit the following report. . . . We remained at Hardeeville eight days on a very bad and wet camp ground; left there on the 28th of January and arrived at Robertsville on the 29th . . . when we left Robertsville . . . we marched toward Lawtonville. . . . About 2:40 p.m. we encountered about 500 of the rebel cavalry deployed in a very thick swamp three-quarters of a mile from Lawtonville. . . . I then drove the enemy through the town of Lawtonville.
>
> The next morning we took up the line of March and arrived at the following points at the time herein specified: at Allendale, February 4; crossed the Big Salkehatchie February 6 and the Little Salkehatchie on the 7th; struck the South Carolina Railroad between Graham's and [Bomberg] the same day at dark. Reached Blackville on the 9th . . . destroyed four miles of the railroad . . . my command has found abundant subsistence in the country, both for man and beast. . . . Distance traveled from Savannah to Goldsborough, about 475 miles.[41]

[40]Davis, *Sherman's March*, 146.

[41]Lamont, *The War of the Rebellion*, 1:47:1:419, 582, 668, 791.

In a postscript to a report that Colonel H. Case of the 129th Illinois Volunteer Infantry, 1st Brigade, Third Division, 20th Corps, had made, he added that he had "omitted reporting the destruction of the following: 1,500 bales of cotton, 70 cotton gins, 4 miles of railroad." He also reported that a forage party near Camden "has captured at least a portion of the assets of the Bank of South Carolina and the Bank of Camden and also a quantity of jewelry and silver plate" and that "the safes were delivered unopened to the Provost Marshall of the Twentieth Corps."

Other Union officers reported at length and with enthusiasm their successes on their Savannah-to-Columbia march. General Barry, U. S. Army chief of artillery, reported that "artillery . . . was advantageously used . . . at Lawtonville on February 2, 1865." Lt. Buckingham, 20th Connecticut Infantry said, "The enemy retired precipitately" before them "on the road to Lawtonville on February 2nd." His unit encamped there, then encamped again on the night of the fourth "one mile East of Allendale." General Cogswell of the 2nd Massachusetts Infantry reaffirmed in his report that "at or near Lawtonville four regiments of the brigade were formed in two lines of battle" and that "after encamping [they] went on to burn 300 bales of cotton and the railroad buildings at Graham's station." Brigadier General Dustin of the 105th Illinois Infantry "marched the enemy from the town," and after "driving the enemy" from Lawtonville moved on to Orangeburg, where "never was a railroad more effectively destroyed."[42]

When Sherman's hordes pushed Confederate forces from the Carolina Low Country, General Joseph Wheeler's Confederate Cavalry was the only fighting force in the area. Wheeler had headquarters for his 6,700 mounted men at the Steep Bottom Church in Lawtonville from January 19th through January 31st. When Union forces took over, they destroyed the town and used the church building, gutted of its oak pews and pulpit, as a field hospital.

Thomas Henry Willingham [II] was apparently safe with his son Benjamin in Georgia when the house he had built in 1829 in Lena, a few miles from Lawtonville, was burned by Sherman's army. Many years later a descendant wrote, "All evidence of Grandfather's handwork has gone except the old hewn timber barn on one side of which a hole was cut through

---

[42]Ibid., 1:47:1:803, 821, 831.

which Wheeler's cavalrymen loaded corn as they passed through, ahead of, or behind Sherman's Army."[43]

Sherman had, indeed, loosed hell on South Carolina, and the most extensive destruction seemed centered on the lands of the Willingham, Lawton, and Robert families. Benjamin Lawton Willingham fled to Georgia in January 1865. At that time most of the Willingham cotton-producing lands were located in South Carolina. Shortly after Lee's surrender, a correspondent of the New York Times wrote, "I hazard nothing in saying that three-fifths [in value] of the personal property we passed through were taken by Sherman's Army."[44] Benjamin's property losses fit within the statistics. Most of his cotton crop of 1864 had been seized or destroyed. All of his many slaves—including the 104 living on his Barnwell District land at the beginning of the war—were now free. The fifty slaves who migrated with Benjamin to Georgia were, as freedmen, working for wages or as sharecroppers, or living as best they could without wage or work. The loss of his slaves, some of whom were valued at $2,000 a head, brought Benjamin to the edge of financial ruin. Benjamin's brother, Thomas Henry [III], was occupying and managing the southwest Georgia lands. Seed was lacking, tools and machinery were gone, work animals were scarce.[45]

At the end of the war, in a proclamation signed on May 25, 1865, President Andrew Johnson granted amnesty and pardon to the Rebels, and provided a means by which property—not including slaves—could be restored to rightful owners.[46] Benjamin's Gravel Hill house was, miraculously, still standing among the desolate, scorched fields. There would be a ready market for cotton and rice whenever the fields could be reclaimed and crops made. Benjamin's father's house was gone, but it could be rebuilt, as indeed it was, with the work being directed by Thomas [II] when he was in his late sixties. He lived his last days in the cottage that replaced his Lena mansion, and he was buried in the old Lawtonville Baptist churchyard in 1873.

---

[43]Pound, Memoirs of Jerome B. Pound, quoted in Thomas Oregon Lawton to Anne Willingham Willis, 1941, 198.

[44]Simkins and Woody, South Carolina During Reconstruction, 4.

[45]Ezell, The South Since 1865, 27, 46, 53, 116. Greene, "The Political Crisis," 468.

[46]Simkins and Woody, South Carolina During Reconstruction, 229.

The abilities and spirit of Benjamin Lawton Willingham remained intact. Together with Elizabeth, he assessed what remained to them. Their "most precious possessions," the children, were unscathed. While they were living in Forsyth, Benjamin and Elizabeth became parents of yet another child, their thirteenth. When Benjamin entered the name "George Milton Willingham" in his Bible and the date, "born 27 January 1866," he added, "Thank God for the boy." In June, Benjamin made yet another entry in his Bible: "I moved from my Forsyth place June the 25, 1866 by R. R. back to Allendale. B. L. Willingham."

Back at Gravel Hill, with the active assistance of his wife and older children, and with as many reliable freed slaves as he could muster to work under the Union laws, Benjamin set about restoring order to the house and land. He had earlier sent his eldest daughter, Phebe Sarah, to Furman University in Greenville, South Carolina. By the time she married her sweetheart from Georgia days, Charles E. Malone, in the fall of 1866, Gravel Hill fields had been cleared and readied for planting the following spring, and the house had been put in order. The bride and groom said their vows in a simple morning ceremony in the front parlor.

Without the slaves to bear the physical burden of planting, tilling, harvesting, ginning, and hauling the crops to market, Benjamin could not restore production. There was land in plenty, but few workers and little cash. The specter of poverty was at bay. There was certainly no risk of his ever-increasing brood of children going hungry. But he had become accustomed to plenty, if not to luxury, and even the devastating results of the war could not deter him from his goal for his children. He continued to pray for his children "to become useful men and women of society." Achieving this objective, he believed, depended upon "Godly living, hard work, and using your God-given talent." Proud father that he was, he believed his children were heavily endowed with intelligence and talent, and that his duty as their father was to see that the native abilities of his children were developed to the fullest. To that end, from the time his first son was born, Benjamin determined to send all his children to college. For this, he needed much more income—coming in regularly and without fail—more than could ever be wrested from the violated land, which never again could be cultivated by slaves that he owned.

In 1870 the Honorable Robert Somers came bearing letters of introduction to British consuls in America from his well-placed English friends, including Robert Dalglish, a member of Parliament. The letters requested that the recipients "should render Somers such assistance as they could properly afford" in his proposed travels to the Southern states. His request was unique; for in the five years since the Civil War, as he stated, "Among the many writers who visit the United States with somewhat similar purposes of observation, one so seldom directs his steps to the South that I am fain to hope there may be found in this circumstance alone an ample warrant of publication." Somers traveled through the South from October 1870 through March 1871. His observations were subsequently published. Of his visit to Macon on November twenty-seventh and twenty-eighth, he wrote:

> The position of Macon, in the heart of Middle Georgia, where all the railways—north, south, east and west—converge as to a common center, renders it probably the most important and promising inland town of this lively and enterprising State. It receives from 90,000 to 100,000 bales of cotton annually, and the drafts of planters in the surrounding country are honoured eagerly by merchants and warehousemen to the extent of their resources, with the view of fostering and increasing the importance of the town as a mart for cotton. . . . [There is] a powerful and permanent impulse to its trade and industry.[47]

Other visitors had noted the cultural atmosphere of the town of Macon, where a college for young ladies was thriving not far from Orange Street; and on the city's western border the tower of Mercer University was being raised against the sky on Tattnall Square grounds, on land donated for the purpose by the city. A Board of Education for Bibb County was being formed to control public schools. They would soon be opening their doors, replacing antebellum academies.

Five years after the last Union Blue Devil had tramped the wasted fields of Gravel Hill, Benjamin made another major decision—to move to Macon. Phebe and her husband, Charles, were left in charge of Gravel Hill. Other Willinghams kept the southwest Georgia lands under cultivation. Benjamin's Bible shows a final notation in his flowing handwriting: "I moved with my family to Macon, Georgia on 9 of Nov. 1870. B. L. Willingham."

---

[47]Somers, *Southern States Since the War*, v, vi, 86.

A wooden signboard bearing the words B. L. WILLINGHAM, COT-TON, was affixed above the doors of his warehouse and factor's office on Fourth Street, erected between Cherry and Poplar streets, close to the loading docks of the Central of Georgia Railroad. This sign was the first of many throughout the business and industrial areas of Macon on which the Willingham name would appear. His advertisement that "I obey Instructions and Do My Best to Please," began to pay off and the business thrived.

Benjamin and Elizabeth bought a house on Orange Street,[48] a structure large enough to accommodate all their many children, of whom fourteen were still living. Three had been born after the family moved to Macon. Nine sons and four daughters, including Caroline—Carrie, their fourth child—lived to establish families of their own.[49]

Some of the family units of which Benjamin and his Willingham relatives were a part—those who made up South Carolina plantation society before 1861—were broken, scattered, and churned into a heterogeneous people. Those who managed to maintain plantations learned to survive by dint of their own hard work, and the dignity of newfound labor was admitted and asserted. The vision of the Southern planter sipping mint juleps on the piazza, if indeed it ever existed, was long gone. Some Southerners lamented "the great *mania* of Southern planters for transforming their sons into lawyers, doctors, and merchants." Others were equally sure that what the region needed were "smaller farms, more villages, less pride, more industry, fewer stores and clerks and more laborers."[50] In deciding to move to Macon, where he became a leader of uncommon stature, Benjamin was to realize his lifelong hope that his children would become useful citizens of society. In fact, he deliberately took his place among those who were accused of having a *mania* for transforming their sons into merchants, lawyers, manufacturers and, in the case of one of Benjamin's sons, ministers of distinction.

Thomas Henry [IV] was the first to contribute to the realization of Benjamin's dreams for his children. Thomas studied at Richmond College

---

[48]McKay, "School in Old Home," 20. An excerpt from this article appears in the Appendix.

[49]See Appendix: Benjamin Lawton Willingham and Elizabeth Martha Baynard Family Group Record.

[50]Ezell, *The South Since 1865*, 220-21.

in Virginia, then completed his education at Eastman Business College in Poughkeepsie, New York. Returning to South Carolina, he married Frances (Fannie) Harper Wright on November 12, 1872, and participated in restoring Gravel Hill Plantation after the war. By 1877, at twenty-seven, Thomas [IV] had also left Gravel Hill, and the name plate THOMAS WILLINGHAM, ATTORNEY was affixed to an office door at 64 Mulberry Street in downtown Macon. Thomas moved Fannie and their children to Georgia, managed family lands at Byron, Georgia, not far from Macon, and took up residence next door to his father's house on Orange Street. Thomas highlighted one aspect of his practice: "Special attention given to collections." He very likely acted as his father's attorney and collection agent in his cotton factorage business.

Also by 1877, Benjamin's sons, Calder B. and Robert J. (Bob) Willingham, opened an office as insurance agents on Fourth Street. Calder, twenty-five at the time, and Bob, twenty-three, were thus initiated into their father's rapidly growing business endeavors. A few years before, Calder had graduated from Washington and Lee University, returned to Macon, married Lila Ross, and opened the insurance office of which he was cashier. His office was near his father's, and he began to take over many of the details necessary for managing the factorage business. Bob brought home a diploma from the University of Georgia, on which were written the words "with high honor." He served as principal of the North Macon School and at the same time worked with Calder in the insurance office. Both Bob and Calder went on to careers that, to their parents, brought "pride to their hearts." Bob, after returning to school and graduating from the Southern Baptist Theological Seminary, filled pulpits in Thomaston (GA), and in Chattanooga, Memphis, and elsewhere. Then for more than twenty years until his death in 1914, he was secretary of the Mission Board of the Southern Baptist Convention, the convention that Richard Furman had spent much of his life working to establish.[51] Osgood, apparently fresh from college in 1877, was working as a salesman, and had moved from the family home to board on Bond Street.

In 1882, Osgood Pierce, twenty-five at the time, and Broadus Estes, twenty, with the backing of their father Benjamin, established Willingham

---

[51]See chapter on Richard Furman.

Sash and Door Company, which a century later was still described as "one of the South's largest such concerns." At the time it was founded, the factory was popularly called the Dixie Works and advertisements boasted, "We are proud of our fine reputation for both variety and quality of products." These included "sashes, doors, blinds, bandsawed scroolwork [*sic*], lumber, & moulding . . . now a full line of building materials is carried & architectural woodwork manufactured." The office and plant were located on Seventh and Cherry streets.[52]

*Carrie and Richard Lawton acquired this house at 620 College Street, Macon, about 1874. All of their children were born here, including their oldest child, Furman Dargan Lawton, in 1875.*

[John J. McKay, Middle Georgia Historical Society]

---

[52]*Macon News*, November 15, 1959, 1:8; 2:6.

Soon the roster of officers for Benjamin's main business, described in 1877 as "Cotton Factors, Warehouse, and Cotton Commissioners," included the names of sons Calder and Broadus, along with reference to himself as president.

Benjamin and Elizabeth's brown-eyed, fair-skinned, willful "Carrie"—after completing finishing school at Tift College in Forsyth, Georgia—on January 11, 1872, married her distant cousin, Richard Furman Lawton, recently widowed. Benjamin deeded a narrow lot, part of his city lot on Orange Street, to Carrie and Richard. From all accounts, he assisted his new son-in-law to build a house there and to become established as a banker and broker in downtown Macon. [53]

The three youngest brothers, Paul, E. Pringle, and Benjamin [II], as well as Edward, all completed college by 1890—at Mercer, the University of Georgia, and others—and were firmly ensconced in a variety of businesses in Macon. Edward and Pringle were working long hours to establish their furniture manufacturing plant on Eighth Street, near Cherry. Their brother-in-law, William S. Payne, Cecelia's husband, later became an executive of the furniture plant that grew to include a complex of buildings: a woodworking machinery shop and finishing and varnishing buildings, as well as what is shown on the land plan as an "enginehouse." A railroad spur track served Payne's property as well as, across the tracks, the Willingham Sash and Door Company. Both businesses provided employment for a number of former slaves.

Osgood, Broadus, and a friend, J. A. Reynolds, whom the brothers had taken on as an owner-operator of the Dixie Works, announced that "about May 1st, 1891, O. P. and B. E. Willingham Sash and Door Co., will move to their new building at 510 Cherry Street." The name Dixie Works seems to have been dropped about that time.

Paul, then twenty-three, joined the Payne and Willingham Furniture Manufacturing Company. Benjamin Brooks, at eighteen the youngest living child in 1890, was working for his father's cotton factorage and ware-

---

[53]*Macon, Georgia, 1890-1891 City Directory*, 414.

house business. All of Benjamin's sons who were closely associated in business were also close neighbors, living within blocks of each other on Orange, College, and Bond streets. About the turn of the century, Broadus broke away from the Orange Street neighborhood to build a handsome, columned house among the magnolias in the suburb of Vineville.

In business, as neighbors, and by close ties of blood, the Willinghams—parents, children, and grandchildren—participated in many activities together. From generation to generation, they were members, deacons, and supporters of the First Baptist Church of Macon. Benjamin's "liberality to the church and its work knew no stint," as one biographer expressed it; the same could be said for his sons. Benjamin was chairman of the Board of Deacons for many years. When he retired from the office, his son Calder was elected to it. Calder's son, Alfred, held the office in mid-twentieth century.[54] At Mercer University, Benjamin served as trustee for twenty-two years, and he was the progenitor of a contingent of children, grandchildren, and great-grandchildren who attended the university. When the Georgia public school system was set up in 1872, Benjamin served on the newly created Bibb County Board of Education. When Central High School, later called Gresham High School, opened its doors in 1873, young Willingham children were enrolled.

On the first warm days of spring, when the peach trees were in bloom, various family members—sometimes dozens at a time—climbed into buggies and carriages and drove to Byron for an all-day outing at the farm. In summer they would make the trek to Byron again, returning to Macon in late afternoon, past the fields white with cotton, to deliver great baskets of peaches to the houses on Orange and College streets, where the black cooks turned the fruit into delectable pies, jams, jellies, and preserves.

When an aging Jefferson Davis spoke in October 1887 at the Georgia State Fair in Macon's fine Central City Park, little Willinghams, uncharacteristically subdued, filed in shy and solemn procession to the bunting-draped bandstand to shake the hand of the former president of the Confederacy. Grandfather Benjamin, getting out a bit after Elizabeth's death in July,[55] accompanied the grandchildren. There was respect and, in the case

---

[54]Batts, *First Baptist Church . . . of Macon,* 169-70.

[55]"Death of Mrs. Willingham," *Macon Daily Telegraph,* July 18, 1887. An excerpt from this article appears in the Appendix.

of Benjamin, deep sadness in their greeting of Davis, the white-thatched symbol of a South that was no more.

Cotton remained the chief stimulus of trade in central Georgia, and Benjamin's method of operating his factorage business—a method that proved to be highly profitable through the years—was to pay the seller when the sale was consummated instead of after the cotton had been disposed of, as was the usual custom among factors. The election of Grover Cleveland to the presidency in 1884 was a further stimulus to Benjamin's business. Cleveland was the first Democratic president since the war, and Macon received the news with jubilation. Under a general aura of optimism, trade of all sorts accelerated.[56]

As each son completed his education and was ready to take his place in the adult world, Benjamin supported and advised him upon entering one or more Willingham family enterprises. The Willingham family—Benjamin and Elizabeth and all their sons and daughters—exemplifies the close-knit, energetic, proud Southern families who found, in the postwar disorder, not insurmountable calamity but challenge and opportunity; not defeat, but triumph.

Benjamin gloried in his sons. As he neared the end of his life, he gathered them all together, summoned a photographer, and with himself in the center of the group, had his likeness struck with his nine sons—all college-trained, all certainly "useful members of society."

After Elizabeth's death in 1887, Benjamin married again. His second wife was Mary Shorter Perkins, daughter of John Gill Shorter, governor of Alabama from 1861 to 1863. Benjamin did not live to see the spindles whirling and the finished twines and webbing loaded on the boxcars at Willingham Mills: he died in 1898. Calder, with an initial investment of $500,000 and with his younger brother Broadus as partner, after many months of planning, building, and trial runs, began by 1899 to produce yarn and warp threads spun from the abundantly available short-staple cotton of the Georgia countryside. Located near the Vineville Railroad Station, the mill complex included a large building to house the spinning machinery, a neat village of clapboard cottages to house the several hundred mill workers, and a small chapel with a tiny steeple, the Willingham Baptist Church. In a way, the mill and its village were comparable

---

[56]*Macon Guide*, 58.

*Near the end of his life, Benjamin Lawton Willingham posed with his nine sons (ca. 1895), all "useful members of society." Back row, l to r: Broadus Estes, Ernest Pringle, Edward John, Benjamin Brooks, Paul Dargon. Front row: Robert Josiah, Thomas Henry, Benjamin Lawton (father of the nine sons) Calder Baynard, Osgood Pierce.*

[Collection of Mary Chambers Dudney]

to Gravel Hill Plantation: the owner's building surrounded by the workers' cabins; the place of worship provided by the owner; the lives of the workers closely bound to cotton produced under a benevolent master. There was a difference, though: the worker, more often white than black, was not bound to the master for life. He earned a wage, placed in his hand every Friday. He was free to buy bread or beer, as he chose, sometimes both. And he could vote, if he could write his name and pay his poll tax.

Calder, who was president, and Broadus, who became vice-president, together with G. F. Kinnett, the superintendent, maintained offices on the mill property. By 1900 Broadus was president; by 1902 the mill was in brisk, often overtime operation, supplying "Ply Twist Yarn on Tubes" to carpet manufacturers such as Worchester Carpet Mills, Palmer Carpet Mills in Massachusetts, and Hightower Smyrna Company in New Jersey. There were weekly shipments of "Numbered Duck" to Illinois Central Railroad Company in Chicago. The Great Western Sugar Company in Denver found use for many shipments of "Hose Duck." "Bootleg" was bought by the half-carload by Mishawakaw Manufacturing Company in Indiana. Glen Alden Coal Company in Scranton, Pennsylvania, bought "Numbered Duck," as did Swift and Company in Chicago. Shipments of "Harvester Duck" went all the way to Toronto, Ontario, where it was used by Massey, Harris Harvester, Ltd. Small shipments of warp thread for toweling went to Muscogee Maufacturing Company in Columbus, Georgia.

When this chapel was erected on the Mercer University campus in 1890, C. B. Willingham's name was chiseled in the cornerstone as "Chairman, Building Committee." In 1940 the building was renovated, a tall tower added, and the name changed to Willingham Chapel, at which time Dr. Spright Dowell, university president, announced, "Although the gift is not a memorial to any member of the Willingham family, it is in a sense an expression of the historical relationship of the Willinghams to Mercer University."

[Historical Archives,
Mercer University]

Business was truly booming by 1922, when motorcars had virtually re-placed the horse and buggy. Willingham Mills supplied rubber companies with "Hose and Belt Duck," used in the manufacture of automobile tires. Goodrich Rubber Company of Akron, Ohio, had a standing order on the mill's books, as did the New York Rubber Company, the Hood Rubber Company of Watertown, Massachusetts, and the Mercer Rubber Company of Hamilton Square, New Jersey.[57]

Only in the 1940s and 1950s when heavy modernization costs and competition from foreign imports imposed insurmountable financial hard-ship on mill operations, did the rails of the mill's spur track become rusty and overgrown with weeds and the spindles stop spinning.

On February 17, 1898, an article appeared on the front page of the *Macon Daily Telegraph*:

> All that was mortal of the late Benj. L. Willingham was laid to rest in Rose Hill Cemetery yesterday morning, while hundreds of sorrowing relatives and friends stood by to pay the last tribute to his memory. The funeral services were conducted at his late residence on Orange Street, in the presence of the largest assemblage of people ever seen at a house funeral in Macon. . . . Dr. J. L. White, pastor of The First Baptist Church, read the burial service.
>
> The cemetery being only a short distance from the house, several hundred people walked behind the long procession of carriages, among them being the faculty and students of Mercer University. A beautifully impressive sight was about thirty grandchildren marching in the proces-sion, bearing floral designs, and at the cemetery when the service was over these flowers were placed around the grave. . . . The casket was low-ered, hidden by the large number of floral offerings from sorrowing friends, and the designs were appropriate to the life of Col. Willingham.
>
> Rev. Robert J. Willingham accompanied the heart-broken widow[58] to the grave, and the other eight brothers were the pall-bearers. It was an impressive funeral as well as a large one, and no better evidence of the love and esteem in which Col. Willingham was held in the community could have been shown than such a large gathering of citizens.

Among the thirty grandchildren bearing floral arrangements were the children of Benjamin's "little Carrie," who at thirty-nine had been wid-

---

[57]Willingham Cotton Mills Account Books.

[58]See n. 48 on Benjamin Lawton Willingham's second wife, Mary Shorter Perkins.

*Willingham Cotton Mills (ca. 1930) was owned and operated by Benjamin Lawton Willingham's sons and grandsons for many decades until the 1950s. Management of the post–Civil War mill village and its mill workers, including the family-owned church (see steeple at the arrow, bottom right) closely paralleled the family's management of their antebellum plantation and slaves at Gravel Hill, South Carolina.*

[Archives, Middle Georgia Historical Society]

owed when Richard Furman Lawton died six years earlier. How Carrie Willingham Lawton reared her nine children is part of the ongoing saga of the Lawton-Willingham-Nottingham-Guttenberger kith and kin.

*Chapter Eight*

---

# THE LAWTON PLANTERS
## (1735-1865)

*. . .and Capital keeps his eyes on the field. . .*

Passed from parent to child, the tale of the "King's Hiding Place" has enthralled generations of young Lawtons. The story concerns an infant, William Lawton, and King Charles II, whose father, Charles I, provoked a civil war that led to his execution in 1649. To save his own neck, for years Charles II fled for safety to the English countryside, France, and elsewhere. Only when he was brought back from France and restored to the throne in 1660 did his throne become less shaky and the political turmoil into which England had sunk ameliorate somewhat.

When Charles I was dethroned and later executed, there were numerous friends known to be faithful to the Crown, to whom his heirs might have turned. But during the eleven years of his banishment, Charles II at times sought less conspicuous friends for refuge and succor.

One hundred sixty miles northwest of London in what was Cheshire County in the seventeenth century, Lawton Hall still stands. Built upon a natural terrace, the three-story-brick central section of the house is flanked by a pair of two-story wings that were added in the past century. A considerable wealth of coal, ironstone, and salt, mined on the estate, supported Lawton Hall in the days of its glory. Shipping and business transactions for the Lawton family were handled in nearby Liverpool. John Lawton, apparently one of the king's less conspicuous friends, owned and occupied Lawton Hall when he gave haven there to Charles II in 1656. Many apartments, greatrooms, and bedchambers comprised the manor, but during his stay Charles II used a small, oak-paneled dining room as a sleeping chamber. To a trapdoor in a passage leading from the chamber to a drawing room, Charles hurried when danger was imminent, emerging when danger had passed.

According to the tale, Charles remained at Lawton Hall for some time and acted as sponsor for his hosts' eldest son, William, when the infant was baptized in 1565. The king presented a drinking cup to his godchild and, when Charles could safely depart Lawton Hall, he left as a memento a "curiously carved boxwood snuff box, bearing the royal arms," to which Lawton arms were later added.[1]

Whether the William Lawton (1723-1757) who is a progenitor of the Lawton family in America[2] is a descendant of William, the godchild of Charles II, is unclear. The first recorded trace of a Lawton in South Carolina occurred when one William Lawton took quill in hand and signed his name as a witness to the will of John Sealy. Two other witnesses put their X on the document. The signature on John Sealy's will is the first evidence that William Lawton, a literate man, was a citizen of Charleston County in 1737.[3] Why William Lawton left England, when and where he arrived in America, and how he decided to take up life in South Carolina remains an enigma. But because he did, and fathered Joseph Lawton (1715-1815)—as well as six other children who were less prolific than Joseph—William became the precursor of descendants who number in the hundreds, if not thousands, who spread and settled all over the States, with the oldest settlements in South Carolina. "Indeed, the Lawtons must be one of the most

---

[1]Omerod, *History of Cheshire*, 11-22. [Editor's Note: The above source was taken from the author's family files, which have been passed from generation to generation. The author's recent attempts to verify the source have thus far been unsuccessful.]

[2]See Appendix: Lawton Lineal Chart #1.

[3]Will Book, 1740-1747, 49.

prolific families in the state [who are] strongly clannish, and who, even among Lawtons of distant relationship [have an] uncanny resemblance to each other."[4]

By the time that William Lawton witnessed Sealy's will in Carolina, the lords proprietor had been routed, George II had been reigning for more than a decade, and the colony was enjoying a period of notable prosperity under royal rule. In 1750, when William Lawton took a third wife, Mary Stone Grimball—the widow of Paul Grimball [II], an Edisto Island neighbor[5]—conditions in general had greatly improved. The coastal islands were no longer plagued by pirates. The Indians John Barnwell had fought were now less threatening. The new colony of Georgia, founded in 1733, provided a buffer against the Spaniards in Florida. German, French, and Swiss immigrants were settling in Georgia. The little colony of Huguenots at James Town had passed its prime, and its citizens were scattering to other parts of South Carolina. Negro slaves, of whom William Lawton owned several dozen, were being shipped in, purchased, and set to work on the rice and indigo plantations. English dissenters and High Churchmen, Irish adventurers and Dutch mechanics were arriving and settling in the coastal areas as well as in the central sections of South Carolina.

William Lawton had long since taken his place among the growing group of settlers whose lands lined the Ashley, Cooper, Santee, and Combahee rivers, or who had settled on the Sea Islands, where great live oaks overlooked the shining stretches of bay and sound. Farther removed from the sound, longleaf pines reached skyward in contrast to the dense growth bordering the dark creeks and streams.[6]

In 1744 William purchased the first of two tracts of adjoining land on Edisto Island, Colleton County—200 acres from the executors of the estate of William Tilley.[7] A second parcel, 460 acres, was conveyed in 1756 to

---

[4]Lawton, *Saga of the South*, 27.

[5]See Appendix: Lawton Lineal Charts #1 and #2, and Grimball and Lawton Family Group Records. Also see Peeples, "A Grimball Plantation Journal," 64-69.

[6]Meriwether, *Expansion of South Carolina*, 4.

[7]Brevard, *Statute Laws of South Carolina*, in Lawton, "Captain William Lawton," 86-93.

"William Lawton, Memorialist."[8] A creek "that comes out of Edisto River" bounded the land on the north and Joseph Palmeter's land bordered it on the south.[9]

William cleared the swamp along the creeks and planted rice. He acquired in all thirty-six slaves to do the arduous work in the boggy swampland. The slaves set the seedlings, tended the paddies, harvested the grain, and ran the rough kernels through one or more of eight rice mills that Lawton owned. Heavy, shining grains poured from the mills, and the chaff of hulls and bran accumulated in bins to be stored in the barns as winter feed for the livestock. Sale of the milled rice redounded to the ever-increasing prosperity of planter William Lawton. In fact, demand for the superior Carolina rice was so brisk that rice became Lawton's leading crop and the chief article of export of most of the other Carolina planters as well.

On plateaus above the rice fields, Lawton planted "pease," corn, and other foodstuffs. Three corn mills, manned by slaves, ground the corn. He continued to cultivate indigo, although the declining market for it made indigo the plantation's least lucrative product. Sixty-five cattle, thirty-six sheep, and six horses grazed the lands. Large flocks of chickens, turkeys, and geese supplied the table with eggs and meat. Fifty "hoggs" rooted in the pens, fattening for slaughter and the smokehouse. Bees from four hives collected honey from the flowering fields.[10] Slaves smoked the bees from their hives in the fall, harvested the honey and beeswax, and sheltered the brood-nests against the coming winter.

William Lawton more than amply provided food and shelter for his family, which in rapid succession consisted of three wives and many children. Although there is little evidence that Mary Stone (Grimball) Lawton—William's third wife—lived up to the expected role of "wife and helpmeet" who directed the household's day-to-day activities, there is also

---

[8]Inventory Book, 1756, 1-8.

[9]South Carolina Memorials, 1731-1776, 7:141-42; 436-37.

[10]Inventory Book, 1756-1758, 189-96. The seven-page inventory of the estate, in addition to the items mentioned in the text, includes household furniture, silver tableware, china, linen, Lawton's personal wardrobe, "a lott of old clothes," a large variety of farm tools, spinning wheels, a quilting frame, "a large and a small sailing canoe," several guns, fishing equipment, horse whips, and saddles.

no evidence that she did not fulfill her traditional duties.[11] "Captain Lawton," as he was referred to when his estate was appraised, represented the family in the outside world: in the community, in elections, in church business, and in public affairs. Like other eighteenth-century Carolina women, Mary seems to have had no identity separate from William. She participated only in family and church-related activities.

As the male head of his family, Lawton represented it as a "sober, discreet, and substantial person." He was selected to fill a position in the parish in which he was expected to provide for the poor—if not directly from the fat of his land, then certainly indirectly by counsel and advice at the monthly meetings that under the law he was required to attend.[12] Samuel Jones and Joseph Phips, as well as "Mr. William Lawton [were] a Pointed Oversears [sic] for the Poor of the said Parish," as recorded in the minutes of the church vestry of St. John's Colleton, the Anglican congregation on Edisto Island. The appointment, made on August 6, 1750, did not necessarily mean that committee members were also church members. Under the statute law, the vestries, church wardens, and rectors of the parishes were elected; and the parish government, besides providing for the church, was charged with the care of the poor and the conduct of elections. The appointed members were required by the statute to meet monthly after church services to report their activities and to "regulate matters pertaining to the poor." If an appointed committeeman refused his appointment or failed in its discharge, he was subject to fine.[13]

To wear to the meetings of the "Oversears of the Poor," Captain Lawton could choose from among a wardrobe of seven coats and pertinent accessories. More than likely for the gatherings, he donned his best broadcloth suit with gold sleeve-buttons, attached his silver buckles to his shoes, arranged his wig on his head, and put on one of his two hats. Pocketing his silver watch, he would be off to meetings in one of a number of conveyances: carriage, buggy, canoe—large or small—or, with English horsewhip in hand, he used Frisk, his riding horse.[14]

---

[11]Norton, Liberty's Daughters, 1-4.

[12]Dalcho, Episcopal Church in South Carolina.

[13]Statutes of South Carolina, 2:123, 127, 287-91, 594; 3:51.

[14]Inventory Book, 1756-1758, 289-96.

In 1757, although he was only in his thirties, William Lawton "considered the uncertainty of this Transitory Life and the certainty of Death" and made his will. In it his wishes were documented "concerning all my worldly Estate and such lands and Tenements Goods and Chattels it hath pleased God to bestow upon me." To his "well beloved wife," Mary, he bestowed nine specific slaves with their issue—axes, hoes, and reap hooks—his riding horse Frisk—with new saddle to be bought for her out of his estate—as well as one-fourth of his stock of cattle, a fourth of his sheep, a third of his furniture, and the use of his large canoe and sails during her life. Significantly, William also willed that for Mary "a Suit of Mourning" be purchased out of his estate. Further, Mary had the "use of my plantation I now live on during the term of her natural Life."

After generously taking care of his children by his first two wives, William Lawton made a special provision for his only child by Mary, his four-year-old son Joseph. After the time of Mary's death, William allotted to Joseph "the Tract of land I now live on to him and his Heirs forever." Joseph also received a Negro girl, Hannah, and a Negro boy, Tom, as well as those treasured symbols of his father's status as a member of Carolina's privileged class: his "Silver watch and Silver Shoe Buckles."[15]

The customs of the times stipulated that widows were to wear black from head to toe as long as they remained unmarried. In little more than a year after William's death, Mary discarded her widow's weeds. A kinsman who kept a meticulous journal of family events recorded that "Samuel Fickling was married to Mary Lawton January 15, 1759, it being Tuesday between 2 & 3 o'clock in the afternoon."[16] After she married Samuel Fickling, Mary moved her children, including Joseph, then five years old, from Edisto to Prince Williams Parish in Granville County, the site of her new husband's lands. Mary lived into her eighties, receiving a legacy from her mother, Susannah Carriere Stone Winborn, upon Susannah's death in 1779.[17] Mary had earlier released to her son Joseph her rights to the Edisto Island land that William had made arrangements for in his will.

---

[15]Will Book, 1767-1771, 507. William Lawton's will was recorded October 9, 1757, and proved December 9, 1757.

[16]Thomas Grimball Journal, Item 194.

[17]Will Book, 1760-1784, 47. Will of Susannah Winborn, widow, Wadmalaw Island, St. Johns, Colleton County. Mentions daughter "Mary Fickling" as well as Mary Fickling's three children: John Grimball, Joseph Lawton, and Mrs. Anne Roberts.

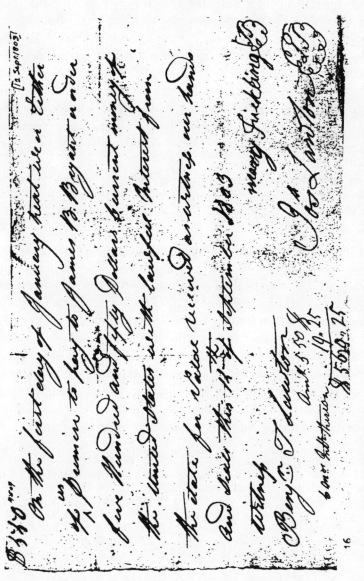

This promissory note, dated September 12, 1803, and bearing the signatures of Mary [Lawton] Fickling (the mother), Joseph Lawton (her son), and Benjamin T. D. Lawton (her grandson), is one of the many hundreds of business papers that survive, and that show the close business and personal relationships of family members in South Carolina during the nineteenth century.

[Manuscript Division, The South Caroliniana Library]

Joseph was reared with his stepbrothers and stepsisters on Edisto Island, but seems always to have been his mother's favorite child, and it was he to whom she turned in her old age. At twenty, Joseph married Sarah Rob-

ert, granddaughter of Pierre Robert, the French Huguenot *Pasteur* on the
Santee. By the time of their marriage on May 18, 1773, Joseph had already
received royal land grants both on the Savannah River (250 acres, St. Peter's Parish, March 2, 1772) and on Edisto Island (200 acres, St. Helena's
Parish, Granville County, March 3, 1772).[18] He received bequests of land
and money from at least six sources: in his father's will; from his three unmarried half brothers, Josiah, William [II], and Jeremiah Lawton; from his
mother, Mary Stone Grimball Lawton Fickling; and from his grandmother,
Susannah Carriere Stone Winborn.[19] By all accounts, he became a very
wealthy man.

Shortly after his marriage to Sarah, Joseph sold his land on Edisto Island and moved to Black Swamp, acquiring the first of the lands that comprised his Mulberry Grove Plantation, near the settlement that by 1812
became known as Robertville.

After the move, Joseph set about managing his lands and establishing
a household. Their first son, William Henry, was born February 23, 1775.
The provinces were already involved in the fight for freedom when a second
son, Joseph James, was born on August 19, 1777.[20] Later, at the time of Robertville's founding, William Henry became first postmaster of the town.

George Washington was named commander of the Continental army
in April 1775, and on March 17, 1776, the British evacuated Boston. Congress shortly thereafter proclaimed the Declaration of Independence. Momentous events that would result in the formation of the United States of
America were occurring in the colonies. Major events were also occurring
in the life of Joseph Lawton, events that had a great bearing on the lives of

[18]Royal Land Grants lists the following transactions for Joseph Lawton: March 2, 1772,
250 acres on Savannah River, St. Peter's Parish; March 3, 1771, 200 acres at St. Helena's
Parish, Granville County; October 28, 1773, 300 acres at St. Helena's Parish, Granville
County; August 19, 1774, 250 acres on the Savannah River, St. Peter's Parish; February 10,
1775, 330 acres in Granville County. Hampton County Land Titles (Book 4-D, 588) shows
Joseph Lawton's Mulberry Grove Plantation, located east of Robertville in St. Peter's Parish,
contained a total of 4,493 acres, made up of parcels of land acquired separately over the
years.

[19]Thomas O. Lawton, "Joseph Lawton." Address, Lawton Family Association meeting,
Atlanta, June 19, 1976.

[20]Children born after the Declaration of Independence were reared at Mulberry Grove
Plantation. See Appendix: Joseph Lawton Family Group Record.

his family and on his descendants—indeed, on the very existence of those descendants.

After independence was declared in July 1776, and until early 1778, the American Revolution was a civil war within the British Empire. After France, Spain, and the Netherlands joined the colonies against Britain, the conflict became more widespread. Americans fought the war on land with two types of forces: the Continental (or National) Army and the state militias. The war was therefore one of small field armies and, according to the sparse records that still exist of Joseph Lawton's military service, he served in both types of organizations. Militia were summoned for periods of usually not more than three months, and Joseph served in the South Carolina Militia in the spring and summer of 1778. As a lieutenant in Colonel Stephen Bull's Granville County, South Carolina Militia,[21] he led the Black Swamp Company of Foot Soldiers in protecting Two Sisters' Ferry, the strategic Savannah River crossing between Georgia and Carolina Low Country.

Brigadier General William Moultrie successfully defended a fort (later named Fort Moultrie in his honor) on Sullivans Island off the coast of Charleston. Shortly thereafter, placed in command of the patriotic forces in South Carolina, he set up his headquarters at Black Swamp, not far from Joseph Lawton's Mulberry Grove Plantation. At Black Swamp, Moultrie conferred with General Benjamin Lincoln, commanding officer of the Department of the South of the Continental Army. It was from Black Swamp that forces were deployed for operations crossing Two Sisters' Ferry in defense of Savannah, and to which the wounded were returned for hospitalization. Moultrie campaigned in Georgia, and dislodged the British from Beaufort, South Carolina, in February 1779. Moultrie was taken prisoner during the war; when released at war's end, he returned to his state, where he served for two terms as governor.

Joseph Lawton's specific service under Moultrie's command in Black Swamp is open to guess, but many years after his death, Joseph was commended for his bravery:

> During the Revolutionary war [Joseph] Lawton owed his life to a
> British officer whom he once befriended. The officer lost his horse near

---

[21]Account Book, 1778, 91; Cash Book, 1777-1779, 123; Treasury Journal, 1778-1787, 115.

Mr. Lawton's, and to his surprise, the Whig Lawton, furnished him one with the remark, "I am not fighting men, but for principles." When the Tories betrayed Mr. Lawton, and he was about to be executed by the British, the officer went to the execution through curiosity, and on discovering his benefactor, saved his life with the expression, "Such a man must not be executed."[22]

Queen Caroline on her birthday in 1735 proudly wore a shining court dress made from eight pounds of the finest raw silk, brought from Georgia personally for her approval by General James Oglethorpe, founder of the colony. She expressed a "great satisfaction for the beauty and the fineness of the silk, the richness of the pattern, and at seeing so early product from the colony." At the time it was classed as "equal to any Italian silk and worth full 20 shillings per pound."[23] In ensuing years considerable quantities of silk were produced both in Georgia and in South Carolina.

When he moved to his new lands at Black Swamp, Joseph Lawton evidently had in mind that he would produce silk on his plantation, named Mulberry Grove for the trees upon which the silk worms were to feed. Joseph actually produced little silk. Whether his operations were doomed because of "poisoned dew or warm weather, late frost, badness of the seed," technical incompetency, "unaccountable backwardness"[24] of his slaves in attending to the worms, or simply that his interests were drawn to other crops, Joseph failed to make silk production a profitable venture. He was not alone in his failure. Many mulberry trees, planted by Carolina Low Country landowners, grew on their plantations. Few planters made silk culture worthwhile, and what had begun auspiciously with Queen Caroline's blessing never materialized.

Although Joseph Lawton abandoned silk culture early at Mulberry Grove—if he had ever undertaken it in earnest—with his ever-expanding acquisition of lands and slaves, he began the production of rice, indigo, and especially cotton. Joseph was among the early planters who developed a significant relationship with his slaves. Starting with only a few (he owned

---

[22]The incident was apparently reported in 1895 to the Savannah River Baptist Association by the Rev. Fred Jones. The author has an undated and unidentified clipping from which the quotation is taken.

[23]Harden, *History of Savannah*, 56.

[24]Ibid., 56-57.

twenty in 1790), he gradually increased their number, managing them with astuteness, firmness, and—it was said—with kindness, so that they drew together in a well-organized, well-functioning community, presided over by the master and his white overseers.

As the only son of Mary Stone (Grimball) and William Lawton, he became the patriarch of five branches of Lawtons through his five sons.[25] Although later scattered throughout South Carolina, Georgia, and elsewhere, they remained close in spirit and in contact with each other. A compact social group, frequently intermarrying and associating in business, in personal matters, and mutually supportive emotionally and financially, they were regarded as typical, wellborn Southern gentlefolk.

In lower South Carolina and Georgia, the network of navigable rivers and their tributaries brings every parish in touch with Charleston, Beaufort, Savannah, Darien, and other coastal towns. In the case of Joseph Lawton and his family and neighbors in Black Swamp, the Savannah River and its branches formed the system of communication that made it easy for them to market all sorts of crops.[26] Transporting his cotton crops to Savannah on the Savannah River with barges built, loaded, and manned by slaves proved to be eminently profitable to Joseph. From Savannah or Charleston, the cotton could be shipped to England to be sold and manufactured into cotton goods. Through the years, Joseph kept in contact with his Lawton relatives in England, who were still serving as cotton factors and maintaining a shipyard at Liverpool. They made profitable disposal of the crops grown by the Lawton kith and kin in the colonies, and in return shipped them finished products—furniture, dry goods, household goods, plantation necessities.

On July 18, 1873, Joseph Lawton bought a 198-acre parcel of land that was "Butting and Bounding Northwestern Land" belonging to his good neighbor, Dr. George Mosse, including the "gardens, orchards, Fences, wells, waters, watercourses, easements, Profits, commodities, advantages, emoluments, hereditaments and apurtenances whatsoever. . . ."[27] In making the purchase, Joseph added acreage adjacent to his already considerable

---

[25]See Appendix: Joseph Lawton Family Group Record.

[26]Dodd, *Cotton Kingdom*, 1-12.

[27]Lawton Papers, collection 415. Sale recorded July 18, 1783 for 594 pounds of 198 acres in St. Peter's Parish, Granville County, by Elias Robert [his brother-in-law] to Joseph Lawton.

holdings at Mulberry Grove Plantation. In so doing, he made an important move, one that had great bearing on the lives of three of his five sons: Joseph James, Alexander James, and a third with that imposing name: Benjamin Themistocles Dion Lawton.

Joseph, Sarah, and their children entered upon a friendly relationship with Dr. Mosse and his family, a friendship that had far-reaching effects through generations to come. At the time of the land transaction, Joseph and Sarah already had four children—the youngest, Benjamin, born December 22, 1872. Three more followed.[28] Their neighbors, George and Phoebe Norton Mosse, had three daughters; four more daughters were born in ensuing years.

George Mosse, a native of Ireland, and educated there as a physician, settled on St. Helena's Island, South Carolina, when he came to America. Although he was a practicing physician, he supported his family largely through the operation of a store and a large tannery on St. Helena's. Many journeymen and apprentices maintained the tanning vats by the riverside. Each month the doctor's slaves rowed him in his twelve-oared boat to Savannah or Charleston where he purchased supplies for his businesses. The tannery, if not his medical profession, proved profitable. Mosse served in the Continental Army during the revolutionary war. Taken prisoner after the Battle of Camden, he was held in May 1781 on board the British prison ship *Torbay*[29] in Charleston's harbor. One night, his shackles loosened to permit him to go on deck from the stifflingly hot shiphold, he evaded his captors and slipped quietly, unnoticed, into the waters. Knowing the harbor well, he swam to safety at nearby Hilton Head Island. Mosse resumed his post as surgeon in the Continental Army, and after the war returned to his home and businesses on St. Helena's Island.

Mosse employed a teacher for his seven daughters and sent the eldest ones to finishing school in Charleston. He purchased lands in the Black Swamp area of St. Peter's Parish and in fine weather he took his wife and daughters for long vacations there. One of the girls' aunts, Hettie McKenzie, kept a boarding school on Bay Street in Savannah. At the turn of the eighteenth century, as his youngest daughters grew older, Dr. Mosse sold his St. Helena property and moved his family to Savannah, where the girls

---

[28]See Appendix: George Mosse and Joseph Lawton Family Group Records; Ancestor Charts A, B, and C; Mosse Lineal Chart; and Lawton Lines #1 and #2.

[29]Another account gives the name of the ship as the *Schooner Pack Horse*.

could attend school at Aunt Hettie's. He practiced medicine more vigorously in Savannah; helped form (October 26, 1880) and became one of the first deacons of the Baptist church there; organized the old Savannah Medical College; became a charter member of the first Medical Society in Georgia; and served as superintendent of elections for mayor and aldermen. All the while, George Mosse kept up contacts with his plantation at Black Swamp and with his friends there, among whom the large family of Joseph Lawton was included. As could be expected, during the summer months when the Mosse family lived in St. Peters Parish, the ebullient, lively Lawton boys, as they reached maturity, were inevitably drawn to the houseful of seven nubile girls on the next plantation. With both sets of parents friends of long standing, and their children playmates through the years, they grew up in an aura of mutual friendship. The parents gave their blessings as first one and then another and then another of the Lawton sons courted and married a Mosse daughter.[30]

Joseph James Lawton (1777-1859) was the first to take a bride. Phoebe J. Mosse (1781-1858) and Joseph were married at her parents' home on St. Helena's Island in 1799. They lived in St. Peter's Parish after their marriage. Benjamin and Jane—the second couple to make a Lawton-Mosse alliance—said their vows in the Savannah home of Dr. Mosse on June 16, 1803, after the Mosse family moved there from St. Helena's Island. Following her father's death, Martha, the third Mosse daughter to marry one of Joseph Lawton's sons, married Alexander James at the home of her Aunt Graham in St. Peter's Parish on November 15, 1809. Through the years the three couples experienced a "drawing thither" to the Black Swamp-Allendale area, as a cousin expressed it in her memoirs of the family.[31] These three couples, as well as all seven of the children of Joseph and Sarah Robert Lawton, generated a great proliferation of Lawton kith and kin through-

---

[30]The narrative of George Mosse and his family is based on the following sources: The *Times*, April 4, 1808; "Morton and Mosse Family Record," as written in 1891 by Mrs. Martha Norton Buckner; "Research Compilations Re Dr. George Mosse," by Mrs. Walter A. Norton—a paper presented to the Georgia Historical Society, November 21, 1963. Typewritten copies of these documents are in the author's possession. Additional sources were: the *Courier*, April 5, 1808; Erwin, *South Carolinians in the Revolution*, 85-86; DAC Lineage Book, Lineage of Mrs. Laura Erwin Lawton Reynolds.

[31]Buckner, ibid.

out South Carolina and Georgia—a teeming growth of large families of
children that continued until well into the nineteenth century.

*Dr. George Mosse (1792-1808) was a close
friend and neighbor of Sarah Robert and Joseph Lawton. Three of Mosse's seven daughters married three of Lawton's sons, thereby
entangling roots and branches of the family
tree.*

[Collection of Cecilia Willingham Grove]

William Seabrook (the eighth of the eleven children of Jane and Benjamin T. D. Lawton)[32] was the one grandchild from among Sarah and Joseph's numerous grandchildren—there were 114 at the time of Sarah's
death in 1839—to move to Macon, Georgia, after first living in Savannah
for a few years in the 1840s. In Georgia, with Lawton relatives among his
principal clients, he "trafficed [sic] in cotton and commercial goods."

When the three Lawton brothers with their Mosse wives experienced
the "drawing thither" to Black Swamp in St. Peter's Parish, Beaufort

---

[32]See Appendix: George Mosse, Joseph Lawton, Benjamin Themistocles Dion Lawton,
and William Seabrook Lawton Family Group Records. Also see Ancestor Charts A and B,
and Mosse and Lawton Lineal Charts #1 and #2.

District[33] was already becoming well settled with Roberts, Maners, Nortons, Jaudons, McKenzies, Bosticks, Rileys, Coles, Lowrys, Boyds, Staffords, and others. Many of these families were related by blood or marriage to Joseph and Sarah Robert Lawton and their children. Plantations run by the various relatives were given over almost entirely to the already big business—especially big since the invention of the cotton gin in 1792—of raising cotton. That cotton would become a tyrannical king was not yet evident in the first decades of the nineteenth century in Beaufort District.

The United States Congress passed an act banning importation of slaves after 1808.[34] The ban apparently irked the Lawtons less than the other slaveholders. Because of the family's stated policy not to separate slave families, the slaves on Lawton lands were encouraged to procreate, and the number of slaves grew apace with demands for "new hands" to cultivate, pick, clean, gin, and transport the cotton crops. Blacks—almost all of whom were slaves—outnumbered whites by almost two-to-one by midcentury.[35]

As the Lawton families grew in size, wealth, and influence, they and their kinfolk drew together and cooperated in all sorts of religious, social, civic, educational, and business endeavors. Their efforts were marked with a certain similarity of conviction and purpose. They founded towns; managed all phases of large plantations; served as ministers, missionaries, deacons, and association officers of Baptist, and in a few instances, other Protestant churches; they were elected to serve numerous terms in the South Carolina state legislature; acted as commissioners, postmasters, surveyors, grand jurors, judges, lawyers, justices of the peace; they entered partnerships with one another, forming businesses that operated in Robertville, Allendale, Savannah, Charleston, Augusta. By the last decades of

---

[33]The area of South Carolina Low Country in which large numbers of the Lawton clan lived in the eighteenth and nineteenth centuries—encompassing the towns of Allendale, Black Swamp (later Robertville), Lawtonville (now Estill)—was known by various names during the course of the two centuries. The area will be referred to here as "Beaufort District."

[34]Wright, *South Carolina, a History*, 162-63.

[35]Ibid., 153ff.

the nineteenth century, many lived out their lives in Macon and in other Georgia and South Carolina towns as well.

All the while, during the pre-Civil War period, the relatives maintained a fierce pride in their religion, their accomplishments, their lands, and their slaves. They took special pride in a "good name," and in untainted bloodlines. Through the generations, since the first slave was purchased by the first Lawton, the story persisted that "you don't see any high-yellow or light-complected darkies on a *Lawton* plantation." And after a pause the raconteur would usually add, "Well, if you *do*, they look like Mr. _____," and the storyteller would name the plantation overseer.[36]

By 1810 cotton was beginning to pass through the ports of Charleston and Savannah at a phenomenal rate to mills in France and Germany, as well as to English mills and mills within the United States. The Lawton planters directed crop production on their various plantations—Gravel Hill, Mulberry Grove, Cypress Vale, Pineland, Transpine, and others—to meet the rising demands for the fluffy "white gold." "Capital," personified by the Lawton planters, "kept his eyes on the field."[37] It paid off. If there were hints that the soil was becoming exhausted and production diminishing, it was not apparent on plantation account books.

On January 13, 1810, Alexander James Lawton, a few months after his marriage to Martha Mosse, made one of the first entries in his new Mulberry Grove Plantation diary.[38] He wrote: "Tom, Moriah, Will Hagan and Son came from Estate [of George] Mosse. These are the Negroes I got by my wife." On April 7 he entered: "Commenced planting cotton on Middle Field."

Alexander maintained the plantation record diligently for thirty years, leaving an accurate account not only of the details of the operation of Mulberry Grove Plantation and the management of his slaves, but also well-conceived specifications and progress reports regarding the building of a summer house that was named "Transpine." Significantly, and perhaps unknowingly, Alexander James Lawton left a record of his character, his generosity and strengths, as well as his foibles, shrewdness, and sagacity. His

---

[36]See editor's note above.

[37]See Appendix for the text of "The Cotton Bloom."

[38]Alexander James Lawton Plantation Diary, collections 414 and 415, vol. 1. Typed copy, 1-100.

relationships to his brothers and other family members emerge in the accounts.

By June of the year 1810, the slaves had planted other fields, and Alexander noted: "Finished 5th & last plowing, hoeing began." In Middle Field the first small leaves of the cotton plants broke the crests of the contoured soil; the leaves enlarged and thickened, and the tight green buds appeared among the dense foliage. The first blossoms appeared, creamy white, and Alexander wrote on June 23: "Saw cotton blossoms in both fields, red and white." By the next morning the cotton blossoms would have been purple-red and dropping from the stems as the cotton bolls began to appear. The plants grew knee-high and the bolls swelled. Beginning with the bolls on the lowest branches, they began to change from green to brown. From the tip of the boll to the stem, the crisp brown cases split along three or four ridged lines, finally gaping wide to show tufts of white lint and seed that had filled the several small pockets of each boll. [39]

Alexander reaped a good crop that year; on August 9 he "made 11155 weight seed cotton & sold it 505$." There were also crops of rice and peas, "75 bushels of corn, potatoes for victuals for the negroes to eat." After Christmas, evidently feeling an obligation to the Black Swamp Baptist Church, he set some of his slaves and "father's negroes, Preston & Martin to work on the Parsonage House [that] I am to build in a plain manner with shed to it; the whole house & lumber to be completed for 400 dollars." By March of 1811, he had "finish'd working on Parsonage House, work'd in all 42 days." Shortly thereafter, he cleared new fields and planted at Transpine, where in a few years he would build a summer home for his family.

The first cotton crop of 1810 was good, but in 1811 "the great rains commenced 9 July & continued from time to time till this day ending with a storm of the greatest fall of water that has been known for many years." Later in 1811, he put the date "Feby. 14" and wrote, "I forgot to mention that on this day my Brothers Joseph [James] & Benj^m & Sister Thirza Polhill set off with their Families for the Mississippi territory."

Alexander stuck with his lands in Beaufort District. Benjamin and the relatives who made the trek to land in Mississippi soon regretted their move. When they returned to South Carolina, Alexander noted on March 19, 1814: "In this year my Brothers Joseph Lawton & Benj^m T. D. Lawton &

---

[39]Phillips, *Life and Labor*, 91-92.

Sister Thirza [Lawton] Polhill's bereav'd Daughters returned from the Western Country, after a disastrous journey to that country for the purpose of settling there—they calculate they sunk about 1800 dollars each. My poor sister Thirza died in that country [Vicksburg] Dec[r] 1811."

When the saddened, poorer, and weary members of the Benjamin T. D. Lawton family returned to South Carolina, they were welcomed back into the "bosom of the family." With the memory of the disastrous venture fresh in his mind, Benjamin made a more cautious decision to settle nearer his relatives. Upon his return he spearheaded a move to more hospitable lands in upper St. Peter's Parish, Beaufort District, less than a dozen miles from his parents, his brother Alexander, and other relatives in the Low Country. Benjamin gave the name Lawtonville to the new settlement. The village, in the center of which was the Republican Baptist Church (later named Lawtonville Baptist Church)[40], soon became the center of business, religious, and social activity. Later other families joined the contingent at Lawtonville, including members of the Willingham family who intermarried with Lawtons.[41] The years softened the painful memories of the Mississippi undertaking as Benjamin and his brothers became caught up in the increasing demands of plantation, family, church, political, and civic responsibilities.

The Lawton brothers, unlike some Southerners who had an interest in obtaining west Florida from the Spanish, seem not to have been deeply involved in the War of 1812, which some considered a war without a cause. The Beaufort District planters had no reason to consider that their lives would be adversely affected regardless of the war's outcome, since it was a war fought mainly in Canada and the Northeastern states. The final action took place on January 5, 1815, at New Orleans, a struggle that came only after the technical end of the war. When directly confronted with the call to demonstrate their patriotism, however, men of the family volunteered or were drawn into military service. In 1813 Alexander wrote in his diary: "On the 13th day of June I marched for a tour of duty in Beaufort in a Military Way: to command in the rank of first Lieutenant. I remained in camp of

---

[40]Johnston, *Two Centuries of Lawtonville Baptists*, 24, 52, 53.

[41]See Appendix: Thomas Willingham, Benjamin Lawton Willingham, and Benjamin T. D. Lawton Family Group Records. Also see chapter seven on Benjamin Lawton Willingham.

Charleston sitting on a Court Martial until 23 August." In all of the wars—
the Indian wars, the War of 1812, the Civil War, the Spanish American
War, World Wars I and II—men of the family performed their duty, often
with enthusiasm and commendable bravery, and in at least two instances
sacrificed their lives to the cause. Still, they did participate in the War of
1812 with less zeal than most.

Perhaps because of his absence on tour of military duty, the year 1813
was, as Alexander expressed it in his record, "the worst year for making
crops I have experienced since I have been planting. I shall make but a sorry
crop; there was a very serious drought and in the fall excessive rains; and
on the 12th and 14th days of October had a frost which stopt the growth of
cotton."

From the time he began developing his plantation in 1810, until 1815
when "this year the 8 March, my hon'd affectionate Father [Joseph] de-
parted this life," Alexander and his father "planted in co[operation] as
usual." The year 1814 "was a good year for crops, the best I have experienced
as a planter." The following remarks are dated 1815, the year of his father's
death: "I planted with my Father . . . with nineteen hands besides the
driver, out of which I draw eight shares. . . . [We planted] corn, potatoes,
rice & 90 acres of Cotton, the last all at Transpine."

When he died, Joseph had bequeathed "unto my beloved wife, Sarah,
during her natural life, the use of my Houses & as much land as she wishes
to cultivate, of any lands I own in this Country," at least thirty slaves, "my
stock of Horses, Cattle, Sheep and Hogs; my Household and Kitchen Furniture, riding chair, waggon & all plantation Tools; the said property, except the land, to be divided equally [among] all my Children." Further, he
had bequeathed to son Alexander James "the tract of land on which I now
live, on which my Houses stand." Joseph made his "beloved sons, William
Henry, Joseph James, Benjamin T. D. and Alexander James his lawful
Executors."[42]

In devising his will as he did, whether deliberately or unknowingly, Joseph had set the stage for Sarah to control Mulberry Grove as an always benevolent matriarch. Mulberry Grove was already being occupied by
Alexander James and his family, as well as by Joseph and Sarah, until Joseph's death. Sarah continued as its mistress in name, if not in fact, until

---

[42]Will of Joseph Lawton, November 16, 1811.

her own death. To her son Alexander, with whom she made her home, fell the direct task of caring for his mother and maintaining the houses and lands of Mulberry Grove according to her wishes.

Sarah was an indomitable soul, devout, fiercely proud, and imbued to her dying day—she lived almost a quarter century longer than Joseph—with a deep conviction that it was her responsibility to run the plantation, to keep up with their seven surviving children and, as far as possible, the numerous offspring of those children. In her later years, on fine afternoons, she had her well-groomed horses hitched to her carriage, and one of her slaves drove her on inspection tours of the plantations, and for visits to the families.

*In her old age, Sarah Robert Lawton (1755-1839) had become a sharp-tongued matriarch who, as her health declined, became more and more demanding of her many descendants, of whom, by the time of her death in 1839, she had many scores, including 114 grandchildren.*

[Collection of Cecilia Willingham Grove]

One of her contemporaries wrote, "Mrs. Lawton was the mother of at least six heads of families in Beaufort District." Sarah was especially concerned with the spiritual health of the children of those families, which she nurtured by setting an example of faithful church attendance and by admonishing those who were not as faithful as she was. She wrote letters of advice, or summoned any miscreants to visit her. They learned to mend their ways when Sarah spoke. On one occasion Sarah wrote from Mulberry Grove to "My dear Grandson" in Savannah.[43] Soon to be married, the grandson, Winborn Joseph Lawton, had been deceived in a business venture, for which Sarah gave him her sympathy: "You being young, and inexperienced, he took you in. But don't let that make you ashamed. . . . You are young and you must be saving and industrious and make every edge cut. Never go above your income if you *never* do well. . . . A young couple married must live as they can afford." Sarah continued her letter with congratulations and love to his intended "amiable companion" and then expressed concerns that were basic to her staunch nature and forthrightness:

> Oh my child what happiness it would afford me to learn that you had embrac'd religion. That I hoped to have heard before this, but all that are grown, except you have made an open profession of religion. . . . Remember your Creator in the days of your youth. . . . I hope when you are married you will try to bring your companion to see me that I may receive her into my family as a granddaughter with the rest of mine.

Upon Joseph's death, when Sarah was still a vigorous sixty, she began to participate actively in running Mulberry Grove, and in managing the slaves—field hands as well as household slaves—that she owned. Astute and methodical in maintaining her personal affairs, she set up cooperative arrangements with her sons for crop production. An arrangement with Alexander seemed to work smoothly through the years, for he wrote in his diary on March 8, 1816: "This year I plant in Co. with my mother. I work Eleven and a half & she Eight hands (inclu^d driver) . . . Mother 5 3/4 acres in cotton . . . with her house servants." The next year the "partners" added 619 acres purchased from Benjamin H. Buckner, which were "situate[d] in St. Luke's and St. Peter's Parishes." In 1817 Alexander made the notation: "I plant as usual in conjunction with my mother. We work as follows—myself: 14 hands, Mother 8 1/2." In that same year, Alexander was elected to and served as a delegate for St. Peter's Parish to the Twenty-Second General Assembly of South Carolina, at which time Andrew Pickens was gover-

---

[43]Sarah Robert Lawton to her grandson, Winborn Joseph Lawton, July 23, 1835.

nor.[44] Also in that year he reported: "So awfully dreadful was the yellow &
bilious fever in Beaufort, that it is said one sixth (1/6) of the population of
white[s] died this year & 200 persons died in Savannah in the month of October." The overall result was that "we made [only] about 3/4 crop of cotton,"
and "we made a late start this spring in consequence of the great & unusual
sickness of the negroes & a very wet winter." But they did get the crops
planted, and later that year "my mother and myself [undertook] to build a
summer house" at Transpine, on acreage within Mulberry Grove
Plantation.

With Sarah's grandchildren rapidly approaching and passing school
age, the brothers Alexander, Benjamin, William Henry, and Joseph James,
together with their sisters and their husbands and other Beaufort District
parents, set about launching an institution to educate their children. They
designed the Black Swamp Academy, Robertville, South Carolina, to be ad-
ministered in two sections: the lowest classes to provide "a plain English
education with English grammar," and a second or higher class, whereby a
"scholar" could obtain a "knowledge of Latin & Greek Languages & every
qualification necessary for entering the Junior Class in the South Carolina
College."

As did most South Carolina planters, the Lawtons and their neighbors
regarded education of their children as a private concern, worthy of their
active support.[45] A nucleus of interested citizens mustered sufficient financial support and enough donated slave labor to build a "neat & comfortable
school house which they have stiled [sic] the Blackswamp Academy." A
meeting was called on July 1, 1818, and the "following seven persons

[44]Edgar, Biographical Directory, 1:192-294. From the Fourth General Assembly of South
Carolina, when Wood Furman represented the "District Eastward of the Wateree River" in
1782, to the Fifty-seventh Assembly, represented by John Lawton in 1886-1887, various family members served in the South Carolina General Assembly, including: Peter Robert, Jr.,
and Joseph James Lawton from St. Peter's Parish, 1804-1805; Alexander James Lawton and
Reuben Roberts, St. Peter's Parish, 1816-1817; Alexander James Roberts served additional periods representing St. Peter's Parish in 1818-1819; Joseph Maner Lawton represented St. Peter's Parish in 1824-1825, 1826-1828, and 1832-1833; Benjamin William Lawton from
Barnwell District, 1850-1851; James Stoney Lawton from St. Peter's Parish, 1852-1853; Winborn Lawton, St. Andrew's Parish, 1828-1829 and 1830-1831; Joseph Maner Lawton, St. Peter's Parish, 1859 and 1860-1861; William John Lawton, Hampton County, 1878-1880, and
John Lawton, Hampton County, 1886-1887. John Lawton was also elected a member of the
South Carolina Board of Agriculture for the Fifth Judicial District on December 22, 1887.

[45]Taylor, Ante-bellum South Carolina, 107-11.

[elected] Trustees to have the Care and Management of the same, to wit: John Robert, William Maner Sen<sup>r</sup>, W<sup>m</sup> H<sup>ry</sup> Lawton, Joseph J. Lawton, James Jehu Robert, John S. Maner & Alex J. Lawton"—all related by blood or marriage. Benjamin T. D. Lawton became a trustee in 1820. Alexander, elected secretary at the first meeting, faithfully kept the minutes for the next five years.[46]

"Mr. Boyd," the first teacher, instructed about twenty-five students, composed mainly of the children of the seven trustees. As the classes grew, in the following years two teachers were required: Alexander Lowry became principal and Thomas Lowry served as an assistant teacher. Pupils whose families lived close by walked, or were brought to school by carriage or wagon; others boarded at a "Steward's House" during the two school sessions, January to June, and June to December. Rules were harsh but fair: "Laughing, talking, whispering & other improprieties are forbidden. . . . Any pane of glass broken, the student shall pay 50 cents . . . willfull [sic] injury shall be punished by suspension, which shall be announced by the principal before all the students, and parents informed." Parents sent wagonloads of wood on a prearranged schedule to heat the building. Young men students brought water from the well, and the girls swept the floors. A "suitable brick collar" contained the firewood, and a "suitable screen" surrounded the "necessary."

At examination time in June, "the performance of the scholars in all the parts excepting writing and arith" proved to be satisfactory to the trustees, and in "some of the branches, very superior." In the evening of the last day of examination, "the male students performed public speaking and dialogues in a handsome manner & very satisfactory to all present, after which honors were conferred on the meritorious." At the next examination time, trustees became eloquent in their praise of the graduates: "It is believed their performance has not been equalled or excelled."[47]

[46]Minutes of the Board of Trustees, Blackswamp Academy, July 1, 1818 to September 28, 1825.

[47]In a presentation to the 1975 Lawton Family Association in Atlanta GA on June 18 and 19, Thomas O. Lawton reported that—based on letters from various schools and universities that he had in his files—planters' sons who had been students at Black Swamp Academy later attended: Brown, Princeton, Madison (now Colgate), University of Virginia, Randolph-Macon, Hampton-Sydney, and the South Carolina College. Daughters attended Emma Willard, Troy NY; Salem Academy, NC; Miss Bonney's School, Philadelphia; and other schools closer to home.

A few years later, Robertville Academy (as Black Swamp Academy was then known) engaged Charlotte Verstille, who had been preceptress of Phillips Andover Academy in New England. Already the school had operated on a firm academic basis. Under Charlotte Verstille's leadership, it attained a reputation for excellence. Students at the academy were accepted at Princeton, Harvard, Madison (now Colgate), Emma Willard's School, Troy, New York, as well as South Carolina College, the University of Virginia, and other colleges and schools closer to home.[48]

Charlotte's brother, Tristam Verstille, a Robertville planter and businessman, lived "within a Biscuit's throw" of the academy, which was situated on a half-acre lot adjacent to the Black Swamp Baptist Church on Sisters' Ferry Road. The academy overlooked "a pleasant green." Charlotte wrote her relatives back in Connecticut from time to time of the little village of Robertville. On one occasion in 1821, she wrote:

> This splendid village contains but six houses, a Church [the Black Swamp Baptist Church], an Academy, and a black-smith's shop. But there are a number of houses situated at unequal distance around it, and inhabited by wealthy planters. . . . Our situation . . . is pleasantest, being at the union of the Savannah, Augusta and Charleston roads, with a green in front of which stand the Church and the Academy.

In 1824 Rebecca Verstille, Tristram's wife, wrote the Connecticut relatives that two houses had been added and that there had been a wedding: Thomas Willingham [II] had married Phoebe Sarah Lawton, Benjamin T. D.'s daughter.[49] A carriage maker opened a shop, and steamboats regularly plied the Savannah River. A "splendid new structure" to house the Black Swamp Baptist Church was built, and in 1829 a parsonage was constructed.

A "mercantile establishment" became part of the village in 1819, when Alexander and his brother, William Henry, "naturally agreed to enter into copartnership under the firm of Alex J. Lawton & Co. for the purpose of purchasing the situation known by the name of Robertville, in said settlement & for the purpose of keeping a store for the sale of goods at said

---

[48]Calendar of the Tristram Verstille Papers, 1811-1860. Also see "The Lawton Family of Robertville," a paper delivered by E. L. Inabinett, director, South Caroliniana Library, to the Lawton Family Reunion, Allendale SC, June 8, 1963.

[49]See Appendix: Benjamin T. D. Lawton and Thomas Henry Willingham [II] Family Group Records, Charts A, B, and C, and Lawton Lines #1 and #2. Also see Willingham Line.

place, for our mutual advantage & interest. . . ." After William Henry's death in 1827, Alexander sold the business to "Messrs Chovin and Willingham."

Alexander continued to note in his diary various plantation management arrangements with his mother: "We work in all 21 hands . . . A. J. Lawton's hands 11 3/4; my mother's hands . . . 9 1/4." In the year 1820, they made "in all 40 bales of cotton. We made also 800 Bushels corn, 50 large Banks Potatoes besides a pretty parcel of Peas, wheat—oats &c. We Fail'd altogether in rice on acct. of worms eating it in that bed. I made in Village 5 or 6 Bushels Potatoes." Finally, in 1825, he vented his true feelings about working "in co." with Sarah:

> I do not count Brister's work this year—mother has many more cattle than I, that cause more work to be lost out of the field than mine, & moreover I have never viewed it unjust that I should pay for half of his work as a field hand, when Mother loses nothing by his attending to my herd with hers & I have never charged her one cent for more than ten years attention to her business. I cannot allow it in future; it is unjust; my family is increasing in numbers & expense for support, & I have no money to pay in this way improperly. I have made a calculation & I find I have paid mother nearly six hundred dollars for Brister's half work since Father's death, which I consider so much taken unjustly from my family, & which I cannot allow hereafter.

Whether Alexander ever resolved his differences with his mother and adopted new, more harmonious management methods with her is not apparent in his diary; but he continued to note her actions, as in 1829: "Mother and self work our hands together this year," or "worked in Co. with Mother." In one of the last entries made in April 1839—with no mention that his mother was seriously ill—Alexander listed "S. L.'s Negroes" by name; and among those to whom he issued a hoe and blankets was "Brister," his mother's field hand, payment for whose work had been a bone of contention.

Alexander did not mention his mother's death in his plantation diary, but in his strong handwriting a notation appears in Sarah's big family Bible: "Sarah Lawton died at Transpine Sunday morning about 10:00 o'clock 6 October 1839, aged 84 years & 6 months of a lingering fever after weeks proceded [sic] by a melancholy affection of the brain of nearly 18 months duration."

After Benjamin Themistocles Dion Lawton returned with his family from the venture in Mississippi, he settled in the pine barrens near the center of the village that he named Lawtonville. He and his wife Jane became the parents of eleven children, including Phoebe Sarah (1808-1862), who married Thomas Henry Willingham [II] (1798-1873), and William Seabrook Lawton (1814-1859), who married Dorothea Furman (1820-1886). [50] Benjamin's brother, Winborn Asa Lawton (1792-1876), and his family became a part of the growing community of Lawtonville when Winborn began serving as pastor of the Pipe Creek Church (renamed Lawtonville Baptist Church in 1884).

As in Robertville, so in Lawtonville. The "woods were full" of Lawton kith and kin in the early decades of the nineteenth century and until the Civil War: Lawtons, Baynards, Brisbanes, Davants, Peeples, Polhills, Grimballs, Maners, Rhodes, Willinghams, and more.

Alexander James Lawton was an extraordinarily talented and industrious man. Available records show he represented St. Peters Parish in the South Carolina House of Representatives. He represented the family in courts of law and was executor and business manager for numerous estates. The many bills, receipts, accounts, estate settlement papers, and mercantile business accounts show that although because of his day-by-day management of Mulberry Grove Plantation in Robertville, he seldom left the Beaufort District, he did carry on a prodigious amount of business outside the Beaufort District through his affiliation with family members and others in cities and towns in South Carolina and Georgia. [51] Records of Benjamin T. D. Lawton and of Lawtonville have not survived as have those of his brother Alexander, but family tradition supports the belief that Benjamin was also adept—after his abortive attempt to settle in Mississippi—as a plantation manager and businessman. With headquarters in Lawtonville, he also had business and family connections, in particular with his sons and daughters throughout the two states.

---

[50]See chapters 1 and 7 on the Furman and Willingham families.

[51]Record of partnership agreement to establish Alexander J. Lawton & Co., February 8, 1819, signed by William Henry Lawton and Alexander James Lawton. In 1833, after his brother Thomas Henry's death, Alexander took his cousin J. B. Jaudon into partnership, and they operated a mercantile firm named J. B. Jaudon & Co. in Savannah.

Benjamin's son, William Seabrook Lawton, who went first to Savannah shortly after his grandmother Sarah's death, thence to Macon, was one of these. At the time, rumblings of Southern secession were already being heard in the halls of Congress, and until his dying breath, South Carolina's John Calhoun was leading the proslavery faction in the debates that led to the Compromise of 1850.

*Chapter Nine*

# WILLIAM SEABROOK
# LAWTON
## (1814/15-1858)

### 'Tending to Business

Between 1820 and 1850, almost anything seemed possible to the enterprising Lawton planters. In common with their neighbors of the Carolina Low Country, they lived with the daily challenge that wealth from the vast region of rich cotton lands was theirs for the taking.[1] Manage your slaves well and work hard. Provide the best for your family. Fear God. Live according to His commandments. Above all, rear your children well. But enjoy life. Be hospitable. Be magnanimous. You could afford to be, or so the records showed.

As members of the plantation gentry, strongly entrenched in public and religious life, Lawton kin took pride in their English antecedents, in high standards of conduct, and in uncompromising guardianship of a dis-

---

[1]Dobb, *The Cotton Kingdom*, 2, 12.

tinct and inviolate color line. With rare exceptions, they were personally honorable, and did what their class and society expected of them. Differences of opinion among family members, which might have developed into angry debate or open hostilities, were handled privately; and if certain factions handled the matter by "silent contempt"[2] of other family factions, that was acceptable. Be always courteous, always politic. The "silent contempt" approach to handling dissension was seldom used. Often as not at family gatherings, the amusing aspects of family differences would become apparent, and the icy atmosphere would melt under animated conversation, bursts of laughter, and hugs and kisses all around.

That characteristic of forgetting past grievances and seeing the humor in potentially explosive issues served the family well—they stuck together, the many dozens of them. They tended to evaluate outsiders, not so much as individuals, but as belonging to a family, as being related to this or that specific family. They forgave much if offenders were "kinfolks."

When Governor B. F. Henegan delivered a message to the South Carolina legislature in session in November 1840, he expressed gratification that "the occupation of planter, always respected among us, has risen in public estimation to a dignity not second to the learned professions."[3] The Lawton planters had a part in raising the occupation of planter to a respected position not only in South Carolina but in Georgia as well. During the early decades of the nineteenth century, cotton cultivation by Lawton and Willingham relatives spilled over South Carolina parish lines to Georgia and, to a lesser degree, Alabama and Mississippi. Those new lands proved to be good regions for cotton. Ties of all sorts between the original family groups in South Carolina and the younger generations of relatives in the port cities of Charleston and Savannah, as well as in the Georgia inland towns of Macon, Albany, Augusta, Forsyth, Atlanta, sprang up and were made strong. To a certain extent, cotton and the plantation system carried, wherever it spread, something of the Low Country culture.[4] By midcentury, Savannah had become as important a business, commercial, and social ad-

---

[2]Winborn Asa Lawton to son Winborn B. Lawton, September 7, 1854.

[3]Taylor, *Ante-Bellum South Carolina*, 41.

[4]Stoney, *Plantations of the Carolina Low Country*, 39.

junct of Carolina Low Country planters as Charleston had been in earlier years.

In traveling to Savannah, the Beaufort District planters could go by either road bordering the Savannah River on horseback, crossing the river at Two Sisters' Ferry. At a slower pace, they could travel the distance by one of their sturdy carriages or wagons. Several times a month, stagecoaches jostled along the roads on irregular schedules. On the river travelers could go by canoe or small boat. In later years, pack boats equipped to carry passengers plied the Savannah, passing through the pine barrens and deepwooded country. Flatboats and rafts received their loads of cotton at wharves that lay at the end of country lanes along the river's banks. To transport their cotton to market, the Beaufort planters used their own flatboats, often built by their slaves, who furnished the motive power with poles and oars. In 1826, with Savannah boasting a cotton shipment of 190,000 bales—this and other crops were thence shipped to Liverpool and other foreign ports—the city had taken its place in the front rank of Southern ports.[5]

The Lawton brothers—the five sons of Joseph and Sarah Robert Lawton—among them had several dozen children who lived to maturity. The parents placed great importance on good educations for them all, in order to establish them as either plantation owners, factors, merchants,[6] or in the professions. Sarah considered the profession of minister of the Gospel an especially appealing vocation for her progeny, one that would contribute to the well-being of their family and society as well. In accord, William Henry, Joseph James, Benjamin T. D., Alexander James, and Winborn Asa, together with their own wives, their two sisters, and their husbands (Thirza and Thomas Polhill; Charlotte Ann and James Jehu Roberts),[7] set up private schools for their children's education. These included Black Swamp, Allendale, and Lawtonville Academies. Upon their children's graduation from the academies, they sent them to colleges or universities, or in the case of the girls, to finishing schools or colleges for women. Then,

---

[5]Stokes, *The Savannah*, 296.

[6]Wright, *South Carolina*, 104: "It should be remembered that the term *merchant* meant a wholesaler, who stood on a different social plane from the retailer, or humble shopkeeper."

[7]See Appendix: Family Group Records for Benjamin Themistocles Dion Lawton and Alexander James Lawton.

well schooled, the men were expected to take their places in the Southern community, as planters, professionals, or in trade, and the women as wives of "upstanding" planters, doctors, lawyers, or ministers.

Among Joseph and Sarah Lawton's grandchildren, there were numbers who stayed on the family plantations in South Carolina, taking over their operation as time went on and as they established families of their own. Others kept their lands in South Carolina, and acquired and maintained additional property in Georgia. Alexander Robert Lawton (1816-1896), son of Martha Mosse and Alexander James Lawton, was one of these. After his graduation from West Point in 1839 and Harvard Law School in 1841, he married Sarah Gilbert Alexander, a belle from Washington, Georgia. They settled in Savannah where he made a distinguished career in law, as president of the Augusta and Savannah Railroad, in the Georgia legislature, in military service as Robert E. Lee's friend and brigadier general on his staff, and after the Civil War as U. S. ambassador to Austria.[8] Another of Joseph's grandsons, Henry Martyn Robert (son of Adeline Elizabeth Lawton and Joseph Thomas Robert), also a West Point graduate (1857), became brigadier general and chief of engineers of the U. S. Army, designed the sea wall for the city of Galveston, was the leading authority on parliamentary law in the country, and in 1876 wrote and published *Robert's Rules of Order*,[9] twentieth-century editions of which still bring in royalties for his descendants.

Several of Joseph's grandchildren combined professional or business careers with plantation management in Georgia and South Carolina. Dr. Benjamin William Lawton—Joseph James's son—after graduation from the Medical College of South Carolina in 1843 became a practicing physician in Allendale, was one of numerous cousins who served as a South Carolina legislator, voting for secession in the legislative session of 1861-1862. Later he moved his medical practice to Augusta, Georgia, and served as president of the Miller-Lawton Insurance Company there, returning eventually to Allendale.

Yet another of Joseph's grandsons, Joseph Alexander Polhill, was born in Natchez, Mississippi (1811) when his parents, Thirza Lawton and Thomas Polhill, made the fateful trek with Benjamin T. D. to settle in Mis-

[8]Candler and Evans, *Cyclopedia of Georgia Baptists*, 2:457.

[9]Miller, *Family Circle*, 261-64.

sissippi. The baby Joseph Alexander was brought back to South Carolina after his mother's death. He graduated from Furman Institute, served for many years as pastor of the Allendale Baptist Church and as trustee of Furman University.

And so, through the generations the lawyers among the kith and kin turned to politics or planting or military service—sometimes all three. The several cousins who became physicians combined "doctoring" with planting, with politics, with "pastoring," with civic and military duties. And the ministers in nearly all instances owned slaves.

The big plantations required abundant supplies of hand tools, clothes, shoes for the slaves (Alexander James Lawton noted in his diary the purchase of dozens of pairs at "$1 per pair for field hands; $1.25 per pair for house servants"), blankets, simple furnishings for the slave quarters. For the big house there were fine wool blankets, as well as plain and fine clothing material, and, occasionally, books, imported from England. And always there was need for gins and mills, buggies and wagons, saddles and leather goods, iron and blacksmith supplies.

Most Southern planters were never very good at accounting and fiscal matters. With the possible exception of Alexander James Lawton, and a few others with his special talents, every planter dealt with a factor, or firm of factors. The factor was the middleman involved in all areas of financing and marketing the Southern staple crops in the decades before the Civil War. The factor traded, held consultations, acted as agent, and had charge of all sorts of transactions and negotiations for his planter-client. He was commission merchant, purchasing agent, storekeeper, banker, bookkeeper, counselor, and in some cases, lawyer. He received the crops and sold them; often saw them loaded aboard ship for their assigned destinations; purchased supplies for the plantations at home and abroad. In short, he got things done—whatever it was that needed to be done for his client, the planter.[10]

Alexander James Lawton, as is evident in his letters, diary, and account books, carried the prodigious burden of business manager, accountant, lawyer, tradesman, for numerous close relatives, friends, distant cousins, and first and foremost, for his strong-willed mother Sarah. In addition, he discharged civic duties as well, and he performed duties as a church officer, Carolina state military officer for fourteen years, and was elected and served on the South Carolina Legislature for a term.

[10]Woodman, *King Cotton and His Retainers*, 5.

After many years as officer in the state militia, he tendered his resignation to Brigadier General William Oswold on February 20, 1823. He wrote that he had been "long in the service" of his state, "to the sacrifice of personal Interest," and that "my domestic concerns are increasing, and require more of my personal attention." There seems no doubt about it; he was indeed a very busy man.

Available documents, especially those in the Southern Historical Collection of the University of North Carolina, support the view that Alexander James Lawton was relieved and pleased when on several occasions through the years various sons and nephews moved to Savannah, Charleston, and elsewhere, and set up law offices, factorage offices, or became merchants and businessmen directly supportive of family plantations in South Carolina. Alexander James, his brother Benjamin T. D., and the members of the older generation could then give full attention to matters on the plantation when several of their sons and grandsons began to "tend to business" in Georgia.

Generation after generation, in its heyday as a city-state, Charleston grew under the intelligent and cultivated rule of a few great Carolina families. The Beaufort District planters of South Carolina, because of their geographical situation and their easier access to Savannah, were drawn more often to the Georgia port city of Savannah rather than to Charleston. They were drawn to Savannah for religious associational meetings, for trade, for political and cultural events, and especially for profitable disposition of their cotton crops.

In the early decades of the nineteenth century, the prosperity of the Charleston port had declined, tied directly to the fluctuating price of cotton.[11] Much of the cotton trade from northwest South Carolina was being channeled through Augusta and the tributaries of the Savannah River to the port of Savannah. Business in Charleston declined; business in Savannah grew. In 1820, in a speech undoubtedly exaggerated, Robert Y. Hayne, later a U.S. senator and prominent spokesman for the South and its doctrine of states' rights, complained to the Senate of South Carolina that the commerce through Charleston had virtually disappeared[12] and that her shipyards were "rotting away in disuse." The break with England and the

---

[11]Wright, *South Carolina*, 161.

[12]Taylor, *Cavalier and Yankee*, 262.

revolutionary war had ended the bounties on indigo, and the market for rice had been all but destroyed.[13] Despite these downward trends, the market for cotton grew.

By 1843 communication, travel, and trade of all kinds between Charleston and Savannah on the Savannah River became brisk, and in the case of passenger travel, pleasant. After an extensive tour of the South, William Cullen Bryant wrote on April 7, 1843:

> I left Charleston on the 30th of March, in one of the steamers which ply between that city and Savannah. These steamers are among the very best that float—quiet, commodious, clean, fresh as if just built, and furnished with civil and ready handed waiters. . . . Our fellow-passengers were mostly planters of the [sea islands and coastal mainland] and their families, persons of remarkably courteous, frank, and agreeable manners. The next morning early we passed up the Savannah River and the city was in sight, standing among its trees on a high bank of the stream. . . .[14]

Commerce increased in both seaports, and based on a burgeoning cotton economy by 1860 South Carolina had a network of railroads that made transportation easier throughout all of South Carolina as well as to Savannah and throughout Georgia.

On that "high bank of the stream" where Savannah stood, William Seabrook Lawton, native of Lawtonville, son of Benjamin T. D. and nephew of Alexander James, took up residence. He opened an office in the Taylor Building, and ran an advertisement on July 24, 1841, in the Savannah *Daily Georgian*:

> Factorage and Commission Business
> The Subscriber will carry on the Factorage and Commission Business after this on his own account, and solicits a share of patronage from the planters.   Wm. S. Lawton

The wording of the advertisement indicates that William may have been a partner in an earlier factorage business—Messrs. Lawton & Co.—from which his brother, James Stoney Lawton, later withdrew; but by 1841 William was in the factorage and commission business in Savannah "on his own account."

---

[13]Craven, *Coming of the Civil War*, 59.

[14]Thorp, *A Southern Reader*, as quoted in Bryant, "Bryant Tours the South," 26-27.

William Makepeace Thackeray, the great English novelist, visited the little city of Savannah in midcentury, at about the time William lived there, and described it as

> a tranquil old city, wide streeted, tree-planted, with a few cows and carriages toiling through the sandy road, a few happy negroes sauntering here and there, a red river, and a tranquil little fleet of merchantmen taking in cargo, and tranquil warehouses barricaded with packs of cotton, no row, no tearing Northern hustle, no ceaseless hotel racket, no crowds.[15]

As a factor, William Lawton represented his Carolina relatives in the "tranquil old city" of Savannah that earlier had been plagued with fevers in the summer months. According to the poet Bryant, when he was there in 1843, the town was "more healthy of late years than it formerly was." Bryant explained that an arrangement was made with owners of plantations in the immediate vicinity, by which the "culture of rice has been abandoned, and the lands are no longer allowed to be overflowed with water within a mile of the city. The place has become much less subject to fevers than in former years."

In Savannah, William Seabrook managed details of all sorts for the plantations back in Robertville, Lawtonville, and Allendale. He ordered a carriage made for his grandmother Sarah, watched its progress as it was built, and finally shipped her the finished product. Now she could make her afternoon inspection visits in and around Robertville in fine style. As June 1842 approached, William ordered trousseau items from Europe, and upon their arrival in Savannah, had them placed aboard the packet *Santa Anna* for his Uncle Alexander James, whose daughter Amanda married Jonathan Miller shortly thereafter. The order included "1 pairs white kid gloves, 1 pair white thibit [sic] stockings, 1 white lace veil, 1 1/2 yds fine-thread lace, and 5 yds white satin."

The principal business that William transacted for the plantations was, of course, in cotton. After the barges that had been loaded with bales of cotton at the plantations had been floated downriver to Savannah, William checked them at the docks, sold the harvest according to his clients' instructions, and had the cotton reloaded on the proper seagoing vessels for shipment to England or elsewhere. He directed slaves in repacking the

---

[15]Harden, *A History of Savannah*, 427.

empty barges and packets with orders of farm provisions, rough cloth, shoes, and with imported goods for the return upstream to the plantations. He also transacted business by letter. On June 11, 1842, he acknowledged receipt of "$800.00 in all" from Cousin Joseph Robert, for "services rendered." He also sent bills: "1 bunch Span Segars $1.00; For sharpening shovel plough, .25¢; mending waggon belt, 12 1/2¢; pointing mill spindle, 50¢." He acted as banker for his clients, and as agent to buy everything from ironing hams to saddle plough eyes; from rocking chairs to finest mirrors, paintings, and books. He collected past-due medical accounts for his cousin, a physician, who also bore the name William Seabrook Lawton.[16]

At her parents' home in Sumter, South Carolina, Dorothea Furman married Factor William Seabrook Lawton in 1839.[17] Lawton's wealthy mother-in-law, Eliza Scrimzeour Furman, reputedly lent William a large sum of money, which he put into his business and which, through "unsound business practices," was lost.[18] Just when and how William lost the money he borrowed, and when he moved to Macon is unclear, but census records for Macon, Bibb County, Georgia, show that in 1850 William and his family were residents of Macon. Two sons, John Marshall, eleven, and Richard Furman, nine, named for his illustrious grandfather, together with Agnes, seven, and wife Dorothea Furman, made up the family. A third son, James Stoney (named for William's brother), was born in Macon, as were several children who died in infancy.

In a printed circular William Lawton once advertised that one phase of his work was "to render every means for facilitating the transfer of his consignments."[19] William surely seems to have discovered most of these. That he was constantly occupied is evident. That he was profitably busy with the basic, more important business of cotton factoring to the exclusion of obtaining "shoelaces and papers of pins" for clients becomes clear only

---

[16]Brother of Alexander Robert Lawton, Savannah lawyer.

[17]See Appendix: Furman Line, Samuel Furman Family Group Record, Ancestor Charts A, D, and D-1. Also see Furman chapter.

[18]See Furman chapter.

[19]The quotation is from a printed one-page circular, a copy of which is in the author's Lawton File.

after he entered a three-way partnership, moved his offices, and opened a warehouse in Macon, Georgia.

In the move to Macon, Lawton improved his lot in life. He managed his affairs more wisely there than in Savannah. Factors who received and exported cotton and other produce for the planters stood in high esteem; factorage was one branch of trade that was not regarded as derogatory to social standing.[20] In partnership with William were Alexander Benjamin Lawton, who had moved from Beaufort District to family lands in Georgia, and Samuel Dowell, who continued the business William had operated in Savannah. William, as third partner, maintained headquarters in Macon.

Royally transported in shining new railroad cars, the mayor, aldermen, and a committee of Savannah city councilmen journeyed to Macon, where they joined Macon officials and citizens in a festival of celebration for the completion of the Central of Georgia Railroad. On that occasion, as reported by the ubiquitous *Georgia Telegraph* on October 6, 1843, eloquent speakers from both cities grew to be friends and exchanged compliments about their cities. The end result was that the two cities through ensuing years grew to realize their interdependence and received "great [commercial] advantages, derived from the extensive railroad and steamship facilities, under the management of the vast transportation system leading to her [Savannah's] very doors." There is no doubt that the "continuous line of 350 miles of railroad, commencing with our largest seaport Savannah, . . . with the object of opening communication with the great West" was a success. The various Georgia railroads in operation by midcentury, including the Augusta and Savannah Railroad, of which Alexander Robert Lawton was president, probably influenced William Seabrook Lawton to establish the factorage business in Macon. With railroads in operation and expanding, shipping the cotton by slow riverboat was no longer necessary. Swiftly the profitable crop could now be transported by railroad boxcar; and Macon, the hub of a network of short railroad lines by virtue of its central location, was the point from which William operated.

Because of its size and importance as a trading center, Macon flourished in a growing prosperity. During the year 1850, the municipal government liquidated a sizable debt without embarrassment. The city placed in operation the first sections of a public water works. The Lamar House

---

[20]Taylor, *Ante-Bellum South Carolina*, 44-45.

opened to receive paying guests who filled the rooms of the luxurious new hotel. The next year two academies for young ladies opened, including one at the residence of the late "Thomas Hardeman, Esq., Vineville, operated by [a] Mrs. Lawton . . . assisted by Miss A. Upson." The *Georgia Telegraph* noted that there were more than a thousand blind children in the state; and in an announcement that proved to be significant to Phillip Gerhart Guttenberger's granddaughter, Emily Lawton, and to future generations of sightless youngsters whom she taught, the Georgia Academy for the Blind was organized and occupied a building on Mulberry and Third streets.

Savannah grew in importance and prestige during midcentury decades, as did Macon. In Savannah entertainments and receptions for visiting dignitaries, including Henry Clay in 1844 and ex-President Polk in 1849—all of whom were lavish in their praise of the thriving seaport—added to the general aura of pride in the city that could "vie in taste and beauty" with any Northern city. The death of Andrew Jackson in 1845 was publicly and officially mourned in Savannah, his "surpassing patriotism and illustrious career" was eulogized, and the city council chambers draped in mourning for thirty days.

The minutes of the city council do not reveal how that body received the news of the death in 1850 of Zachary Taylor, whose troubled presidency was highlighted by his support of the Wilmot Proviso, which excluded slavery from all the territory acquired as a result of the Mexican War. However, there is a brief notation in the council books stating that the mayor and aldermen shall "adopt suitable messages for the solemn commemoration of the death of Zachary Taylor, late President of the United States."[21]

Dr. William S. Lawton and his older brother, Alexander Robert Lawton, living in Savannah, and cousins of William Seabrook Lawton, living in Macon, all became deeply involved in the concerns of the seaport city of Savannah. Dr. Lawton could be counted on to minister to the slaves of his white patients in Chatham County, as well as to the families who owned the slaves. He did so even during sporadic outbreaks of the dreaded yellow fever, which even in the best of years took a few lives in Savannah. Alexander Robert in his thirties became one of the foremost citizens of Savannah through his well-managed law practice, and his counsel and active assistance in all sorts of civic and political endeavors. In 1849 he accepted the position as president of the

---

[21]Harden, A *History of Savannah*, 391, 401, 405, 409, 415, 427.

Augusta and Savannah Railroad. As a designated member of the "Committee on Arrangements," Alexander set up a perfunctory ceremony to commemorate Zachary Taylor's death, and "carried it out as arranged," in sharp contrast to the widespread mourning for Jackson and Calhoun.

Decorated with drawings of neat bales of cotton, and placed between an advertisement giving rules for "transporting Negroes" on the Macon and Western Railroad and an advertisement for the "newly and beautifully furnished Ladies Department of the Floyd House Hotel in Macon," a special notice appeared in the *Georgia Telegraph* on November 25, 1851:

A. B. LAWTON & CO.,
Ware-House and Commission Merchants.
Oglethorpe, Ga.

WM. S. LAWTON & CO.,
Ware-House and Commission Merchants.
Corner of Second and Poplar Streets Macon, Ga.

LAWTON, DOWELL & CO.,
No. 210 Bay Street
Savannah, Ga.

A. B. LAWTON — — — W. S. LAWTON — — — SAM'L L.
DOWELL

Tender their services to their friends and the public, hoping from their long experience in business to be able to give satisfaction.

They beg leave to refer to Samuel J. Ray, Macon, Ga.; Judge B. F. Porter, Charleston, S. C.; T. Willingham, and E. H. Peeples, Esqs., Lawtonville, S. C.; Col. W. J. Lawton, Screven County, Ga.; W. A. Cumming, Coweta County, Ga.; N. Dudley, Esq., Rome, Ga.; Gov. C. J. McDonald, Marietta, Ga.

So, with references and endorsements from Georgia Governor McDonald to Judge Porter of Charleston, and including Georgia and South Carolina planters—most of them related to one or more of the three partners—William launched his new enterprise in Macon.

As William tended to business at his office and warehouse on Second Street, and while Professor Guttenberger and his music students serenely prepared for examinations at the Wesleyan Female College, citizens of Macon became more and more involved in animated conversations, discussions, and meetings on the question of slavery and Southern rights. The year 1850 marked the beginning of a period of tense feeling and excitement in Macon. Clay's Omnibus Bill, considered for the first time by Congress in December 1849, presented features of slavery that were the subject of heated discussions in Macon throughout the following months. Only a few months later, in April 1850, John Calhoun died. Macon, as had Savannah, felt the loss of a great champion, and the *Georgia Telegraph* reported that "our whole community was filled with mourning . . . the melancholy tidings of the decease of John Calhoun, the favorite, the beloved, the cherished son of South Carolina."

There were frequent meetings of both parties—proslavery and antislavery—in Macon throughout the year 1850. On August 31, delegates from all parts of Georgia as well as representatives from South Carolina and Alabama attended a mass meeting to hear "brilliant addresses" on the subject of states' rights.[22] On December 10, Macon sent delegates to Milledgeville, then the state capitol, where representatives from every Georgia county assembled and every appointed delegate was present. There the gathering adopted a report declaring that the "state of Georgia will and ought to resist even to the disrupting of every tie that binds her to the Union, any action of Congress incompatible with the safety, rights, and honor of the slaveholding state." The resolution foreshadowed Georgia's stand which, although not openly declared until a decade later, festered and rankled in the hearts and minds of Maconites for all those years.

As the Southern states drew nearer and nearer to civil war, cotton trade became its most active in years. Good times had returned to Macon. Goods were in abundance; crops were good; sounds of sawing and hammering could be heard throughout the city as stores, warehouses, and dwellings were erected. The well-appointed Grand Theatre attracted some of the most distinguished actors of the day, and Joseph Jefferson's oldest son was born in Macon while his father was appearing onstage at the Grand. Wesleyan lent an air of gentility and culture to the town when the well-dressed young ladies walked in a group on Sunday mornings the few blocks from the college to Mulberry Street Methodist Church. Trainloads of cotton rolled into the Macon freight depot and, under the management of Messrs. Lawton, out again, en route to Savannah or Charleston. From there it was shipped to European markets or to one of many cotton mills

---

[22]*Georgia Telegraph*, August 31, 1850.

now in operation in Georgia, in other Southern states, and throughout the Eastern United States.

William Seabrook Lawton, at forty, was recognized as a well-born, highly successful, respected new citizen of Macon, with "excellent connections" throughout Georgia and South Carolina. Promptly, William had been accepted into the business, civic, and social life of the town.

Until 1850, as cotton production and trade became the main business of Georgia and the South, a great agricultural fair had been held in Atlanta, at Stone Mountain, in October of each year. Macon city officials, representative planters of surrounding central Georgia counties, as well as merchants and enthusiastic citizens, including William Lawton, made prodigious efforts to have the fair moved to Macon. Their efforts paid off. With the Southern Central Agricultural Society as the sponsor, the fair was scheduled to open at Central City Park, in Macon, the first week in October 1851. With the dates set, the Cotton Planters Association made plans to meet at a convention in Macon during Fair Week. As fall weather and time for the fair approached, energies and activities of hundreds of Central Georgians centered on Macon and the fair. The fair grounds became a beehive of activity. Exhibition halls were built, a bandstand erected. The Macon and Western Railroad reduced its rates for exhibitors and visitors. A great soiree, planned by twenty of Macon's foremost citizens, complete with dinner and dancing in the Apollo Room of the Lanier House, opened Fair Week with revelry.

As a member of the Executive Committee, one of William Lawton's responsibilities was to perfect the Premium List, which was said to "excel any offered in any other state, except that of the New York State Agricultural Society, and to be inferior to that *only* in the premiums offered for Horses and Cattle." At the end of Fair Week, William and his fellow Agricultural Society members, exhausted after the months of work and preparation and the feverish activities of the week itself, closed the gates behind the last visitor on the last day. The Executive Committee assessed the fair. Their phenomenal efforts had been richly rewarded. Seven thousand people had come by train, which deposited fairgoers directly on the fair grounds from a spur track; six thousand additional tickets were sold at the gate. Visitors to the fair and the Cotton Planters Convention had come from throughout Georgia, South Carolina, Kentucky, New York, New Jersey. Moreover, three thousand new members had joined the Southern Central Agricultural Association.

Premiums and awards lists, published in the *Georgia Telegraph* on January 31, 1852, included the names of the winners for best wheat, corn, rye, oats, barley, peas, hay, rice, and cotton. There were awards for livestock and leatherwork, for homemade agricultural implements, and for "elegant specimens of axes and hatchets." F. A. R. Scott of Knoxville, Tennessee, took home an award for the "best bottle of Castor Oil"; Wm. Moffett & Co. of Knoxville for best "Cast Iron Grate for Houses." James Hubert & Co. of Augusta received a cup for best buggy as well as best carriage. Dr. Ross of Columbus was adjudged the best bookbinder. Henry, the servant of John Woolfolk of Columbus, received a cup and $5.00 for the "best Stocked Plow, for work done by a slave." The fancy poultry award went to Dr. Battery of Rome. In the fine arts category, Miss Mary E. Rose of Macon received a silver cup for a drawing of Rose Hill Cemetery, and C. C. Ordeman of Montgomery, Alabama, received a cup for a drawing of the residence of E. T. Pollard.

One of Lawton's duties in connection with the fair was as judge of cotton. William and his committee awarded Dr. William Terrell of Hancock County the most coveted award of the entire fair: a silver goblet and $20.00 for the best twenty bales of upland cotton. It was a hard decision for the committee to make. Dr. Charles Thompson's cotton grown in Bibb County was almost equally excellent: his second-place prize was a silver cup and $10.00.[23]

With William's brother, Alexander Benjamin, handling operations in Oglethorpe, and partner Samuel L. Dowell occupied with Lawton & Co. affairs in Savannah, William expanded his business as commission merchant in Macon to include a readily available inventory of commodities and household goods and supplies "on consignment." With his ever-expanding circle of business associates, relatives, and friends, William did a brisk business in all sorts of commodities, including Knoxville Annexation and Empire Cooking Stoves—"A great favorite with Georgia housewives"— Halston Window Glass, prime imported tea, granny bagging, feathers, and bacon, hams, sides, shoulders. Griswold's Superior Cotton Gin also sold especially well.

---

[23]*Georgia Telegraph*, October 21, 1851; January 31, 1852. *Georgia Journal*, October 29, 1851; November 5, 1851.

With Dorothea and the children comfortably settled in a pleasant house, well staffed with faithful servants, among friends and neighbors to whom she could turn if emergencies arose, William made train trips to Savannah and Charleston when his work required it, and less frequently journeyed by stagecoach or other means to the family plantations in South Carolina. Esteemed by his business associates, engrossed in Agricultural Society matters, in civic and church concerns, and in family and home, William went about his daily affairs with enthusiasm.

The summer of 1854 was very hot, and although Savannah suffered a terrific scourge of yellow fever, Macon was unaccountably free of the plague. As soon as word reached Macon of the dangers of remaining in Savannah, William and Dorothea invited friends and relatives in Savannah to visit them until danger had passed. Refugees from Savannah did come to Macon; some, possibly, stayed with William and Dorothea. Some Savannahians died in Macon, but curiously only a few Maconites contracted the disease and none died. When cool weather arrived in the fall, an indication that there would be no more yellow fever that year, the mayor declared a holiday and Maconites gathered at their churches for prayers of thanksgiving that Macon had been spared.

Business in the autumn of 1857 began auspiciously. Cotton was selling at 12¢ and 15¢ per pound: a good price. Every enterprise and industry in the state of Georgia was said to be in "a prosperous condition." Then came a series of crashes on Wall Street. Many Northern and Western companies declared bankruptcies, but Georgians were generally free of debt, and the reaction was rapid. The panic passed. Lawton & Co., as did other Georgia firms, seemed to have recovered easily.

The record is not at all clear why William moved from Macon, but by 1857 the William Seabrook Lawton family was living in Charleston; for when William's sixteen-year-old son, Richard Furman Lawton, was admitted to the preparatory department of the Citadel in Charleston on January 1, 1858, his address was noted in the school records as Charleston District. Late in the summer of 1858, the city of Charleston was suffocatingly hot. The Lawton families most often left the muggy cities of Savannah, Macon, and Charleston in the summer and sought refuge at north Georgia and South Carolina mountain resorts, or at Transpine, or one of the family's other summer places located in the cooler uplands of the two states. Dorothea and the children may well have been at a summer place, but William was in Charleston in late summer.

The September 9, 1858, issue of the *Charleston Courier* gave a frightening report of a yellow fever epidemic that was sweeping the city. "For the five weeks just ending," the report read, "the number of deaths has jumped thus: 4, 20, 26, 70, 127." On September 14, 1858, William Seabrook Lawton became a statistic in that macabre tabulation. At fourty-four, he was dead of yellow fever.[24]

The widow, Dorothea Furman Lawton, received the tender ministrations of her Furman and Lawton relatives in South Carolina. William's youngest son, James Stoney Lawton, had been named for his uncle, Dr. James Stoney Lawton, his father's brother. Dr. Lawton adopted his namesake, and young James took his place as son in the doctor's family, which included a wife and four daughters. James attended Mercer University and later Macon Law School.[25] Dorothea's oldest son, John Marshall Lawton, twenty at his father's death, was in college. Ironically, he too died of the disease by nursing yellow fever patients in Louisiana, thus cutting short a career as an attorney. William's only daughter was fifteen when her father died. After her marriage to John F. Cargile, she lived in Macon.

Dorothea Furman Lawton took another husband after William's death. Scholarly, earnest, trained in law, devout and deeply loyal to the little Monroe Female College in Forsyth, Georgia, that he served as president, Dr. Shaler Granby Hillyer with pride married the granddaughter of Richard Furman as his third wife.[26] At the college (later named Bessie Tift College by benefactors) Dorothea was his "helpmeet" in a period of disorganization at the college in 1880-1882 after a devastating fire. In the summer of 1881, he "closed labors as an educator to devote the rest of his life to the ministry so long as God should give him strength."[27]

Richard Furman Lawton completed his preparatory year at the military school in Charleston, and only a few months after his father's death was transferred on January 1, 1859 to the Citadel, the Military College of South

---

[24]*Georgia Telegraph*, September 14, 1858.

[25]*History of the Baptist Denomination*, 324-27.

[26]See Appendix: William Seabrook Lawton Family Group Record, and Ancestor Charts A, B, C, D.

[27]Stone, *Yesterday at Tift*, 16-17.

Carolina. On April 8, 1862, he graduated at twenty with the rank of cadet captain.

On March 3, 1862, Richard addressed a letter to the Honorable J. B. Benjamin, secretary of war, Richmond: "I hereby make application for the position of Lieutenant in the Confederate Army." Accompanying the letter was another: "[Lawton's] stand in his class is high & his moral character and military bearing unexceptionable [sic]. I therefore take pleasure in recommending him to the Secretary of War of the Confed. States." This one was signed by I. B. White, superintendent of cadets, and endorsed by J. D. W. DeBow: "The applicant is a young gentleman of excellent attainment, high moral character, and in every respect qualified for a commission." The youthful cadet had his picture taken in uniform, showing a "young gentleman [of] military bearing."

Richard Furman received his commission and assignment: first lieutenant and adjutant, Second Georgia Cavalry. A later assignment was as inspector general of cavalry. After the war and his marriage to Elizabeth McLeod, he returned briefly to South Carolina. The marriage was short-lived. Elizabeth died shortly after childbirth, leaving Richard a widower with two infants. He is believed to then have brought his babies and their nurse to Macon, where his mother was living about the time of her marriage to Dr. Hillyer, and where she could supervise the care of the children as Richard entered into business with relatives in Macon. It was an unhappy life for Richard for a few months, but soon with his distant cousin Caroline Willingham as his wife, he entered into a new life in Macon, the town of his childhood.

*Chapter Ten*

# RICHARD FURMAN LAWTON
## (1841-1892)

I n late December 1860, Alexander Robert Lawton,[1] first cousin of Cadet Richard Furman Lawton, then a student at the Citadel in Charleston, returned to his home in Savannah from a heated session of the Georgia Senate in the state's capitol in Atlanta. As the elected senator from Chatham County, Senator Lawton measured swords with Benjamin H. Hill, an antisecessionist. Lawton deported himself well, and supported Georgia Governor Joseph E. Brown in secession debates. A popular governor, Brown, after his initial election to the post in 1857, was reelected by increased majorities in 1859, 1861, and 1863.

Abraham Lincoln had been elected to the presidency and would be inaugurated on March 4, 1861. Lincoln's election was the signal for secession.

---

[1]See Appendix: Lawton Family Group Records, Charts A and B, Lawton Lineal Charts #1 and #2.

All compromise plans had failed. And President James Buchanan still occupied the White House in December 1860.

Throughout the preceding months from Atlanta, as well as from his home in Savannah, Alexander wrote cryptic letters and sent telegrams to his wife, Sarah H. Alexander Lawton, who was on an extended visit to Eastern spas, to Virginia friends, and to Washington. Finally, after a commanding "Come home!" telegram, Sarah was safely home when she wrote a letter on December 30, 1960 to her "Dear Friend," Alex's sister, Adeline Lawton Robert,[2] in Burlington, Iowa.[3]

> Our life was so tranquil six months ago. Public events moved on & cast scarcely a shadow over our quiet lives. Now, private affairs are forgotten, & and their interest merged in the engrossing nature of those political strifes which threaten to change the face of everything around us. You have learned of course of the events in Charleston which have startled *everybody at last*, into the knowledge of those inevitable conflicts which [are] before us.
>
> I learned in Washington that the die is cast. The day that I was there, Mrs. Toombs[4] took me to see the President.[5] He was not receiving, but came down to see us in a state of such evident discomposure and perturbation that we made a very brief call. We did not then know the cause of his disturbance . . . Mr. Breckenridge gave us the tidings of Major Anderson's evacuation of Fort Moultrie, S.C. . . . It was, he said, entirely opposed to the President's views! . . . The Cabinet were called

---

[2]Adeline E. Lawton (1810-1865), daughter of Alexander James Lawton and Martha Mosse, married her cousin, Joseph Thomas Robert (1807-1852?). A Yale graduate, he also studied medicine and later became a minister. Adeline and Joseph moved to Ohio and later to Iowa (see Miller, *Family Circle*, 259-62). Adeline's brother, Alexander Robert, handled business matters in Savannah for her through his law office, and did the same for other family members far removed from Savannah.

[3]Sarah Alexander Lawton to Adeline Lawton Robert, December 30, 1860. This is one of many letters in the Southern Historical Collection in which Sarah corresponds with her father-in-law (calling him "Dear Father"), Mary C. Wilkins, and others to discuss the political situation, and events in Charleston and Savannah, as well as business and family matters. The narrative of the Lawton family related in this chapter, unless otherwise noted, is based on the letters and papers in the Southern Historical Collection (folder dated 1860-1863).

[4]Her husband, Robert Toombs, U. S. senator from Georgia. Later he played a leading role in Georgia's secession and in organizing the Confederacy.

[5]James Buchanan, the "lame duck president."

together & great excitement prevailed. Everyone said, "It is a declaration of war." Just as I was leaving at 6 P.M., the President sent in haste for Mr. Toombs. Since then we have learned nothing, except that we are telegraphed from Charleston that three members of the Cabinet have resigned. . . . I heard in Charleston that tomorrow Fort Sumter will be attacked & it is almost resolved on, here, to seize Forts Pulaski & Jackson.

When I reached the depot in Savannah, my husband was the first man on board, and almost the first thing he said to me was, "I feared I would be off in barracks before you would come home." I know now the meaning of those anxious letters.

I find my husband a very important person here. I am told he was the most influential member of the [Georgia] Legislature & much relied on by Gov. Brown. Owing to that, & to his position as Commander of the Battalion, he is consulted in everything. . . . Even my old father-in-law wears a Blue Cockade! Alex shall have one tomorrow. . . . If you see Dr. Barker, tell him of my safe arrival home, & remember me to him. Alas, that my Northern friends are soon to be Foreigners!

On January 4, 1861, Sarah again wrote to Adeline in Iowa:

Now I know you want the political news—well, you will see by the papers that Fort Pulaski is occupied. By the Governor's order, Mr. Lawton went down yesterday in command, with part of 3 companies, accompanied by Major Wayne, who is Adjutant General of Georgia. Many of the most influential citizens went also & they carried a large negro force, to clear out the ditches. . . . All the cotton states intend to seize their forts & hold them until the question of secession is determined, merely to prevent their being held by federal troops.

As for the capture of Fort Pulaski, Sarah failed to report—if she even knew—what one historian called "an element of the ludicrous about it." He said, "Aglow with warlike zeal, and with flags flying and drums beating, on January 3, 1861, three companies of volunteers [commanded by Alexander Robert Lawton] marched into Pulaski—to find that its defense force consisted of one elderly U.S. Sergeant, who surrendered without a struggle."[6]

Robert E. Lee opposed secession, but when Virginia seceded from the Union in April 1861, he cast his lot with the South. From November 1861 to March 1862, Lee was in Charleston and Savannah, organizing the defense of the South Atlantic seaboard. Throughout those months, on many occasions the Savannah home of General and Mrs. Lawton was filled with

---

[6]Martin, *Georgia, a Bicentennial History*, 91.

*Sarah H. Alexander Lawton, a Washington, Georgia, belle before her marriage to Alexander Rob-*
*ert Lawton, charmed her husband's business and military associates, including General Robert E.*
*Lee, under whom Lawton served as quartermaster general. This photograph of Sarah in a stylish*
*new gown was taken in Paris by A. Liebert & Co. on one of her several shopping jaunts to France.*

[Southern Historical Collection, University of North Carolina]

people "in high places." Sarah wrote to her father-in-law, Alexander James, in Robertville, that "these are busy times with us . . . almost every day last week we had a dinner party, and today [March 18, 1861] we are not alone." Alexander Hamilton Stephens, vice-president of the Confederacy, "dined here last week. He came quietly and spent the evening here." Alexander Robert Lawton, commissioned brigadier general in the Confederate army, was placed in command of the Military District of Georgia, and charged especially with the defense of Savannah and the neighboring coast. General Lee, during his five-months' stay in the Charleston and Savannah area, met with his officers, including General John Clifford Pemberton in Lawton's law offices, and often "spent an evening" with Sarah and Alex at home in Savannah. To show his appreciation for their friendship, Lee gave a small picture of himself to Sarah, which he inscribed to "Mrs. Lawton, with sincere regards, R. E. Lee."

*During the months of 1861 and 1862 that General Robert E. Lee spent in Savannah organizing the defense of the Southatlantic seaboard, he met with his staff in Alexander Robert Lawton's law offices and dined with Lawton and his wife Sarah in their home. At the end of his stay in Savannah, as he was about to depart, Lee gave this photograph of himself to Sarah, which he inscribed to "Mrs. [Alexander Robert] Lawton, with sincere regards."*

[Southern Historical Collection, University of North Carolina]

As it became more and more apparent to General Lawton that he would be deeply involved in the brewing conflict, he divested himself of many of the responsibilities of his law practice and personal business. On January 6, 1862, he transferred his interest in twenty-four of his slaves to his brother, Dr. William S. Lawton. At another time, he arranged for Sarah to "carry on financial business matters" and for all her checks to be honored by his bank "without any trouble to you, my dear wife."

To his aging father, Alexander James, Alex wrote on March 6, 1862:

Gen. Lee has gone to Richmond, & my private opinion is that he will not return to this Command. Maj. Gen. Pemberton is next in rank & I have seen him since Gen. Lee left. He told me he declined to advise planters near the railroad whether to remove their negroes or not—that the State authorities had that matter in charge. I am sure he never thought of planters as far off as Robertville deserting their places.

In June 1862 General Lee ordered Brigadier General Lawton to Virginia, where he commanded a brigade in the Seven Days Battle around Richmond. At Sharpsburg in September, Lawton was critically wounded, and his horse was killed. Two months later, on November 23, 1862, from a hospital in Richmond, where Sarah was permitted to come and be with him, he wrote with a shaking hand:

> My dear Father, I have not been able to write a line since I was wounded. I now feel . . . for the first time I am fast recovering from the wound and the series of surgical operations which followed. . . . I hope to be able to leave for Georgia on Wednesday, the 26th. Our children are [in Washington, Ga.] . . . I hope it will be convenient for you to meet us in Savannah (though I have no longer a home there in which to welcome you) or to pass some time with us in our first efforts at rough country life at Kiakee.

The letter ends in Sarah's handwriting: "His writing shows the effect of long sickness, but I know it will be a welcome sight to you. Most aff-ly Sarah."

Alexander James received much sadder news next month from his daughter-in-law Sarah when she wrote on December 20, "We have received . . . sad tidings. A dispatch [came] from Colonel Gilmer that Captain Edward Lawton was wounded dangerously and in the hands of the enemy." Alexander Robert survived; his brother Edward, youngest son of Alexander James, died December 26, 1862, mortally wounded at the Battle of Fredericksburg. His body was returned to Robertville, where he was buried.

From encampment at Fredericksburg on May 11, 1863, General Lee wrote to General Lawton:

> I am very glad to learn that you have sufficiently recovered of your wound to return to duty. . . . After the death of your estimable brother, your [Lawton] brigade suffered so much for want of a permanent commander & fearing from the accounts read of you that you would not be capable of undergoing the Campaign this Summer, Brig. Gen. Gordon was assigned to its command. . . . In view of your present condition, should there be any other duty you may prefer, it will give me pleasure to advocate your wishes. . . . I hope you left Mrs. I. & your daughter well. . .
>
> Very truly yours,
> R. E. Lee, Gen'l

Shortly after he wrote to Lawton in May, Lee commissioned him to be quartermaster general of the Confederate states, and Lawton served in that capacity until Lee surrendered at Appomattox in 1865. After the war Alex and Sarah took up life again in Savannah, where he resumed his law practice. For five years (1870-1875) he was again a member of the Georgia House of Representatives, and president of the American Bar Association in 1882 and 1883. Lawton's appointment as United States ambassador to Austria (1887-1889) crowned his career, and his "full and salutary life" vindicated in some measure the criticism he had received earlier. Before he became a general on Lee's staff, Alexander Robert Lawton had been in command of the Military District of Georgia. Rev. Dr. Charles Colcock Jones, evidently with strong feelings of animosity toward Lawton, wrote on November 14, 1861: "A resignation of General Lawton, if not graceful at the present time, would certainly be altogether agreeable to the great body of our people civil and military." The mystery of Jones's bitterness toward Lawton remains unsolved, but he did not resign; and when he died in Clifton Springs, New York, on July 2, 1896, Lawton was eulogized by Yankee and Southern friends and associates alike. He was buried at Laurel Grove Cemetery in the city of Savannah. To commemorate his life, Lawton Memorial Hall was dedicated in 1899 for the use of the public without charge.

In early January 1861, Alexander Robert Lawton "seized" Fort Pulaski at Savannah, and went on to become a trusted staff officer of General Lee. The name of General Lawton can be found on pages of Southern histories more frequently than the name of any other Lawton Rebel. But in all there were scores of cousins from South Carolina and Georgia—all grandchildren or great-grandchildren of Joseph and Sarah Lawton—who raced one another to join the fighting, most often as officers, smart companies of cavalry, or as enlisted men. They were, in any case, all bent on battling the Yankees for the "Honor of the South." By 1861 the Southern planting class as a whole was entangled in slavery in all its aspects. Lawton families were no exception. Financially, socially, intellectually, and especially morally, they were committed by "God's will" to the institution of slavery. Anything that threatened that institution was unthinkable. At first, fired by their zeal, the cousins believed that shoulder to shoulder they would quickly bring a victorious end to the "holy war."[7] They almost welcomed the first shots.

---

[7]Henry Watson, Jr., to Dr. John H. Parrish, August 9, 1861.

Throughout the war years, the needs of the plantations clashed with demands to supply Lee's army. In such instances, the Lawton and Willingham planters chose cotton and corn for the home plantations over crops, tools, and supplies for the army. When hard pressed by the Confederacy to furnish foodstuffs and supplies, the planters responded, but always their first loyalties were to their families and their lands. In the final analysis, planters' faith in Southern victory rested on their estimation of the economic power of their staple crops, particularly cotton.[8] They subscribed to the belief that cotton ruled at home and abroad. If the South stopped producing cotton, Northern textile mills must, perforce, stop. Lacking foreign exchange earned by the sale of cotton overseas, the financial structure of the North would come tumbling down. Thousands of bales of cotton were turned out at this time, although this was production on a much smaller scale. Much of the cotton produced in war years eventually smoldered and blackened in the fields or on the wharves and in the warehouses following Sherman's marches.

Family members fought for the preservation of the cotton economy, for the continued ownership of the slaves who produced it, as well as for their "moral" obligations to protect and care for those slaves. Economic survival was foremost in their minds. A slave was a commodity, worth many hundreds of dollars—in some cases, thousands—depending upon his potential as a worker or producer of more slaves. If their slaves were taken from them, the economy would collapse. So the cousins rode to war with unprecedented zeal. They were in a very real sense fighting for their lives and the lives of their slaves.

Among the cousins, besides Brigadier General Alexander Robert Lawton, there was Dr. Benjamin William Lawton who, well before he put on the gray uniform, had championed the cause of secession. Although the outcome of the war proved his efforts to be of little avail, Dr. Lawton in 1860 mustered substantial pledges of financial support from South Carolina banks to arm the state. "So as to feel its temper," Lawton first solicited the support of his own bank, the Merchants Bank of Charleston, of which he was a board member. Pleased with the response, which was "beyond my an-

---

[8]Roark, *Masters Without Slaves*, 29.

ticipation," Lawton persuaded other banks to follow,[9] so that many Carolinians were lulled into a false sense of hope that the financial requirements of the impending war could be met.

Dr. Lawton served the cause of the Confederacy in numerous other ways. He was one of the cousins who had formed a "smart company of cavalry"—the Barnwell Dragoons, designated as Company D, South Carolina Volunteers. Only a few years into medical practice in Allendale after his graduation from the Medical College of South Carolina in 1843, he had represented Barnwell District in the South Carolina Senate. Further, he was a delegate to the Secession Convention, where with a flourish he signed his name to the Ordinance of Secession. During brief periods when the South Carolina Senate was in session between 1862 and 1865, he was given leave from his command of the Barnwell Dragoons to fulfill his duties with the senate. But on March 3, 1863, torn between his military duty and the protection of his family—especially against the ever-present danger of slave uprisings—he wrote from Camp Moultrie to his commander, Col. C. I. Colcock:[10]

> Annexed you will find a copy of a petition recently handed me by one of the [more than fifty] signers. . . . This appeal has more than once been made to me and I have resisted it; but I cannot under existing circumstances refuse to yield to the wishes of a community who are to be left wholly destitute of Medical Assistance. . . . Small pox, that dread Scourge of the human family, is now prevailing within four miles of my wife and children. I have a widowed and a Maiden Sister, whose slaves together with my own number over one hundred, yet on neither of our plantations (all of which adjoin) is there a white man to discipline the negroes. . . .
>
> In leaving my company, I feel assured that I yield the command to a Lieutenant whose tastes and abilities peculiarly fit him for the position which I have so imperfectly filled.
>
> Without enlarging on the other motives which tend to influence my decision, I herewith most respectfully yet unconditionally tender you my resignation. . . .                     B. W. Lawton, Capt.———
>                                      Co. D, 3rd Regt. Cav., S.C.V.———

---

[9]Channing, *Crisis of Fear*, 261.

[10]Captain B. W. Lawton to Colonel C. I. Colcock, March 2, 1863.

Although his resignation was accepted, Dr. Lawton continued throughout the war to serve in an important way both through his medical skills and in the South Carolina legislature.

Two of the sons of Benjamin T. D. Lawton were commissioned as cavalry officers: Colonel Winborn Joseph Lawton, who served under General N. B. Forrest, and Captain Alexander Benjamin Lawton. Then there was Dr. James S. Lawton, who adopted Dorothea and William Seabrook Lawton's son after William's death in 1858. After service as a South Carolina legislator from 1851 to 1853, Dr. Lawton volunteered as a private and went with his company to the coast of South Carolina. Because of his skill as a physician, he was soon made surgeon of the regiment until he too, at the urgings of his old neighbors in South Carolina, returned to his home in Allendale to resume his medical practice.[11]

William John Lawton (1824-1912) was still another of the cousins who discharged his duty to the Confederacy. As colonel, William was placed in command of the Second Georgia Cavalry Regiment. Significantly, Richard Furman Lawton—Benjamin T. D.'s son—was regimental adjutant of the same regiment. Already closely related, the cousins became close friends and cohorts in the cavalry regiment, and when the war ended they went into business together in Macon, Georgia. William John found his summer home, "The Pineland" at Garnett, South Carolina, still standing when the smoke cleared. Most Lawton men who wore the gray were not so fortunate.

Those Confederate officers and soldiers were among numerous Lawton men who caused the hearts of the now elderly brothers Winborn Asa and Alexander James to swell with pride. Two other brothers, William Henry (d. 1827) and Benjamin T. D. (d. 1846), had they still been alive when Sherman was setting his torch to Georgia and South Carolina, would surely have rejoiced with the family over the "courage and bravery" of their progeny who fought for the Confederacy. But there were a few—a very few, the brothers were thankful to say—who, in the eyes of their relatives in Georgia and South Carolina, brought infamy to their erstwhile good name.

At Mulberry Grove Plantation, Alexander James wrote his will on February 21, 1862. At the same time, he wrote a letter to his son, Alexander Robert, in which he explained certain provisions in his will, which ended with the following statement:

---

[11]*History of the Baptist Denomination*, 326.

Should Henry Robert, or any of my daughter Adeline's sons have
engaged in this unrighteous war against the South, I only wish you to pay
your sister her interest on her portion . . . during her life, and then to
cease entirely.

He sent copies of his will and his letter to his sons, but not to his
daughter Adeline "up North," who was the wife of Joseph Thomas Robert,
and mother of Henry Martyn Robert, chief of engineers of the United
States Army. During the Civil War, Henry Martyn Robert was in charge of
the defenses of Philadelphia, and later (1865-1867) was professor of prac-
tical military engineering at West Point and treasurer of the Military Academy.[12] His grandfather—and most of his other Southern relatives—never
forgave Robert and a few other misguided cousins for engaging "in this unrighteous War against the South." It was an unforgivable sin, a source of
inestimable shame that *any* kin wore the Union Blue. But the family's
shame of their members who wore the blue never overshadowed their pride
in those noble, brave cousins who wore Confederate Gray.

Sarah continued her correspondence with her sister-in-law, her dear
Adeline, now a "foreigner" up North. There is evidence that some letters
were written but never mailed.

When General Alexander Robert Lawton wrote his father in 1862 that
General Pemberton "declined to advise planters near the railroad whether
to remove their negroes or not," and that "I am sure he never thought of
planters as far off as Robertville deserting their places," he was giving only
one small example of lack of communication between the planters and civil
and military authorities. Sherman's invasion of South Carolina was imminent in late 1864, but authorities made no serious attempts to organize,
warn, or assist the people to prepare. When word finally reached the planters of the Low Country, terror bordering on panic swept the towns and
countryside.

With many cousins off to the fray at various battlefields, and with only
the old men, women, children, and a few slaves who had not deserted left
on the lands, Lawton, Willingham, and Robert plantations, along with
other Low Country lands, lay vulnerable before the invaders. Confederate
General Beauregard begged President Davis for reinforcements to protect

---

[12]Miller, *Family Circle*, 262-63.

South Carolina from the Union advance. Davis could supply few of these.[13] Robert E. Lee could assign few men to the defense of South Carolina. Lee had, in fact, depended on the Carolina planters as his source of supply for his forces in Virginia. With supply lines to Virginia still expected to be maintained; with the Confederate military command almost impotent in the emergency; and with Confederate General Wheeler and his "band of thieves" moving through the countryside buying up all the food they could find, the families of the men in gray faced starvation. The Rebel army in Sherman's path was demoralized, and the vulnerable remnants of family and slaves left on the land either fled, hid, or tried with apprehension and feverish haste to stash valuables. With no instructions from authorities and little protection from the military, they were on their own: each family made its own decisions and acted accordingly.[14]

Some of the families moved farther north, ostensibly out of Sherman's path. Three families who lived in the area south of Allendale fled to the plantation of Dr. Benjamin William Lawton. An occupied house was less subject to being burned; deserted houses, left vacant, were usually torched.[15] But the three families who set up housekeeping in the basement of Dr. Lawton's house in Allendale were no safer than they might have been in their own homes. Sherman's forces routed out the families, and set fire to the house of that signer of the Ordinance of Secession, Dr. Benjamin W. Lawton. All Lawton's possessions dissolved in flames.[16] Lawton's wife, Josephine, was warned that because her husband had signed the Ordinance of Secession, their house would surely be burned by the forces of General Kilpatrick advancing in the area. For that reason, she hastily took her children and house servants to Gaffney, South Carolina, where they were given haven by friends—the family of William Curtis, president of Limestone College. There, Josephine's seventh child was born. Two "good negro houses" still stood on Dr. Lawton's plantation after Little Kil and his cavalry had passed through Allendale, and it was in them that the three refugee families lived until Lee's surrender. After the war the doctor and his

---

[13]Davis, *Sherman's March*, 141.

[14]Ibid., 143-45.

[15]Peeples, "The Memoirs of Benjamin Spicer Stafford," 100-105.

[16]Reynolds and Faunt, *Biographical Directory of the Senate*.

family occupied the slave cabins while he reconstructed the "big house." In early 1865 another Lawton, Dr. James Stoney, quickly left Beaufort District for Oglethorpe County, Georgia. In the fall, he too returned with his family to find his house in ashes.

At least one Lawton home escaped destruction by fire. Major General Hugh Judson Kilpatrick, the Union's "hard-driving little dandy,"[17] ordered his men to keep their issue of matches in their pockets while he occupied Rose Lawn, the home of Reverend and Mrs. Joseph A. Lawton in Allendale, as his headquarters during days of battle and destruction in the area. With his mistress said to have been ensconced in a large front bedroom— she accompanied Little Kil from one headquarters to another in his sweep from Savannah to Columbia—he delegated a small back room to the elderly owners. To the godly couple who had to stand by while the woman of "ill-repute" occupied their bedchamber, this must surely have added basest insult to dastardly injury.

At long last the war was over. Lee had surrendered, and Sherman in South Carolina had left his sentinels behind—blackened chimney stacks.[18] Just days after Lee's surrender on April 15, 1865, Abraham Lincoln's four-year presidency ended with an assassin's bullet. He had led the Union in conquering the twin evils of secession and slavery. Healing the wounds and rebinding the Union remained a task for others. Even after a century, ministrations continue. Scars are still apparent on the face of the land, and in the souls of the black and white man.

All the major campaigns, with the exception of Lee's well-deported invasion of Pennsylvania, took place in the Southern and border states. Large areas of Virginia, Tennessee, Louisiana, Arkansas, Georgia, and South Carolina lay in ruins, and the Southern cities of Richmond, Atlanta, Charleston, and Columbia were blackened rubble. In Georgia, Savannah was relatively unharmed, and Macon and Columbus suffered far less injury than Atlanta. But from the crossing at Two Sisters' Ferry on the Savannah River, in a wide swath through the countryside of South Carolina and into North Carolina to Goldsboro, Sherman's men under the command of Little Kil had used their issue of matches to fire countless towns,

---

[17]Davis, *Sherman's March*, 26-27.

[18]Woodward, *Mary Chestnut's Civil War*, 734.

villages, plantations, farms, and railroads; open fields and pine forests were reduced to shambles.[19]

Before the war Lawton kith and kin lived under the rule of cotton and prospered by it. After the war most of them wanted nothing more than to resume the pattern of their antebellum lives. After the first months of shock and grief, they began to seek ways to restore their lands to cotton production. In 1860 South Carolina planters had contributed to a record cotton crop of five million bales, and although through uncommon effort and management they continued to cultivate cotton in the war years, in 1865 only 300,000 bales were produced. With the surrender of Lee, the three and a half million slaves that in 1860 had made possible those phenomenal crops were now joyfully free, and their former masters had to use their ingenuity and brawn in ways they had never known before if they would restore and maintain their former prosperity—indeed, if they would even survive.

The elderly Alexander James Lawton long since had stopped making entries in his Mulberry Grove Plantation diary, but he was active during the war in collecting clothing, funds, and supplies for the Confederate armies in Virginia. After the war he carried on plantation life at Mulberry Grove and Transpine Plantations with the encouragement and support of his son, Alexander Robert, who returned to Savannah to rebuild his law practice. Alexander James hired a few of his former slaves who were willing to work on his lands. He seems to have maintained throughout the war years such attributes as religious piety and staunchness coupled with an unwavering belief in the "rightness" of the Southern cause. (He never restored his Union officer grandson, General Henry Martyn Robert, to his will.) His days continued to revolve around cotton, blacks, Mulberry Grove, and Transpine. "The more the freemen resumed the habits and postures of slaves, the better the planters were able to accept the new system."[20] Until his death on April 8, 1876, Alexander James maintained his paternalistic attitude toward the former slaves who remained on his lands; and on more than one occasion, he championed their cause with the Freedman's Bureau, which had been set up by the new Union government to assist freedmen in moving from slavery to freedom.

---

[19]Castel, *The Presidency of Andrew Johnson*, 12-13.

[20]Roark, *Masters Without Slaves*, 159.

With the assistance of his lawyer—his son Alexander Robert—Alexander James presented a petition to the bureau through the courts of Chatham County, Georgia, on June 25, 1969, in behalf of Isabella Graham, his former slave. "After the arrival of womanhood," the petition read, "Isabella legally married Moses, a slave on an adjoining plantation." By Moses she had four children: Amelia, William, Richmond, and Leavinia. Moses Graham quit his master's plantation at the oubtreak of the war, leaving Isabella and their children behind at Mulberry Grove. He joined the United States Army, served as a private in Company C, 125th U.S. Cavalry, and he died in the service of the United States Army sometime after 1864. Alexander James swore to the accuracy of facts in the petition, and said that Isabella was then "still living and planting on the plantation of the said deponent, where she had lived the most of her life & and has not married since the death of her husband, Moses." He further petitioned that Moses' widow should receive his death benefits and back pay for his service in the Union army.

Two years later, on May 26, 1871, Isabella Graham put her x-mark on a receipt: "Received from J. W. Brinkerhoff, Agent of Bureau R.F. & A.L. Three hundred seventeen 55/100 dollars in full for arrears of pay and bounty due deceased husband, Moses Graham." In a wavering hand, "Alex. J. Lawton" affixed his signature as witness.

Clearly, among the cousins in gray, and among their families who stayed on or soon returned to the land at war's end, the traditional set of ideas—the convictions that God had placed the black man in their care, that slavery was right, and that the black's salvation lay with their protective masters—still remained. Hence in dealing with the Freedman's Bureau in behalf of Isabella Graham and her fatherless children, Alexander James Lawton was seeing that justice was done for his charge.

Richard Furman Lawton (1841-1892) is the next family member of concern to this history.[21] In school at the Citadel when his father William Seabrook Lawton died, Richard immediately received a commission as lieutenant in the cavalry of the Confederate army upon his graduation at twenty. As mentioned, he became adjutant under the direct command of his older cousin, Colonel William John Lawton. William seems to have

---

[21]See Appendix: Richard Furman Lawton Family Group Record, Lawton Lineal Charts #1 and #2, and Ancestor Charts A and B.

been mentor, friend, business partner, and father-figure to Richard throughout his life. Although younger than William by many years, Richard died twenty years before William.

Apparently Richard had no slaves when he entered the Confederate army, although perhaps he had a servant to attend to his personal needs in camp, as was the wont of young, well-placed officers. He was with Colonel Lawton and their commander, General Alfred Iverson, in the Tennessee and Georgia campaigns, and records show that Richard was paroled at the end of the war from prison camp in Albany, Georgia. Richard had no lands of his own to which he could return. He was spared the problem of freeing slaves, for he had none. He had no wife, no children. His widowed mother Dorothea had survived the war; she would soon marry again. He came out of prison camp in relatively good health. And he had youth, the admiration of family and friends for his "brave service," and the tangible support of his cousin William John Lawton,[22] who, as senior partner, took Richard into a wholesale and retail grocery business. Richard had spent his childhood in Macon, and in 1866 he returned to enter business there.

In 1865 Macon was a town of about 8,000 people. Business there revived relatively quickly. Some of the refugees who had crowded the city during the closing stages of the war stayed on and were absorbed by the town, subject to restrictions that the "courteous and gentlemanly" General Wilson endeavored to enforce.[23] By late 1866, rail shipments in and out of Macon were again brisk. With a large fund, said to be a million and a half dollars, reserved from prewar earnings and safely deposited in England, the Central of Georgia Railroad could now draw upon the fund to meet costs of repairing the tracks. Contracts were let and engines purchased from England. In a remarkably short time, before the year 1866 had closed, many miles of tracks were reopened, wooden station houses rebuilt, and Macon again was the recipient of daily freight shipments,[24] including shipments of provisions and produce for the fledgling Lawton & Lawton grocery firm.

Before William moved his family from South Carolina to Macon, business arrangements between William in South Carolina and Richard in

---

[22]Davidson, The Last Foray, 219.

[23]Conway, The Reconstruction of Georgia, 28-29.

[24]Thirtieth Report of the Georgia Railroad, 278-79.

Georgia were at first similar to arrangements made before the war between older-generation Lawtons, Willinghams, and Roberts on the plantations and younger-generation relatives in business in the towns and cities. In South Carolina, William, mainly through his owner-and-tenant share-cropping agreements, began producing crops again, ones that brought in a flow of cash. He could assist in financing the new business: "Lawton & Lawton: W. J. Lawton & R. F. Lawton, Grocers and Produce Merchants, Wholesale and Retail, at No. 63 Third St., Macon, Ga. (next door to Hardeman and Sparks)."[25] William's land in South Carolina and the rich red soil of middle Georgia, tilled in large part by sharecropping freedmen under contract to their former owners, provided the food crops that were the staples of Lawton & Lawton, Grocers. Richard worked hard. He learned about sweat and aching muscles, and he determined that if he exercised his brain as well as his muscles, he could very well make a go of anything he undertook. He learned about retail and wholesale business practices of bor-rowing and lending. He kept up his inventory and soon had the "carriage trade"—by then a euphemism since most carriages had long since col-lapsed—depending on Lawton & Lawton for household provisions.

When William returned to Pineland before his move to Macon, he found the house still standing and some of his former slaves (the 1860 cen-sus showed that he owned 100) still living in the cabins, making feeble at-tempts to till the land. They were now free under the law, and as free persons they remained on the land. William kept his plantation in opera-tion, and although he had moved his family to Macon by 1868, he devised a scheme whereby his South Carolina property would be profitable to him. Laboriously he prepared a contract and on June 15, 1868, had the document duly signed, sealed, and recorded in the Beaufort District records.[26] The contract was drawn between "W. J. Lawton & the freedmen whose names are attached." Nineteen names, written for the blacks and witnessed by Ste-phen E. Blount, appear at the end of the document, provisions of which include:

> Article 1st. The said freemen agree to hire themselves as laborers on the plantation of the said W. J. Lawton from the 1st of Jan. 1868. They agree to conduct themselves honestly and civily [sic] and to perform any

[25] A *Directory of Macon*, 1866, 14.

[26] Lawton Papers.

labor on the said plantation or connected therewith that may be required
of the said W. J. Lawton or his agents.

The freedmen further agreed to perform such tasks as "listing, bedding, splitting rails, cultivating, ditching, and cutting grass; to labor diligently ten hours per day." They were to forfeit "50¢ per day for absence from
work, 50¢ per day for bad work. If absent without leave, $2.00 per day; if
absent more than one day, to be banished from the plantation." Further
agreements included "taking care of all utensils with which they may be
entrusted . . . to be kind and gentle with animals under their charge . . . to
keep their houses and premises in repair and order, subject to inspection at
any time . . . to bear all their expenses & to return any advances that may
be made during the year from their respective shares in the crops."

In return, the said W. J. Lawton agreed "to treat his employees with
kindness and respect, to do all in his power to elevate and improve [their]
condition . . . to furnish each family with a comfortable house, and the
fourth part of an acre for a garden . . . to allow them to raise poultry and
one hog to each laborer to be kept within their own enclosures."

The next agreement was most important; the whole system of tenancy
and sharecropping, not only for W. J. Lawton but for hundreds of other
Southern planters, was based on a similar agreement between planter and
freedman. Many former slaveowners as well as former slaves became desti-
tute trying to make the system work. Sometimes it did.

In the case of W. J. Lawton, he agreed "to divide the crop with [the
sharecropper] at the end of the year, in the following proportion per hand.
. . . One-third of the net proceeds of all cotton, and one-third of all other
crops raised on the plantation." There were additional agreements that the
employer would provide medical attention, medicines, and bread shares, to
be paid for out of the tenant's respective shares, and furnish work animals,
wagons, carts, and plantation utensils "such as cannot be made on the plantation." That first year Lawton's fields were to be planted in cotton, corn,
potatoes, peas, rice, turnips, and slips; and all the profits from them were
to be shared according to the articles of the agreement.

In working out the intricate provisions of the sharecropping compact
with his former slaves, Lawton demonstrated that he was among that large
number of planters whose passionate fidelity to slavery and to proslavery be-

liefs had survived the actual destruction of the institution.[27] In Georgia and in other Southern states, variations of the share system became widespread. It was an expedient arrangement that satisfied neither landowner nor share-cropper, but it was a compromise that offered planters without cash a means of making their lands productive again. It offered the blacks something they had never had before—a modicum of money in their pockets. Through ensuing years and well into the twentieth century, unsavory as the system was, it was an economic arrangement that redounded to the survival of both planter and freedman.

As an alternative to sharecropping, to take the place of the freedmen laborers, South Carolinians were among the most vigorous proponents of immigrant labor, but they had little success in luring immigrants to the region. Still another cousin, another William Lawton, as chairman of the Committee on Chinese Immigrants for the South Carolina Agricultural and Mechanical Society, was a staunch proponent of imported Chinese labor to allay the crisis. Lawton, in letters to the editors of the *New York Journal of Commerce* on July 17, 1869, and to South Carolina officials two days later, declared: "I look upon the introduction of Chinese in our Rice lands, & especially on the unhealthy cotton lands . . . as new and essential machines in the room of others that have been destroyed. . . ." In his 1871 letters, written seven years after emancipation, Lawton said that Negro labor was "*dying out*, and becoming year by year, less efficient and reliable."[28] Little came of Lawton's efforts and of the efforts of the various agricultural societies to introduce foreign labor into the postbellum plantation system of the Southern states. The few workers who came—from China, Germany, Italy, and elsewhere—seldom remained long on the plantations, often deserting them to find work in the cities and on more prosperous Northern farmlands.

But William John Lawton's contract with the freedmen to sharecrop served his purpose. It was an expediency that permitted him to stay solvent, if not affluent, in the years immediately following the war—something that could rarely be said for Low Country planters. Moreover, to sharecrop in

[27]Roark, *Masters Without Slaves*, 94.

[28]Ibid., 166-67. William M. Lawton to the editors of the *New York Journal of Commerce*, July 17, 1869; William M. Lawton to Robert Mure, July 19, 1869; William M. Lawton to James R. Sparkman, August 2, 1869.

this way salved his conscience. He still "took care of" at least a few of his former slaves. And Richard Furman Lawton managed Lawton & Lawton Grocers for the partners while William initiated the contract and made intermittent trips to his South Carolina lands after he moved to Macon.

When Richard first launched the grocery business, he had found a boarding house with a good table for himself at the corner of Poplar and New streets in Macon, within walking distance of his business on Third Street. He took his place among the respected young business and professional men of the city, since by then to be "in trade" was quite socially acceptable, if not laudable.

Apparently, to assuage some of the pain, sorrow, and privation of the demoralizing war years, social activity and entertainment of all kinds increased in Macon. And Richard was drawn into the goings-on: he attended germans, musicals at Wesleyan Female College, poetry readings, and especially performances of the "First Genuine Negro Minstrel Troupe in the World" on the occasions when the boys of "Macon's own Minstrel" appeared on their home stage at Ralston Hall. Troupe members, composed of former slaves, had been "the petted servants of rich Southern people." Their young masters had encouraged their "boys" to perform their antics of singing, dancing, guitar picking, and drum beating for the amusement of assembled Maconites at the Lanier House or at old Concert Hall. With gags brushed up, music strengthened, and the act smoothed down to a professional polish, on July 4, 1865—only two months after Lincoln signed his proclamation—the boys gave a rousing performance for a filled house at Ralston Hall. General Wilson, in residence in Macon while the city was under military control, was said to have been in the audience, as was W. H. Lee, a sutler who had "made enough to retire" by following Wilson's troops, selling them provisions, liquors, and the like.

Sutler Lee, so the *Telegraph* reported, "saw on the stage before him an opportunity to leap into fame and fortune on the backs of the dusky darkies." He outfitted the troupe and took them on the road. As his instinct told him they would, thousands of Northern people, including New Yorkers and Bostonians, "willingly shelled out the shekels to see the negro, that great bone of contention." The troupe stayed on the road for several years, and whenever their boys returned for performances at Ralston Hall, the house filled to capacity. Lawton may possibly have been there, laughing at the gags and slapping his knees in time to "Plantation Jig," danced by the champion, Master Neil, or to "Banjo Duet," played by Josh and Julius. The concluding grand burlesque circus performance topped off by "Dixie" brought the audience clapping and stamping to their feet, requiring, no doubt, the services of the provost marshall's guards who were on hand to maintain order.[29]

Richard, after proving he could make a living for himself and a family, soon married. Elizabeth McLoud, according to the story passed to the present generation, was the widow of a Confederate soldier who had been killed in battle. They married in South Carolina, and Richard brought her to Macon, where they bought a home. Two babies were born in rapid succession. After the birth of the second child, Elizabeth, already in frail health, soon died.[30] Richard received an inheritance from Elizabeth's estate, and he husbanded it carefully as he made plans for caring for his motherless babies and for expanding his business endeavors. Still dealing in groceries and provisions in 1869 and 1870 in partnership with his cousin William, Richard resided during his marriage at the corner of New and Poplar streets. In 1871 he organized the Exchange Bank with Samuel G. Bond and became the bank's cashier. The bank grew and prospered for the next ten years, and Richard with it.

Caroline (Carrie) Willingham, who came with her parents (Elizabeth and Benjamin Lawton Willingham) when they took flight to Albany and then to Macon to live,[31] after the war attended Tift College in Forsyth, Georgia. Back in Macon after her graduation, she joined her family in expressing sympathy to their distant cousin, Richard Furman Lawton, for their families had long been friends and business associates in South Carolina as well as in Georgia. She fell deeply in love with Richard and felt a particular pity for his two babies. It seemed the most natural thing in the world that Richard should ask Carrie to marry him and help him rear his children.

So they were married on January 11, 1872. The couple went on a wedding trip, afterwards returning to Richard's house. By then he was living on Orange Street where servants, under the watchful eye of Carrie's mother

---

[29]*Macon Telegraph*, July 4, 1865.

[30]Bibb County Court Records, 1882 Term. Petition of Richard Furman Lawton to be appointed trustee for Elizabeth Lawton's child, March 31, 1880, 131-32.

[31]See Appendix: Willingham Line, Willingham Family Group Records, Charts A and B, and Lawton Lines #1 and #2. Also see Willingham chapter.

who lived close by, cared for the babies until the honeymooners returned. Carrie entered the large bedroom upstairs and went to the two small cribs to gather her "new babies" in her arms. She was appalled to find them feverish and limp. All of the first night in her new home she spent ministering to the seriously ill children. They both died shortly thereafter.

*Richard Furman Lawton (here in his cadet uniform, left) distinguished himself at the Citadel in Charleston. After his graduation from the military school, he was appointed lieutenant in the Confederate army, in which he served until war's end in 1865.*
*This photograph (r.) of an uncharacteristically solemn young Caroline (Carrie) Willingham was taken when she was a student at Tift College, Forsyth, Georgia, before her marriage to Richard Furman Lawton in 1872.*

Carrie and Richard became the parents of eight healthy children of their own: five boys and three girls,[32] of whom Furman Dargan Lawton, born in 1877, was the oldest son. The same year that his son Furman was

---

[32]See Richard Furman Lawton Family Group Record.

born, Richard was listed as cashier of the Exchange Bank; and on the fine new map of the city, published that year, the residence of R. F. Lawton on Orange Street is shown as neighboring that of his father-in-law, B. L. Willingham, next door. Out on Vineville Avenue, the lot of Mrs. E. Guttenberger, widow of the blind professor, is depicted between the properties of Mrs. Sorrel and Mrs. J. P. Lamar. Emily Jane Guttenberger was also living in the house on Vineville with her husband, John Jacob Nottingham. Their daughter, Mary Elliott (May) Nottingham, was born there two years later in 1879.

In common with most South Carolina and Georgia plantations, by 1880 the fragmentation of the Lawton cotton plantations was complete.[33] Under the systems of sharecropping and hired help, portions of some of the Lawton and Willingham lands were still under cotton cultivation, including lands in Beaufort District and Bibb and Screven Counties in Georgia. The former masters coped with debts and shortages of all sorts—laborers, tools, and livestock. There was little resemblance between the farms of the 1870s and the antebellum plantations. Only those owners who had cash were in a position to continue production. It was to supply cash and credit that by 1880 Richard Furman Lawton entered into the biggest venture of his life. In so doing, apparently unknowingly, Lawton became entangled in an injurious credit system that eventually became his downfall.

But in the Reconstruction years of the late 1870s, Richard was on the upward climb, and the future of his venture looked bright. With a base of profits realized from his grocery business, and by solicitations of family and business friends, he is said to have made a voyage to the banking houses of France to round out the funds necessary to incorporate in 1887 the Merchants National Bank, with offices located at 356 Second Street in Macon.[34] In 1891 capital was listed at $100,000, surplus $10,000, with R. F. Lawton as president, C. M. Boisfeuillet, cashier, and directors, besides Lawton, included W. W. Brown, L. P. Hillyer, W. A. Davis, Roff Sems, A. B. Small, W. T. Johnston, and J. E. DeVaughn. At that time Lawton was also listed as president of the Guarantee Company of Georgia, of which H. M. Smith was secretary. Capital assets were $50,000. Lawton kept an interest in the grocery store, which now bore the name Winn, Johnson &

---

[33]Roark, *Masters Without Slaves*, 179.

[34]*A Directory of Macon*, 1891, 49.

*After his marriage to Carrie Willingham in 1872, Richard Furman Lawton and his bride lived in a house next door to his father-in-law, Benjamin Lawton Willingham, on Orange Street in Macon, on a lot Willingham gave to the bride and groom, as shown in this early map. For many years the Orange Street-Georgia Avenue-College Street area was populated by Willingham and Lawton kith and kin. Schools, banks, and churches were nearby, and "downtown" Macon was an easy walk down Mulberry Hill. Richard and Carrie lived next door to Benjamin until their children were born, at which time they moved to a larger house at 620 College Street.*

[Archives, Middle Georgia Historical Society]

Co. Another significant affiliation of his included partnership in Lawton & Smith, Loan Negotiators.

The Merchants National Bank checks, printed for his clients, bore a pen and ink portrait that had been made of Lawton's beautiful young daughter Elizabeth—Furman's older sister—on her sixteenth birthday. On the bank letterhead a legend appeared that gives some clue as to the eventual downfall of what began as a propitious banking establishment: "Five Year Loans on Improved Farms—Negotiated." Business was good, and the loan negotiation aspect of the bank was especially busy. However, the Merchants Bank unwisely lent money to a number of farmers whose farming efforts failed. The difficulty of producing cash crops by their own labor or with hired or sharecropping labor was simply beyond the abilities of many Georgia planters. They could not repay their loans. Again and again Richard was forced to foreclose,[35] and his bank was on the verge of bankruptcy at his death in 1892 when the incorporated bank was only four years old.

There was only a hint of the embarrassing involvements and "hardening circumstances" Richard Furman Lawton experienced in the operation of his bank in the long, glowing obituary in the *Macon Telegraph* of January 14, 1892.

> Major Richard F. Lawton, president of the Merchants National Bank of this City, and one of the best known men in financial circles in the state, died at 8 o'clock yesterday morning at his residence on College Street. . . . Wife, children and relatives mourn one of those rare men who in spite of a busy life and hardening circumstances that surrounded the career of the successful financier, had never been anything but the gentle, loving, kind, brave protector from whom they learned. . . . His valor on the battlefield . . . acts of friendship, and prowess in the field made him popular and respected. . . . He graduated with high honors from the Military Institute at Charleston [became] Adjutant of General Iverson's Division of Cavalry. He distinguished himself on many occasions by his acts of bravery. . . . He faced death with the same bravery. About a year ago he was recommended to go to New York, where it was discovered he had a malignant tumor. . . . From New York he went to Europe where he consulted all the leading physicians. But it was all to no avail. . . . His bright mind remained unclouded until the end.

The next day the *Telegraph* reported: "The remains of Major Richard F. Lawton were interred in Rose Hill Cemetery."

---

[35]Bibb County Court Records, October Term, 1882, 102.

Under W. T. Johnston as proprietor and C. M. Boisfeuillet as cashier, the bank kept its doors open for a while after Lawton's death; but by 1894 the Merchants Bank had become another victim of postbellum griefs and Reconstruction hard times.

By shrewd management of his personal finances, Richard Lawton managed to leave Carrie a "well-fixed" widow.[36] She reared her children in the house at 626 College Street that Richard willed to her, and on the proceeds from a large life insurance policy she educated her children. Yearly she took her brood away from the summer heat of Macon to nearby Indian Springs, or to a cool north Georgia or South Carolina "watering place." At the Elder House at Indian Springs one June, an elderly black porter is said to have stood on the wide hotel porch, shaking his head in dismay and counting his fingers as eight Lawton children trooped from the carriages that had brought them from the train station to the rambling old hotel. His face relaxed a bit as he saw a black nurse and houseboy begin to unload the baggage wagon, piled high with trunks and boxes.

There is also a story of how, another summer, comfortably settled with the children on the train chugging to north Georgia, Carrie came back to reality with a start when Furman asked, "Where's Walter, Mama?" Weary from the long wait for the train to depart, the tot had climbed on a long wooden bench in the station waiting room, and there he slept on and on, oblivious of the departure bustle, and the family unaware of the sleeping child.

Carrie now considered that Furman, the oldest of eight, was the man of the house. A photograph made shortly before their father's death shows Furman standing protectively by three of his four little brothers—Calder, Richard Jr., and Osgood—who were clinging tightly to each others' hands, enduring the ordeal of picture taking. Walter, the baby, is not pictured. Of the girls, there was beautiful Elizabeth, who married George Call Johnson and moved to Atlanta. After her marriage to Albert Vaughn, the ebullient Caroline, the youngest daughter, also left Macon. Corinne, intellectually bright and full of the joy of life, attended Wesleyan College where she graduated with honors, as did her best friend there, May Nottingham. Corrine

---

[36]Bibb County Probate Court, 1889 Term. Will of R. F. Lawton, March 28, 1889, probated after Lawton's death on January 13, 1892.

married Robert Greene Jordan, and they lived with their family in a big columned house on Vineville Avenue.

At fourteen (ca. 1890) Furman Dargan Lawton (l.) was the oldest of the five sons of Carrie and Richard Lawton. Clinging tightly to each other are Calder, Richard, Jr., and Osgood. Walter is not pictured. Their father died shortly after this picture was made.

When she was at Wesleyan, Corrine arranged for her brother Furman to meet her best friend. Romance blossomed, and May Nottingham and Furman Lawton formed an alliance that lasted through wars, grief, penury, despair, and the Great Depression into serenity and peace with themselves and the world. This was a remarkable achievement in the early decades of the twentieth century.

*Chapter Eleven*

---

# MAY NOTTINGHAM AND FURMAN DARGAN LAWTON
## (1900-1934)

*Proud mind, empty purse*

W hen rebels took up guns against their Spanish masters on the island of Cuba in 1895, American sympathies quickly settled on the rebels, and Georgians almost forgot the Civil War in their zeal to support the Stars and Stripes by expressing outrage against Spain. When Joseph Wheeler, native Georgian and the only man to serve as a corps commander in both the Confederate and United States armies, spoke to a Confederate reunion in Atlanta in 1898, nattily outfitted in his U. S. Army uniform, the crowd warmly applauded "Fighting Joe." Although as many as 3,000 Georgians volunteered for service in the Spanish-American War, few went to battle. Encamped at Central City Park in Macon, then called Camp Ray for the regimental commander, or at Griffin or Athens or on drill fields throughout the state, most Georgia volunteers lost their enthusiasm endlessly marching back and forth.[1]

At the end of the brief conflict, when President McKinley visited Georgia for a Peace Jubilee in December 1898 in Atlanta, he also came to Macon. There Confederate veterans joined the celebration, pinning a Confederate badge on his lapel, which he wore throughout the day. On his Georgia visit, McKinley rallied the citizens solidly behind him when he declared in an address to the legislature that Confederate graves were "graves of honor" and it was "the duty of the United States government to keep them green."[2]

At the turn of the century, Georgia was still a one-crop state; King Cotton maintained his tyrannical rule over tenant, sharecropper, and landowner. But on July 18, 1900, Edward John (Ned) Willingham, from his carefully tended young orchard near Byron, loaded a railroad boxcar with luscious peaches for shipment to a Northern market. This first shipment of Georgia-produced peaches marked the beginning of a venture that in ensuing years became a mainstay of the financial and agricultural economy of central and south Georgia, in some instances displacing cotton. As usual, the editors of the Macon Telegraph caught the significance of the event, and the newspapers that were published in June and July of that year frequently mentioned the maturing peach crop and forthcoming plans for marketing the fruit.

On December 2, 1900, the Georgia House of Representatives approved a new charter for Macon, calling for the annexation of suburbs. Shortly thereafter, when the governor signed his name to the document, Vineville, Georgia, became part of Macon, and with the stroke of a pen the city's population increased to almost 35,000.

Descendants of slaves lived and worked on Willingham and Lawton lands as tenants and sharecroppers or wage earners in the cotton fields, and more often now in peach and pecan orchards, along with fields planted for a diversity of vegetable and melon crops. Bibb County and the town of Macon, the "Heart of Georgia," absorbed the children of former slaves into a system of segregation. It was a necessary device, the white people believed, to make possible harmonious relations between blacks and whites, who

---

[1]The Macon Guide, 59.

[2]Coulter, Georgia, A Short History, 429.

through a strict code of conduct were unalterably separated.[3] The blacks who lived in Macon—many hundreds of them—lived on dirt streets parallel to the main avenues where the whites lived, or in clusters of shacks and cabins—always well separated from the houses where the white people lived. In the mornings the blacks assumed their smiles and impenetrable masks of affability in passing from Pecan and Ward and other back streets to the big houses on Vineville Avenue and College and Orange streets, and on to the business houses, mills, and trading places where the colored maid worked for $3.00 per week. The black man, for not much more, worked in the cotton warehouse, fertilizer plant, hardware store, lumber mill or, in rare instances, in the yards, or as houseboy or butler.[4]

Furman Dargan Lawton (1877-1955) grew up in the household with his widowed mother Caroline—her friends called her Carrie—and his sisters and younger brothers, with a cook and yard boy coming from a back street to work for Miss Carrie. Carrie moved the family from 626 College Street to Lamar Street in Vineville before 1900, and a couple of black "help" worked for her there too. Furman attended the Macon public schools, as did his brothers and sisters, and when the time came, he enrolled at Mercer University. A quiet boy, not given to roughhousing, Furman loved books—history, novels, books on travel to faraway places. When he entered Mercer, he joined the Phi Delta Theta Social Fraternity, and displayed a jeweled fraternity pin on his lapel. But there was little time for fraternity hijinks; he applied himself to his studies. As the end of his freshman year approached, Furman became unaccountably more and more listless. He took to spending many days at home, quietly reading. His face grew haggard and pale. His distraught mother and his puzzled doctor finally decided that an operation was necessary, one that could be performed only by a well-known New York surgeon. With heretofore unrecognized fortitude, Furman went alone by train to New York, entered the hospital, and submitted to an ether cone over his nostrils and hours on the operating table. After weeks alone at a hospital in the big city, he returned to Macon to the arms of his anxious mother and an enthusiastic welcome by his siblings. He

---

[3]O'Brien, *Idea of the American South*, quoted in Davidson, "Preface to Decision," 394-412.

[4]Lambdin, *History of Lamar County*, 136-37.

was received home as a hero, as much a hero in the eyes of his family as his father had been when he returned as a freed prisoner of war in 1865.

*Hair neatly combed, in stiff collar with silk tie impeccably knotted, Furman Dargan Lawton displays his jewelled fraternity pin shortly after his induction into the Phi Delta Theta Fraternity at Mercer University (ca. 1896).*

Furman recovered; the deep, inches-long wound in his abdomen healed. But beneath his handsome, pale face and deepset eyes were unfathomable contradictions in his character. He had irrevocably changed. Only his "Dear Sweetheart," May Nottingham, whom he married in 1900, came close, years later, to understanding the depths of his hurt. She saw the vagaries of his character and, as he neared the end of his life, the extent of his remorse in not being able to provide a "comfortable living" for his family. His children were wont to burst into tears and run away from him when, after a real or imagined hurt, they would come to him for comfort. "There, now," he would say, "you won't know the difference a hundred years from now."

When Furman returned from New York, he rested at his mother's home for a few months, recovering and reading. He did not return to Mercer. He had an inheritance from his father safely tucked away in a bank, and felt no immediate compulsion to earn a living. Eventually, he accepted a genteel position. Every day he donned a white starched shirt with hard, detachable cuffs and stiff-winged collar, a three-button coat, waistcoat, narrow trousers, and polished, high-button shoes. His impeccable costume with slight variations in the summer and winter versions, and with slight changes in style, was worn throughout the years. Thus attired, he sat at a high writing desk at "Johnson, King & Co., Manufacturers, Importers, and Jobbers; Candies, Crackers, Confectionery, Soda Fountain Requisites." In the graceful curves of the "Spencerian Style and System of Penmanship," Furman recorded the business transactions for the company, kept the accounts, and wrote the business letters as required to the specialty wholesalers that furnished the company with Lowry's chocolates, Beach and Clarridge's flavoring extracts, and Wankesha ginger ale. Furman's Spencerian flourishes were a model of handwriting legibility and beauty. The basic business of specialty wholesalers seems not to have interested him, but through his work there he found artistic expression. He made art works of columns of figures, bills of exchange, and orders for Lowry's chocolates.

Now in good health, with a sparkle back in his brown eyes, his inheritance known to be drawing interest in the bank, and his work affording him remuneration and a feeling of achievement, Furman became one of the most sought-after young blades of the town. There was no doubt about it, Furman had a way with the ladies. For a Sunday afternoon spin, he handed a young lady into his smart buggy with just the right light touch to the elbow. And for soirees at Wesleyan, he graciously invited a mother first, then included her daughter in the invitation almost as an afterthought. He had his pick of Macon, and he chose May Nottingham, his sister Corinne's best friend at Wesleyan College.

Tethered to a sapling elm tree at the ornamental front gate of the white house on Vineville Avenue, Furman's horse and buggy could often be seen on a fair day. On starry evenings, gallantly escorting the ladies, first Mrs. Nottingham, then May, down the steps and into the waiting buggy, the trio would be off to Chautauqua or an entertainment at the college on the hill. Upon their return, while Furman lingered over a cup of hot chocolate, his impatient horse took to nibbling at the green bark of the young tree to which he was tethered. Years later when Furman saw the great lump of scarred bark on the mature tree, it reminded him of his courting days, and he would regale his children with tales of his horse that "ate the tree."

Throughout the years of May's childhood, years after her Grandfather Guttenberger's death, the house on Vineville still rang with the sound, if

not of music, at least with the sound of attempts to make music. Emma continued to teach piano in the front parlor. But in 1898, prodded by the need
for more income, Emma accepted an offer to become "Music Professor" at
Gordon Military Institute. It meant leaving the house on Vineville and
moving to Barnesville, a town on the Central of Georgia Railroad forty
miles northeast of Macon. Emma turned the house over to renters, and
May, recently graduated from Wesleyan and now engaged to Furman,
moved with her mother to Barnesville.

In Macon at that time, as was true elsewhere in the South, there were
certain families with which one had to be associated in order to be numbered among the elect. Those were the old, tradition-bound families, the
pillars of church and charities. The widowed mothers in such families were
treated with particular deference and respect, and their mature children
throughout their lives looked to them for advice and counsel, which more
often than not they heeded. Although the various stratifications of society
were generally taken quite seriously in the little city of Macon, a gentleman
whose family was of the caliber of Furman Lawton's family[5] could choose
without detriment to his own social standing, and always with prior approval of his mother: a well-educated, well-brought-up young lady of "impecunious circumstances." So with Carrie's approval of May Nottingham,
who, Carrie said, "has a fine character and the most lovable disposition of
any girl I know," Furman asked May to marry him.

Gordon Institute[6]—a secondary school for girls as well as a military
school for boys—received sizable grants from the city of Barnesville in
1897: a new auditorium and armory had been built and, significantly for
Emma, six new pianos were purchased, and a faculty of six music teachers
assembled. Emma Nottingham was placed in charge of the expanded Music
Department. The new auditorium brought orators, musicians, and educa-
tors for special appearances, and for annual meetings of the Georgia Teachers' Institute.

In the small cottage across the street from the institute, May sewed a
trousseau for herself and awaited the date of the wedding, which was set for
July 24, 1900. Furman, at every opportunity, boarded the train for Barnes-

---

[5]See Appendix: Furman Dargan Lawton Family Group Record, Lawton Lines #1 and
#2, and Ancestor Charts A and B.

[6]Now Gordon Junior College of the University System of Georgia.

ville—there were several runs a day between Macon and Atlanta, with stops at Barnesville and other small towns along the way—and he wrote dozens of letters to May in his Spencerian handwriting on the Johnson, King & Co. letterhead. He did so even on days he would later see May in Barnesville. Throughout the weeks before the wedding, "a quiet home affair at the home of the bride in Barnesville,"[7] Furman wrote:

> It will be the happiest moment of my life when I can claim you as my bride. . . . I very proudly showed your picture to some visitors at home yesterday. The comments were something like this: "A fine profile, such a pretty mouth, a mighty fine looking girl." I am being congratulated on all sides . . . have not fully, but almost decided to secure rooms at Mrs. Leggs. . . . As I write, someone at Prof. [Ferd] Guttenberger's is playing the wedding march. It is very inspiring, and my thoughts naturally turn to you . . . am coming up Tuesday. . . . Corinne reached home safely and said that she enjoyed every minute of her visit with you. From what she said, I'm sure the girls must have teased you unmercifully. . . . This is my last week of labor before you and I will be one.[8]

After a long honeymoon by train from Atlanta for the purpose of "sightseeing in the cities," including Washington and New York, where they had their first ride in a "horseless carriage," they went by steamer up the Hudson, then had "a run over to Niagara Falls," afterwards returning to Mrs. Leggs's to board at the "fashionable boarding house" Carrie had selected for them.

In 1902 Dorothea was born and, sadly, soon died. There were other children: Emily, named for Grandmother Emma Nottingham; Carolyn, named for Grandmother Carrie Willingham Lawton; and Elliott Nottingham, named for his Virginia-born grandmother. Another son, Furman Jr., died in infancy. Emma was still living in Barnesville when May and Furman reclaimed the house from the renters, moved from Mrs. Leggs's, and settled in the house at 417 Vineville Avenue. In 1904 Furman opened a real estate and insurance office at 456 Second Street. It seemed a wise move, and in his artistic handwriting he documented insurance contracts, real estate deals, and rent receipts. Bibb County records show that Furman was busy in the early years of his marriage. Among his clients were May's Gut-

---

[7]*Macon Telegraph*, July 26, 1900.

[8]Furman Dargan Lawton to Mary Elliott (May) Nottingham, April 17; June 14, 20, 27; July 6, 11, 14, 16—1900.

tenberger and Nottingham relatives and Furman's Willingham and Lawton relatives, who were variously occupied in businesses of their own—music store, lumber mill, hardware store, law office, warehouse office, furniture store, cotton mill. For a while, Furman was partner with F. T. Vincent in another insurance office at 417 Second Street. Furman's brothers, Osgood P. and Richard F., joined their sister Corinne's husband, Robert G. Jordan, in a wholesale candy manufacturing company. Furman had an interest in that endeavor also, but the candy company foundered, and the partnership was soon dissolved.

*Handsome Furman Lawton cancelled his place as one of Macon's most eligible bachelors when he became engaged to May Nottingham in early 1900 and gave her this photograph of himself.*

*Demure and lovely May Nottingham gave this photograph to her "intended" shortly before her marriage to Furman Lawton on July 24, 1900. She summoned her courage to inscribe on the back, "with love from your sincere friend, May N."*

The businesses of various Macon kith and kin were improving right along in 1910. Guttenberger Music Company advertised with pride that "the firm has recently been appointed agents for the Victor Talking Machines and records," and that "every kind of record can be had from Rag-

*The house on Vineville Avenue where May and Furman Lawton set up housekeeping about 1902 is pictured as the house appeared then. Four generations of family members were born here. It passed from family ownership at May's death in 1966, and an office building now stands on the spot.*

time to Grand Opera. The Victor, as everyone knows, is the greatest talking machine in the world. . . ."[9] On the "Automobile Page" of the *Telegraph*,[10] the Wheeler-Willingham Auto Company advertised the Speedwell Special 50, which will "meet the demands of the most critical at $2,500," and the "Velie 40, at $1,800, the car that 'takes all hills on high.'" Corinne's husband, whose Jordan Realty Company was operating a bur-

---

[9]*Macon Telegraph*, February 24, 1911.

[10]Ibid., April 2, 1911.

geoning business at 607 Cherry Street, found many takers when he advertised "Own Your Own Home." Furman's realty and insurance business was
also at its best in the 1910s. Mainly on commission, he sold small city lots
and houses, and a few acres of rural lands to struggling farmers—black and
white. He also sold property insurance and life insurance, and collected
rents on houses and buildings for clients. Emma, now back in Macon,
through her piano lessons provided a bit for the family till. The house in
which they all lived, and which Emma later willed to May, provided shelter
for the family.

Like many homes in Georgia, their home was untouched by genuine
poverty,[11] although memories of past grandeur in South Carolina might
make their modest gentility seem like deprivation. May and Furman did not
feel deprived, at least not in the first years of their marriage. In some of
those years Furman's business brought in quite a tidy sum each month, so
that there seemed always enough for May to have a Negro maid in the
kitchen who could also help with the children and keep the silver shined
and the floors polished. Each Saturday through the years, Lena, tall and
straight and black, came bearing a big wicker basket on her head, filled with
Furman's clean, starched shirts, along with Emily and Carolyn's cotton pet-
ticoats and panties with the scalloped ruffles that she had ironed with a fluter. There were coins for Lena; and there were a few dollar bills each
Saturday for Reuben, who came with his two husky boys from the farm he
owned on River Road, bringing molded pats of sweet butter, brown eggs,
roastin' ears in their husks, butterbeans, turnip salad, and stalks of sugar
cane. On some Saturdays, for a few extra coins, the colored boys worked all
morning, beating the carpets, pushing the recalcitrant hand mower, and
raking the grass.

Furman's real estate business was going particularly well when Carolyn
was born. It was a good thing, too. Immediately after her birth on April 10,
1911, Furman made plans for the entire family, including baby Carolyn and
Nurse Mattie, to have a splendid vacation: a luxurious steamer trip to Cuba.
Carolyn was three months old, and Emily six years old when the family
boarded the ship, Mattie proudly displaying the baby for all the ship's passengers to admire. A picture made later—when Carolyn was two—shows
Mattie with the wan little girl recently recovered from an illness, through

---

[11]O'Brien, *Idea of the American South*, xi-xvii.

which Mattie nursed Carolyn day and night. After that time May and Furman often said, "We'd surely have lost the baby, if it hadn't been for Mattie."

*May and Emily on board the SS St. Louis bound for Cuba. Furman took May, Emily, baby Carolyn, and nurse Mattie for a cruise in 1911. It proved to be one of the last long vacation trips the family made together.*

The church and all it represented was of great importance to May. Its impact was less important to Furman. With her mother, May had signed her name to the roll of thirty-seven members who made up the congregation of Vineville Presbyterian Church when it received its charter on January 24, 1904. May placed the names of the children on the Cradle Roll of the church: Emily in 1906, Carolyn in 1911, and Elliott in 1913. With the church on the same side of the street, in the same block as the house at 417 Vineville, May saw to it that the children were present for services whenever the church doors were opened. From the time they could learn to sit still on the hard pews, they *sat* on them. No arguments. No questions. They were *there*. Only real (not feigned—May always knew) sickness or dire emergency prevented May and her three children from occupying their usual seats on Sunday mornings. Most often Furman was in the pew too, although he kept his membership in the Vineville Baptist Church, which was "right next door" to the house on Vineville.

With two churches, the Joseph Clisby Grammar School and playground across the street, and Middlebrooks Grocery Store only a few blocks farther out Vineville, "food for spirit, mind, and body" were all close at hand, as Furman often liked to point out. Everybody knew everybody else in all the pleasant houses up and down the avenue where the trolley clanged, as well as in the houses on the shady side streets: names such as Lamar, Clisby, Rogers, Corbin, and Callaway. On weekday afternoons Mrs. Beggs, with the respected title of playground supervisor, kept an eye on the children from those houses as they seesawed and whirled on the merry-go-round. Elliott played basketball with the boys and Carolyn slid down the slide with the girls, until the day she came home at suppertime with two small round holes worn in her best Sunday panties with the ruffles that Lena had starched and run through the fluter.

The First World War, although the mightiest war in history, affected Georgians and Maconites much less than had the Civil War. Through all the years there had never been any question in a Georgian's mind as to the meaning of *antebellum*.[12] But in the First World War, Georgians merged their efforts with the rest of the nation, and with enthusiasm backed President Woodrow Wilson as he made the decisions that could affect them all. In May 1915 the *Telegraph* printed the terrible account of a German submarine that sank the *Lusitania* without warning, killing 1,198, including 128 Americans. Maconites rallied to the cause, and military life quickened. By 1917 Camp Wheeler—named for Georgia's own Joe Wheeler, who had served as a commander in the Confederate army, later in the U.S. Army— was in full operation on land a few miles from Macon. Troop trains rolled in day and night, bringing militia units from throughout Georgia and other Southern states to comprise the 31st Division, proudly called the Dixie Division. After the Dixie Division sailed for France, the 99th Division took over the encampment and, until 1919, after the Armistice was signed, the streets of Macon were often filled with khaki-clad doughboys.

On one memorable summer Sunday afternoon, Furman and May took Elliott and the girls for a visit to the camp, and to take part in a specially arranged entertainment for the soldiers. Furman lifted Carolyn, five, and Emily, eleven, to the bunting-draped bandstand. Emily climbed on the piano bench and carefully rendered the accompaniment, while in a soft lit-

---

[12]Coulter, *Georgia, A Short History*, 430.

tle voice Carolyn sang "Little Maria." Then with Emily fingering the first
few bars of "Over There," Carolyn foundered on the second "over there,"
and was about to dissolve into tears when one soldier leaped on the stand,
took up the beat, and led the crowd in the final rousing phrase, " . . . and
we won't be back 'til it's over, over there!" Then he shushed the crowd, and
presented a long-stemmed rose to the by now beaming Carolyn and to the
triumphant Emily, who had not missed a beat.

Following the First World War, there was a short period of unsurpassed
prosperity when cotton was still an important mainstay in Georgia and the
South. Furman did a brisk business in small real estate sales. And then,
almost without warning, prosperity evaporated and in Georgia, as elsewhere, mortgages on homes and farms were foreclosed. Furman's business
almost came to a standstill. But he hung on, even as his capital—the inheritance from his father—began to dwindle alarmingly. The family managed to survive into the mid-twenties, with May having been known to say,
"Well, we may not have anything to eat but cornbread and turnip greens,
but I'm always going to have a cook to cook them!" Indeed, that cook kept
the silver polished and the crystal sparkling and, in her basket on Saturday,
Lena kept bringing the fresh starched linen for the table.

Without anybody thereabouts seeming to sense the eventual devastating effects of the invasion, a little snout-nosed insect was working its way
from Mexico through Texas, Louisiana, Mississippi, and Alabama. The
boll weevil thrust its way into Georgia about 1915, and by the time it had
done its worst, laying its eggs where the larvae fed on the maturing bolls, it
had devastated the cotton in the fields. Between 1919 and 1923, cotton production in Georgia plummeted from 1,660,000 bales to 588,000.[13] The boll
weevil and the practice of one-crop farming, which caused the soil to wash
away, and with it the fertility of the land, all but destroyed the economy of
the South and brought dire poverty to the region. Money became extremely
scarce in the Lawton-Nottingham household. But Emma kept on teaching
piano—somehow parents in the neighborhood found the cash to pay for lessons; and May, with skill and enjoyment, made the bright plaid cotton
school dresses with matching panties for the girls, as well as Elliott's shirts
and knee britches, and the high-necked shirtwaists and ankle-length skirts
for herself. On a few occasions she stitched up black cotton dresses and

[13]Ibid., 431. Martin, *Georgia: A Bicentennial History*, 158-59.

white aprons and caps for the current maid. When the maid served those turnip greens on the Haviland, she looked *good*. Corinne, who bought her children's clothes from Burden-Smith's, said everything May made was so much nicer, and fit so much better than store-bought clothes. May never learned to cook, her theory being that what you didn't know how to do, you didn't have to do. Still, she was good at warming up leftovers for supper, and she did love to sew, especially the baby things, all done by hand on fine nainsook. When Carolyn was born, as a gift for the new baby, May received a little machine-made, lace-trimmed cap. It fit the baby so well, and she looked "so adorable" in it, that it soon wore out. So May ripped it apart, made a pattern from the pieces, and sewed a new cap of fine organdy, edged with Valenciennes lace and with her own featherstitching and tiny embroidered flowers adorning the turn-back. That baby cap was the first of thousands that would pass through May's hands, each bearing her own special touch, and making possible not only roast beef, asparagus, homemade rolls, and lemon pie for the table—and a black cook to prepare and serve them—but tickets for Chautauqua and Victor Herbert Festivals at the Grand, along with college educations for all three children.

When the time came, they would replace the iceman and the icebox with a purring General Electric Monitor Top; the gas-jet lights with a glaring electric bulb hanging from the center of the ceiling; and the wood-burning stove with an enameled gas stove. When Emma's pupils were not making interfering noises on the piano, Elliott could tinker with his "bought" crystal radio set, bringing in WSB in Atlanta, and maybe even Philadelphia, New York, or Pittsburgh.

As Easter approached, a few weeks before Carolyn's eleventh birthday, early one morning, Viola Norris appeared at the front door asking for a job. "I works for Miss May, and that's *my* job," she would say later, as indeed it was, for forty-one years and three months, until May's death.

Viola Norris was born February 7, 1905, near Tobesofkee Creek, a few miles south of Macon in Bibb County. Her mother, stepfather, and the children, as did so many descendants of slaves, lived in unpainted shanties on farms while they labored in the fields. Viola and her family lived first on a farm in Jones County, later on one near Walden. When she was in her teens, the family moved to Macon and lived on a back street parallel to Vineville Avenue. Viola told about the move:

Mr. Joe Edwards' son, he say, "Irene, you got one of the smartest little girls to be eleven years old I ever seen." I could pick hundreds of pounds of cotton. He says, "I gonna give her more than I do you." In those days ladies were getting 60¢ a day and the men 75¢ and I got 75¢ a day every day I worked. I did some of everything that could be done of work. I could cord wood. I could hoe cotton and plant corn—feed the mule—anything. And when Mama and us moved to Macon when I was 'bout seventeen, I didn't want to go to school, I wanted to work. Mama said she was gonna take me to school next day. I couldn't give her no back words, so I prayed and asked the Lord to give me a good job. . . . That the peoples would be nice to me.

Next morning I got up real early and made up my bed. Mama got up and went to the kitchen to fix breakfast, and I said, "I'm goin' on across here and I'll be back tereckly." She thought I was goin' across to get some paper to write my boyfriend I left back in Jones County. But I went right on up to Vineville Avenue. I never had been on Vineville Avenue and I went on out and crossed the street and passed by two big houses and come to the third, and I went up the walk and I rung the doorbell. It was Miss Corinne Jordan's big house and Valley came to the door and I didn't know her and she said to me, "What do you want?" And since I saw her with an apron on, I knowed she was the cook. I said, "Do they want a maid here? Somebody to clean up? A nurse?" She looked at me and she said, "What can you do?" I said, "I can do any kind of work," and she said, "Wait a minute." She never did come back to the door anymore.

Miss Corinne was sleeping upstairs and she come to the window and she called out to me, "Get out there in the walk and let me see who you is." I looked up and she says, "You lookin' for a job?" and I say, "Yessum," and she said, "My sister-in-law needs somebody, and you go on down the street to the house by this big church and you tell her I say to hire you." And when I got there Miss May asked me to come on in and she said, "I'm trying to get the children off to school," and she showed me each one: Miss Emily, Miss Carolyn; and Mr. Elliott weren't going to school 'cause he had the measles. Miss May said, "Have you had the measles?" and I said, "Yessum," and she told me what time to come back to work tomorrow.

I went on down the street walking fast, and I said, "Thank you, Jesus!" And I went on back home and went on in and Mama had the breakfast cooking and I said, "I've got a job." "You've got a job?" she says, "Where?" And I told her. And the next morning I went on to my job, and Mama asked me good where it was. I looked around after I got there and there was Mama and she had Aaron tight by the hand. And I said, "Mama, what you doin' here?" and she said, "I come to see where you workin' at." So I said to come on in, and I carried her down the hall and

I said to Miss May, "This here's Mama," and they got acquainted with one another. Mama said, "She ain't grown. She think she's grown, but she ain't. I come to see where she workin' at and who she workin' fer." And Miss May say, "I don't blame you," and Mama say, "She's a hard worker and she never has give me a back word, and if she ever give you any kind of trouble or gives you a back word, I want you to let me know." And Miss May said to her, "I don't think she is, she seems to be mighty nice and I think we gonna get along fine."[14]

Every Saturday May put three dollar bills in Viola's hand, until Viola got married a few years later, and then she put four.

Emily attended Sidney Lanier High, a coed, all-white school. The blacks attended Ballard-Hudson, their "separate but equal" school, far removed from Lanier. Emily went from Lanier to Wesleyan College and Conservatory on College Street, and after her graduation, began to teach music—piano, organ, chorus, theory, harmony. She learned Braille somewhere along the way, the better to communicate with her students at the Georgia Academy for the Blind, which was within walking distance of home.

By the time Carolyn entered high school, Lanier, already segregated by color, had become segregated by sex. A new, large Lanier High School for Boys was many blocks removed from the Lanier for Girls. Carolyn attended the girls' high school, still taking classes in the old building. May and Furman are said to have breathed sighs of relief at the arrangement, as did most white parents. With white boys now separated from white girls, rumored "sexual problems" in the school could be assumed to have been mitigated; and more important, if desegregation of whites and blacks should occur at some later date (already being considered as a remote possibility), the mingling of black girls with white girls would be much less objectionable than would the mingling of both sexes of both races. So Carolyn conjugated Latin verbs with the girls in Mrs. Pulliam's Latin class at Lanier for Girls, and Elliott blew his baritone horn in Mr. Marshall's band class at Lanier for Boys. When the boys and girls got together for well-chaperoned parties, school plays, sporting events, and parades of the R.O.T.C. battalion on the drill field at Lanier for Boys, those get-togethers were very special indeed.

---

[14]Viola Gantt and Emily Lawton, taped conversation, September 1980.

Susan Myrick's physical education class—gym, the girls called it—was in itself a special event, a special respite in a day of indoor classes. On fair mornings she would say, "All right, girls, our daily exercise today is a walk to Tattnall Square; now step briskly, and keep up." And off they would go for the ten-minute walk to the park. Out of breath when they arrived, the girls sat cross-legged on the grass under the trees, while Miss Myrick beguiled them with Joel Chandler Harris's tales of Uncle Remus's Br'er Rabbit and Br'er Fox, and of the plantation near Milledgeville where, she would say, she was "born and bred in the briar patch."

She would tell of how the farmers around her father's plantation were raising cotton and little else, and how her father produced many crops—not just cotton—including fruits and melons and peas and beans and more. In winter, she informed the girls, he would plant grasses in the fields—lupine and fescue—as feed for the livestock and to enrich and hold the soil; in the spring he would plow under the grasses and plant other crops. She told of how she would ride behind him on his horse when he went to inspect the fields, and how in the hot summer she helped pick the Georgia Belle peaches, and in the fall gathered the Schley pecans. Then she would repeat some of the stories the white-haired old Negroes who still lived on the place had told her about "the ole days" when they were slaves on that very land. Carolyn liked those stores best of all, and back at her desk at Lanier for Girls, she would sit bemused through Miss Marie Hazelhurst's English classes.

Susan Myrick could write even better than she talked; she received fine training at Georgia State College for Women in Milledgeville. She was not long teaching at Lanier for Girls. Soon she wrote straight news for the *Macon Telegraph* and the *Macon News* and, in addition, under the name of "Fannie Squeers" wrote one of the first columns of advice to the lovelorn. She was made promotion manager and director of public relations for the combined *Telegraph* and *News*. When asked by the paper's officials, "What is the major public service that the papers can render?," she immediately replied, "Soil conservation."

Myrick inaugurated a Sunday Agricultural Page, presenting story after story of successful middle Georgia farmers and explaining how they produced their money-making crops using crop-rotating methods. She worked closely with state and national conservationists. She made hundreds of talks on radio and to FHA, FFA, and 4-H clubs. She was eminently successful through the years, receiving the plaudits of T. L. Asbury—conservationist for the state of Georgia—when he said, "With her supersonic jet-propelled lilac and old lace personality and attitude, she is a modernized spirit of the Old South, doing a great job for the land she loves so well." Years later, Carolyn and other former pupils in Susan Myrick's gym classes, as well as practically everybody else in Macon, felt that "they couldn't possibly have made a better choice" when the movie producers hired Susan Myrick to come to Hollywood for six months to serve as technical director of *Gone with the Wind*. [15]

In the early twenties, people were buying up Florida real estate at a great rate—often sight unseen—hoping for a quick turnover at a big profit, or at least a place in the sun for their old age. [16] At first, all you needed was a little cash; but during 1925, sandy, palmetto-dotted land six or eight miles outside Miami sold for more than twenty thousand dollars an acre, and you needed a lot more for a "piece of the action." During the same year, almost a thousand new subdivisions were laid out, and 174,530 deeds and purchase papers were filed by the county clerk. [17] Up North *everybody* was going, it seemed: business executives, retirees, the rich and famous. The smart ones went as tourists, just to have a look at what was going on; the not-so-smart ones went to have a late look at the sandy stretch of land they had already contracted to buy, sight unseen.

The *Macon Telegraph* began reporting that this couple or that businessman had "gone to Florida"; a Macon banker sold his Coca-Cola stock and bought acreage he had not seen near Miami. On one occasion the clerk of the Georgia House of Representatives, meeting in Atlanta, read a statement on the floor that said five members of the House had resigned their offices and moved to Florida. Whereupon a representative from Wilkes County rose and said, "Praise the Lord, may their tribe reach one hundred!"

In Macon, the real estate business was anything but booming. Furman was having more and more trouble providing for his family. His inheritance had long since vanished. May had quietly continued to make the handsewn and embroidered baby caps and now added matching sacques. She com-

---

[15]Harrell, "Susan Myrick—Conservationist," 22, 42, 43.

[16]Andrist, *American Heritage History*, 142.

[17]Daniels, *The Time Between the Wars*, 142-44.

pleted a few sets each week, and with Carolyn in tow, she took them to the Woman's Exchange on Cotton Avenue. There, the two elderly sisters who managed the exchange always exclaimed, as they lifted the garments from their tissues, "How perfectly exquisite! What dainty embroidery, what lovely silk!" Then they would display them in the big glass case near the front of the store. From here, they sold themselves to new grandmothers, who were seduced into buying "that lovely cap and sacque" that "dear May" made. Each week May took home a few dollars. On rare occasions, when Carolyn pleaded hard enough, one of "Cousin Odele's coconut cakes" would be substituted for part of the cash. In 1923 and 1924, it seemed that these dollars May brought home from the exchange must go more and more often for food, purchased from Middlebrooks's or Sowell's. May thought fleetingly about letting Viola go. Then she would pick up her sewing basket and make her needle fly.

Furman read all the reports he could get his hands on regarding fortunes being made in Miami, and all the people crowding the new Halcyon Hotel in Miami just waiting to buy Florida land. With his own background of experience in the real estate business, and his heretofore persuasive talents, Furman *knew* he could do well if he "got into" real estate in Florida. As he discussed it with May, though, it would mean being separated from the family awhile; then after things were going well, he would come back to Macon and take them to Florida to live. So Furman went to Miami, and May continued her sewing.

Within a few weeks a check came from Miami and, within a few months, checks arrived rather regularly. There were many letters back and forth. Christmas 1924 came and went; a check arrived for gifts all around. In 1925 Sinclair Lewis made a dark prophecy. "Within a year," he said, "this country will have a terrible financial panic. I don't think, I know."[18] Furman was very busy in the general goings-on in Miami during 1925 and into 1926. New apartments, hotels, and stores opened, and new blacktop streets spread through the scrub palmettos. Furman began to make plans to bring his family down.

It was early spring, 1926, and young peach orchards that now were thriving on hundreds of acres across middle Georgia were about to burst into bloom, covering those acres in a pink cloud, and filling the soft air

---

[18]Ibid., 158.

with delicate fragrance. It would be a long time before revolutionary farm-ing methods, intelligently and diligently applied year after year could lift Georgia out of economic stagnation. Champions of soil conservation and diversified farming practices were only beginning to make their voices heard: Susan Myrick's crusade came later. But a number of farsighted, large landowners in central Georgia, including Edward John Willingham, who had shipped that first boxcar load of fine quality peaches in July 1900, and members of the Rumph family, who developed the Elberta and the Georgia Belle peach, had nurtured, improved, and enlarged their orchards through-out several decades. In March of 1926, Fort Valley, the little town in the midst of the orchards, was priming itself for the "Fifth Annual Peach Blos-som Festival" that "stands in a class to itself as an artistic advertising triumph."

Nature cooperated, the sun came out, and the peach blossoms opened right on time for miles and miles along the roads throughout what came to be known as the "Peach Belt." There was scarcely a citizen of Fort Valley (or of Macon and the surrounding towns) who was not involved in preparations for the week-long Peach Blossom Festival. Fifty floats were prepared. Five hundred people sewed costumes and practiced their parts for the pageant to be performed each day of Festival Week. Coals glowed in barbecue pits for days, as tempting aromas mingled with the delicate fragrance of peach blos-soms on the Twin Oaks Estate of King Allen and his queen. The 28th In-fantry Army Band and Orchestra came from Fort Benning to lead the parade each day and to play dances for the royal court in the Twin Oaks ballroom and for lesser dignitaries at the Winona Hotel and the Citizens Bank.

Many Wesleyan students came, including Emily, who stopped practic-ing for her senior piano recital to drive with her friends from Macon one day for the parade, the pageant, and the barbecue. The governor, his staff, and 100 Georgia legislators, escorted from Atlanta by state troopers, also arrived. Many visitors on special trains from New York, Washington, De-troit, and Chicago stayed in Macon at the Lanier or the Dempsey Hotel, some going first to Porterfield, the summer home of Macon philanthropist James H. Porter, to see the more than six hundred varieties of roses in bloom there. Former President William Howard Taft attended the festival one day, as did dozens of important personages from throughout the nation.

Those people for whom the festival was planned in the first place were specially entertained at sumptuous luncheons served each day in the big

dining room of Twin Oaks by beaming black cooks and maids. The special
guests included officers and representatives of fruit houses from principal
cities around the country.[19] In late afternoon, with contracts (often for
their entire crops) tucked in their pockets, hosts escorted their special visitors to the dances.

The 1926 Fifth Annual Peach Festival was a huge success, with almost
the entire peach crop "spoken for" while trees were still in full bloom. The
Peach Festivals were, indeed, advertising triumphs, and Georgia peaches
became almost as well known as another Georgia product, Coca-Cola.

Emily's time off from practicing for her Wesleyan senior recital did not
jeopardize her performance. Carolyn, especially, was awed at the way Emily
could fill the auditorium with the sounds of her spirited rendition on the
Steinway of Liszt's Hungarian Rhapsody. Now Emily was eager to get a job
and start teaching. Yet when Furman decided it was time to have his family
with him in Florida, Emily was packed into the Dodge with the rest—Carolyn and Elliott, as well as May and Furman. The trip took three days.
When they unpacked, their suitcases and boxes and bags practically filled
the tiny apartment Furman had rented in Miami. Immediately they put on
their modest bathing suits and took a first dip in the surf. Afterwards, they
hung their suits on a line in the backyard. Next morning, the suits had disappeared. Their first swim was their last. There was no money for new
suits, and things went steadily downward from there. The family had been
in the apartment only a few weeks when Furman's wan hope of fast riches
in Florida real estate reached its nadir.

Quietly, early one morning, May took a selection of her baby caps and
sacques and spoke to the buyer at Burdine's Department Store in downtown
Miami. He gave her an order for dozens of caps and sacques. She gulped.
She would never be able to make that many—not in a whole year. But he
bought her samples, and she accepted a check for them. Then she explained
she could not give him a positive delivery date. He smiled and said, "You
need to increase your asking prices," and they agreed that she would deliver
"as soon as possible, considering the extra time required to provide such
quality, handmade items." The check was enough to buy gasoline for the
return trip to Macon, where waiting on Vineville Avenue was a mortgage-
free, rent-free, big, beautiful, high-ceilinged, cool house. Soon after their

---

[19]*Macon Telegraph*, March 9, 1926.

return, Emily started teaching at the Georgia Academy for the Blind only a few blocks from home on Vineville Avenue.

May called Viola back to work. She phoned Corinne and friends: Mrs. Skelly, Mrs. Forbes—a dozen others. She ordered bolts of white and pastel pink and blue of finest Skinner's silk, sheer imported organdy, Valenciennes lace by the dozens of yards. Sarah Martin thought the name "La May" sounded right; it had just the right intimation of high fashion. May ordered tiny labels made. The friends went to work, fired with May's enthusiasm for the project, and the opportunity to make what they euphemistically called "pin money." (*They* knew and *she* knew they needed the money, and not just for pins.) May carefully instructed them in the intricacies of hand-sewing La May garments.

After breakfast was cleared away each day from the big dining table, with Viola's assistance May cut material to the pattern, then issued the cut pieces with thread and lace and ribbon and tiny La May labels for the ladies to take home. By week's end, Mrs. Skelly—she was usually first, and also the best and fastest worker—came bearing the finished garments. Then very, very carefully Viola and May would inspect each tiny garment and pack them for mailing. May filled that first order within three months. She sold to other stores as well. A New York dealer asked to handle La May items, and then orders began to pour in, all the way from Hawaii to Maine, and from Burden-Smith and Davison's in Macon, to Marshall Field in Chicago and fine stores on New York's Fifth Avenue. For many years, up to 12,500 baby garments were sold each year—every stitch handsewn and embroidered, every one passing the strict inspection of Viola and the special touch of May Nottingham Lawton.

One day, years later, after reading a complimentary feature article about herself in the *Macon Observer*,[20] she grew wistful. "You know," she said, "somehow we never could get Neiman-Marcus to buy."

The family reached home from Miami in late summer, 1926. On September 14, 1926, a tropical storm gathered strength in the Antilles. With incredible force the storm raged across Florida, demolishing central and southern Miami. Two hundred were killed; $111,775,000 damage was done. The Florida boom burst with the storm. Months later, the Macon banker who had sold his Coca-Cola stock to buy Florida land picked his way

---

[20]*Observer*, July 30, 1948.

through debris to stand on what he had been told was the property line of his lot. He looked out over the smooth sea as the water lapped lazily over his feet.

Elliott blew his baritone horn and beat the drums in the high school band, and also played in a jazz orchestra. Then after violin lessons with Glenn Priest Maerz at Wesleyan Conservatory ("I think I was the first male co-ed"), he played violin "in the first row" of the Macon Symphony Orchestra in Macon and went with them "on tour" to Milledgeville. In 1932 he entered Mercer on a music scholarship, supplemented by monthly stipends from Emily's small salary and by WPA funds for which he mowed the campus grass. He played with the Mercer Collegiates for fraternity and tea dances, and on one memorable occasion for a big street dance in nearby Dublin. In the summer of 1933, upon the instigation and flattering recommendations of Emily, who had just made a trip on the Ocean Steamship Company's *City of Chattanooga* from Savannah to New York, Elliott was hired to play dinner and dance music on shipboard, being one-fourth of an orchestra of four. He deftly switched from saxophone to drums to violin to clarinet, and from jazz and the Charleston to semiclassical and back again; at times he even picked up the megaphone to croon a bit, like Rudy Vallee. It was a great summer. Even playing during the summer at the Sea Island Yacht Club and at the George Washington Hotel in Miami Beach, which somehow had weathered the storm and the end of the land boom-burst, never overshadowed those weeks of playing on board the *Chattanooga*. With help from the scholarship, WPA, and earnings from playing, rounded out with stipends from May's business and Emily's earnings from teaching, Elliott made it through Mercer.

The love of music and the love of travel was in his blood. He earned his living as a travel agent; he earned his pleasure with his violin and his horns. Years later on many Saturday nights, and especially on New Year's Eve when Elliott made his saxophone moan with "the bunch" at one of the clubs, friends were likely to say, "Takes you back to the good old days, doesn't it?"

May saw to it that Carolyn also made it to college. Carolyn had delightful visits during her sixteenth and seventeenth summers with Furman's affluent brother, Richard, and his wife, Mattie. These took place in New Orleans and at their summer home in Waveland, on the Mississippi coast. Mattie and Dick were so entertaining and so indulgent of Dick's niece— they had no children of their own—that Carolyn wanted to stay in New

Orleans with them and go to Tulane, but she never gathered enough courage to talk about it with them or with May and Furman. So she returned to Macon where she dutifully attended Wesleyan with borrowed funds, worked in the Registrar's Office and as Wesleyan correspondent for the *Macon Telegraph*, for which she was paid ten cents per column inch.

By the time Carolyn enrolled at Wesleyan, the college had been moved from College Street—the Conservatory of Music still occupied the in-town building—to rolling acres located a few miles north of Macon. Columned and porticoed, the new Candler Memorial Library was the first building on the right after you passed through the main gate where the sign proclaimed, "The World's First Chartered College for Women." Emory University and Wesleyan were beneficiaries of Asa Candler, developer of Coca-Cola and founder of the soft drink company.

When Carolyn went through those gates for the first time, she already seemed to fit the college-girl mold: flat chest, flat hips, dress to the knees, waist around the hips, boyish bob, with a flat curl stuck to each cheek. After classes were in full swing, she found to her surprise she was enjoying the challenge of working to learn; and on the weekends she began to have dates with Mercer boys—a giddy experience. She was the product of a girls' high school, and now as a student in the rarefied atmosphere of a woman's college, simply to be asked to the Kappa Alpha Fraternity tea dance brought incredible delight.

She went to the dance at the armory where, with the fraternity emblem and motto, *Dieu et les Dames*, emblazoned over the bandstand and the winter twilight hovering outside, she was passed from arm to arm. The more arms she passed through, the more "breaks" she got, the better she liked it. May never quite accepted that a daughter of hers was going *dancing*. Furman didn't notice. So Carolyn would rub the lipstick off before she went into the house ("Young *ladies* don't wear lipstick") and tell May what a "nice time" she had at the party, not mentioning what was done there.

One summer day Carolyn went with May to the bank, the Continental Trust Company on Third Street where Lamar Harrell, as he had for years, attended to May's banking needs while Carolyn stood by. Then he said, "Mrs. Lawton, I'd like for you and Carolyn to meet my brother," whereupon a blond, blue-eyed young bank teller, Glover Harrell, smiled and asked Carolyn to go with him to the party the bank employees were having at Idle Hour Country Club. After that, he asked her to go canoeing at Lakeside, where he had a slick white Old Town canoe, and later invited her to play miniature golf. *She* then asked *him* (she was getting very bold) to come out to the Girl Reserve Camp where she was a counselor and assisted with handcrafts for Sunday afternooon—Visitors' Day.

Eventually (after he had paid for the tuxedo he had bought at XV Clothes Shop) he asked her to go every night and Wednesday afternoon for the whole week of performances by the San Carlo Opera Company, which was giving first performances in the new copper-domed, velvet-curtained Macon Municipal Auditorium. Of course, Glover had to usher to earn two season tickets for the performances; but after the first intermission, attired in his natty new tuxedo, he could sit beside Carolyn as the voices of Tini Paggi, Amund Sjorvik, Mario Valle, and Ethel Fox filled the auditorium.[21] By midweek, after *Aida*, *Rigoletto*, and *Madame Butterfly*, she was mesmerized. By week's end she was in love with opera, and with Glover.

In 1933 when Franklin D. Roosevelt was inaugurated president, America was racked by long bread lines of the unemployed. The New York Cotton Exchange quoted a price of five cents a pound, but the Georgia growers received even less.[22] Despair and hopelessness were rife, mortgage foreclosures were mounting. Whatever little real estate business Furman had been able to recoup in middle Georgia after his return from Miami no longer existed; now the commissions from occasional insurance policies he sold were his only income. Somehow May continued to receive orders through her agent for her baby caps and sacques. Doting grandmothers were still the same, and La May garments maintained their appeal at Maison Blanche in New Orleans and Marshall Field in Chicago.

On March 4, 1933, Roosevelt issued a proclamation declaring every bank in the country closed for four days. While they were shut, people lived on checks and credit. Glover, in his teller's cage at the bank in Macon, worked through the nights on those dreadful days, preparing script that would be honored by merchants in Macon who agreed to accept the bank script for food and necessities until the banks could reopen. Glover had held his job through the depths of the Depression—through 1929, 1930, 1931, 1932—and he held on now, through those bleak days in March 1933. He and Carolyn, after it was over, talked earnestly about it all, and decided to keep their plans to be married in June. In the front of her journalism note-

[21]*Macon Telegraph*, January 4, 1919.

[22]Clark and Kirwan, *The South Since Appomattox*, 230.

book, she pasted a calendar. She put a ring around June 10 and another around June 17. Every morning she drew a line through the day's date, and finally on June 10 she was graduated from Wesleyan. On June 17 she was married to Glover Harrell.

Corinne helped May put on what she called "the biggest little wedding I ever saw," meaning there were lots of friends present at the ceremony, for which there was the least outlay in cash of any wedding she had ever attended—and she had not missed a big society wedding in Macon in years. Corinne telephoned a long list of friends, inviting them in May and Furman's name to Carolyn and Glover's wedding (no costly engraved wedding invitations). Isabelle Kinnett placed a simple arrangement of spring flowers from her garden on the altar of the Vineville Presbyterian Church (no florist's bill). Fliss and Ferd Guttenberger played suitable music, including Lohengrin's wedding march, on violin and piano as their gift to the bride and groom (no musician's fee). Emily, the bridesmaid, wore a simple blue dress and so did the bride (no costly wedding gown and veil).

Afterwards, Carolyn and Glover took off for Silver Springs and Daytona Beach in "Bouncer," Glover's secondhand Chevrolet coupé. At Silver Springs they had a ride in a glass-bottom boat, holding hands and watching the marine life that passed in the clear spring water below. As they stepped out of the boat, Carolyn said to the captain, "That was wonderful! We enjoyed it!" He replied, "Glad you did, ma'am. Come again. We always like to have newlyweds." Startled, she asked, "How did you know?" "Well," he smiled, "you both have new shoes at the same time." He shook his head. "It will never happen again!"

In 1934 there were already superficial signs of recovery. They were within reach of the employed only,[23] and Glover was still one of the employed. Franklin Roosevelt was still the buoyant spirit in the White House. The roomy house on Vineville enfolded the newlyweds in the two-room apartment upstairs. Emma, in her lifetime, had converted the second story of the house. Rent from the apartment there had supplemented her income from piano teaching.

Hardly were they settled when Carolyn suspected what Dr. Thompson later confirmed. She was pregnant. Silently at night she wept at Glover's side. She wasn't *ready* to be a mother. But she visited Martha Alman and

---

[23]Jenkins, *The Thirties*, 20.

her new baby, and cuddled the child against her shoulder. Under May's guiding hand, she sewed a layette. She read all the material she could find about baby and child care. Somehow, she felt there was something wrong with Dr. Spock's child-care methods. Carolyn thought about how she would be with her baby, and she began to long for the day when she could hold it in her arms. Glover put his hand on her swollen belly, and they could feel life quicken within her. Both were filled with wonder and love and eagerness for the baby to be born. When Furman read aloud from the *Telegraph* for all to hear, "Dionne Quintuplets Born in Callander, Ontario, on May 28, 1934," then turned to Carolyn and said offhandedly, "Looks like you'll be having five, too," somehow she could see no humor in it.

The day arrived, and Bouncer conveyed Glover and Carolyn to the waiting Dr. Thompson at Middle Georgia Hospital. Carolyn labored through the dawn and into the day. Mary Elliott Harrell, squalling and healthy, was born that afternoon.

Glover spent the next day with Carolyn in her hospital room. Periodically, the nurse brought Mary and laid her by Carolyn's side. Glover pulled up a chair to the bed, and they sat and gazed and touched and admired and exclaimed at the wonder of her. Carolyn curled the fingers of one tiny hand around her thumb; Glover curled the fingers of the other hand around his thumb. Silently, they watched the sleeping baby's chest rise and fall. The door opened and a small basket of rosebuds appeared on the bedside table. The spell was broken. Glover held up the basket and said, "Hey, wake up, new citizen! Look what somebody's brought you!" Tied to the handle in red, white, and blue ribbon was a miniature American flag.

A firecracker popped in the distance. It was July 4, 1934.

# Appendixes

Section A
*Abbreviations*
*Appearing in the Notes*
*and Family Group Records*

| | |
|---|---|
| A/MU | Archives, Mercer University Library, Macon GA |
| A/USMC | Archives, U. S. Military Academy, West Point NY |
| BHC/FUL | Baptist Historical Collection, Furman University Library, Greenville SC |
| CB/NCV | Census Books, Northampton County, Eastville VA |
| CC/NCV | Chancery Causes, Northampton County, Eastville VA |
| CO/BCG | Minutes of the Court of the Ordinary, Bibb County GA |
| CPCR | Charleston County Probate Court Records SC |
| CP/GHS | Cunningham Papers, Thomas Grimball Journal, Georgia Historical Society, Savannah |
| DAC | Daughters of the American Colonists |
| DB/NCV | Deed Books, Northampton County, Eastville VA |
| FFSC | First Families of South Carolina, Charleston |
| GDAH | Georgia Department of Archives and History, Atlanta |
| GHR/WML | Genealogical and Historical Room, Washington Memorial Library, Macon GA |

| GHS | Georgia Historical Society, Savannah |
| HF/WC | Historical Files, Wesleyan College Library, Macon GA |
| HSSC | Huguenot Society of South Carolina, Charleston |
| MD/SCL | Manuscript Division, South Caroliniana Library, Columbia SC |
| M/OFC | Annie Elizabeth Miller, *Our Family Circle.* |
| PCR/BCG | Probate Court Records, Bibb County, Macon GA |
| RCO/SC | Records of the Court of the Ordinary, Charleston SC |
| SCDA | South Carolina Department of Archives, Columbia |
| SCHM | *South Carolina Historical and Genealogical Magazine*, Charleston |
| SC/MGHS | Special Collections, Middle Georgia Historical Society, Macon GA |
| SCHS | South Carolina Historical Society, Charleston |
| SHC/UNC | Southern Historical Collection, University of North Carolina, Chapel Hill |
| VHS | Virginia Historical Society, Richmond |
| VSA | Virginia State Archives, Richmond |
| VMHB | Virginia Magazine of History and Biography, Richmond |
| WB/NCV | Will Books, Northampton County, Eastville VA |
| WL/SC | Warrants for Lands in South Carolina, SCDA |
| WR | *The War of the Rebellion: Official Records of the Union and Confederate Armies* (Washington DC: Government Printing Office, 1895) |

*Section B*
*Footnote Additions*

### B. 1. WILL OF PETER (PIERRE) ROBERT [II]

In the name of God the Father, the Son and the Holy Ghost: Amen. I, Peter Robert [II], born in Basle, Switzerland, and now living in Craven County, South Carolina, being by the grace of God, of sound mind and understanding, but unwell in body, not knowing when and what it shall please God to take me out of this world, do declare to have drawn up this my Testament which I hereby order to be enforced and executed as being my last will.

I commend my soul unto God my creator who redeemed it by the blood of His Son Jesus Christ, beseeching Him to have mercy upon me and receive me on my leaving this life into His eternal Tabernacles. As to my body I commit it to the earth to be therein interred in such a place as my heirs see fit.

As to my world goods which shall be found in my possession at the time of my death, I order that all of my debts shall be paid off first and prior to any legacy.

Secondly I give to Judith Robert, my dear wife, her bed and all of its appurtenances, a press with all of the linen that shall be found in the house, a table, a warming pan, a chest and a mirror.

Thirdly, as my son, Peter Robert [III], has inherited my late father's property, therefore and in consequence of the heavy losses I have undergone for some years, moreover believing that I cannot possibly leave to my other children more than he inherited from my late Father, I do give and bequeath unto my aforesaid son, Peter Robert [II], the sum of one shilling sterling, or the value thereof in currency of this country, for his portion and share in all present and future possessions without him or his descendants ever having any further claim under the pretext of primogeniture or under any other pretext to my plantation or any other real estates that might be found in my possession after my death.

Fifthly [sic], I will and order that in case my herein aftersaid execution deem it advisable for the best interest of the Family to sell all our real estate if they could get a reasonable price, they should do it for the sake of my debts, and I by this Testament and will do empower them to do so; but if on the contrary they could get only a very low price, then I give and bequeath those real estates unto my son James [Jacques] Robert and his heirs to enjoy them, and dispose of them as they please forever, but I also will and intend that my aforesaid son James Robert shall be obliged to deliver the price and therewith pay up my debts . . . my said son James Robert shall inherit the rest of my real estates without any reserve to enjoy them and dispose of them forever as he sees fit. . . .

Sixthly, I do give and bequeath unto my dear wife, Judith Robert one third of what shall remain of my possessions after my debts have been paid up to dispose of as she pleases and the other two thirds I give and bequeath unto my son James Robert and my daughters Magdalene Robert and Elizabeth Robert and all other children that I might have hereafter by my aforesaid wife. . . .

I also recommend and order that my children shall obey their mother and show her every possible respect according to the precepts of the Gospel of God's commandments in order to draw upon themselves His blessing.

I order and intend that my aforesaid wife Judith Robert shall have the use of the home all of her life, if the Plantation is not sold, on the condition that she shall not remarry.

I order and appoint both Judith Robert my dear wife and Mr. Gendron as Executors and Administrators jointly with my son James Robert, when he shall be twenty-one years old, that is to say, on the third of April, one thousand seven hundred and thirty two as it appears from the Baptism certificate delivered by the late Mr. Peter Robert, my dear father.

I revoke and annul any other Testament heretofore drawn up, signing this with my own hand.

Done in Santee, this ninth day of March, one thousand seven hundred and thirty one.

*Pierre (S.) Robert*

Witnesses:
Andre Rembert, Jean Robert, Pierre Guerry, Jean Baxott

Translation quoted from *Transactions of the Huguenot Society of South Carolina*, 29:38-41.

## B. 2.

"Whereas a marriage is intended to be had between Thomas Willingham and Sarah Chovin, both of the Parish of St. James Santee and State aforesaid in consideration of which the said Thomas do hereby agree to secure and settle upon the said Sarah that part of her deceased Father's Estate which she is entitled to by his last will also the following negroes the property of the said Thomas, viz. Judy, Isabella, Tennant, Elsey, Hector, Telly, Peggy, Hannah and Betty, together with their issue and increase as also the issue and increase of those she may receive from her Father's Estate so that the said Property nor no part thereof should be subject to the controul [sic] or disposal of the said Thomas or liable to his debts reserving to him nevertheless the right to receive the profits thereof during the Joint lives of him and the said Sarah and wereas [sic] it is agreed that if the said Sarah should die without leaving issue alive at the time of her death, then and on that case that part of the property she may receive from her Father's Estate and one half of the above named Negroes shall remain and be inherited by nearest Relations. NOW THIS

INDENTURE made on the Fifteenth day of November in the year of our Lord One thousand seven hundred and ninety-six in presence of the said Agreement and in order fully and to all intents and purposes of the said Agreement to carry it into Execution between the said Thomas on the one part and James Jaudon of Santee in the said State on the other.

"WITNESSETH that the said Thomas in consideration of said intended Marriage and of the said above recited agreements has bargained, sold, delivered, and by these presents doth bargain and deliver unto the Said James Jaudon, Se. the aforesaid mentioned negroes with issue and increase, and also all that part of her Father's Estate which she is entitled to in trust for the said Sarah Chovin. IN WITNESS WHEREOF the said Thomas Willingham to those presents hath hereunto set his hand and seal in the year of our Lord one thousand seven hundred and ninety-six. Thos. Willingham. . . ."

### B. 3.

". . .The house [at 272 Orange Street, Macon, Georgia] was built by Col. William S. Moughn of Jones County, who bought in 1860 Lots 29 and 30, Northwestern Range, uniting the two in one ownership for the first time, both continuing as one property in the Willinghams' hands. . . . Benjamin L. Willingham in 1870 bought the house, then with grounds extending below it to Bond Street and above it to encompass several of today's properties, as trustee for his first wife, Mrs. Elizabeth Martha Baynard Willingham, and their children. It was described in the deed then as the house and outhouses on the Hille in Macon lately occupied by the Rt. Rev. Bishop [John W.] Beckwith [Bishop of the Diocese of Georgia in 1867].

"Mrs. Elizabeth Willingham for whom her husband bought the house, died in 1887. Mr. Willingham died ten years later, leaving his second wife who had been 'the widow Perkins.' She was formerly Mary Shorter, daughter of Governor [John Gill] Shorter of Alabama [1861-1863] and she had no children. [Stratford Academy acquired the property at 272 Orange Street in 1964.]"

### B. 4.
#### A GOOD WOMAN GONE TO HER REST
#### THE FUNERAL TO BE THIS MORNING

"Mrs. E.[lizabeth] M.[artha] Willingham died at her residence on Orange Street yesterday morning at 4 o'clock.

"Mrs. Willingham was a daughter of Archibald Baynard, a very wealthy planter of the old regime on the Coast of South Carolina, and wife of B.[enjamin] C.[sic], the well-known cotton factor. Her mother, Martha Sarah Chaplin [Baynard] at the age of 82 still lives in Albany, Georgia. She was born in Beaufort, S.C., September 15, 1830. She passed her girlhood in South Carolina, beginning her education in Beaufort and completing it in Charleston. She was married in Beaufort in 1846 by the Rev. Robert Fuller, and after marriage settled in Lawtonville. In 1870 she moved to Macon, and for seventeen years has made this place her home. Thirteen children, nine sons and four daughters survive her death. Her life was wrapped up in the raising of her children, and she could have left no better testimonial of the purity of her teachings and examples and the perfection of her discipline than is found in the lives and standing of her children. Her sons are well known as the most energetic citizens and the most successful business men in Macon.

"At the age of 14 she was baptized in the Baptist church by Rev. Dr. Fuller late of Baltimore. Today all her children are members of the same church. Of nine sons, five are officers of the Baptist Church, and one a useful minister of the same denomination.

"Mrs. Willingham was of that type of Southern womanhood which feels that home is the true sphere of womanly usefulness and all who know Mr. Willingham have seen reflected in his face and life the sunshine which was never absent from his home.

"Mrs. Willingham was in failing health for a year preceding her death, but only for the past five weeks has her condition been considered critical. Yesterday morning at 4 o'clock, as the darkness was brightening into dawn, she passed away.

"The funeral services will be conducted at the family residence this morning at ten o'clock. Her sons will be her pall bearers. Mr. Willingham and family have the sympathy of the community in their affliction."

*B. 5.*
THE COTTON BLOOM

The rose has a thousand lovers because
Of her delicate grace and perfume,
But lovers for sturdier reasons give
Their hearts to the cotton bloom:

It grows in a dazzling ample land
Of measureless breadth and room—
And the wealth of a splendid tropical sun
Dowers this cotton bloom.

And Capital keeps his eyes on the field
While he hears the hum of the loom,
And his anxious visage glows and pales
At the nod of the cotton bloom!

—Howard Weeden

*Section C*
*Lineal Charts*

*THE BARNWELL LINE*

Matthew Barnewell (?-1690)
Margaret Carberry
‖
John Barnwell (1671-1724)
Anne Berners
‖
Paul Grimball [II] (1703-1750/51)
Mary Barnwell (1709-1738)
‖
William Baynard (1732-1773)
Elizabeth Ann Grimball (1735-1773)
‖
Thomas Baynard (1763-1805)
Sarah (Sally) Calder (1760?-?)
‖
Archibald Calder Baynard (1797-1865)
Martha Sarah Chaplin (1805-1889)
‖
Benjamin Lawton Willingham (1829-1898)
Elizabeth Martha Baynard (1830-1887)
‖
Richard Furman Lawton (1841-1892)
Caroline (Carrie) Willingham (1853-1921)
‖
Furman Dargan Lawton (1877-1955)
Mary Elliott (May) Nottingham (1879-1966)
‖
Glover Futch Harrell
Carolyn Willingham Lawton

*THE BAYNARD LINE*

William Baynard (1686-1746)
Mary Splatt

‖

William Baynard (1732-1773)
Elizabeth Ann Grimball (1735?-1773)

‖

Thomas Baynard (1763-1805)
Sarah (Sally) Calder (1760?-?)

‖

Archibald Calder Baynard (1797-1865)
Martha Sarah Chaplin (1805-1889)

‖

Benjamin Lawton Willingham (1829-1898)
Elizabeth Martha Baynard (1830-1887)

‖

Richard Furman Lawton (1841-1892)
Caroline (Carrie) Willingham (1853-1921)

‖

Furman Dargan Lawton (1877-1955)
Mary Elliott (May) Nottingham (1879-1966)

‖

Glover Futch Harrell
Carolyn Willingham Lawton

## THE FURMAN LINE

John Firmin (1588-1648)
Mary (last name unknown)
‖
Josiah Furman (or Firmin) (1625-1705)
Mary Beers
‖
Josiah Furman [II] (1652-?)
Sarah Strickland
‖
Josiah Furman [III] (1685-?)
Sarah Wood
‖
Wood Furman (1712-1783)
Rachel Brodhead (1722-1795)
‖
Richard Furman (1755-1825)
Dorothea Maria Burn (1774-1819)
‖
Samuel Furman (1792-1877)
Eliza Scrimzeour
‖
William Seabrook Lawton (1814-1858)
Dorothea Furman (1820-1886)
‖
Richard Furman Lawton (1841-1892)
Caroline (Carrie) Willingham (1853-1921)
‖
Furman Dargan Lawton (1877-1955)
Mary Elliott (May) Nottingham (1879-1966)
‖
Glover Futch Harrell
Carolyn Willingham Lawton

## THE GRIMBALL LINE

Paul Grimball (1645-1696)
Mary (last name unknown) (?-1720)
‖
Thomas Grimball (?-1722)
Elizabeth Adams
‖
Paul Grimball [II] (1708-1750)
Mary Barnwell (1709-1738)
‖
William Baynard (1732-1773)
Elizabeth Ann Grimball (1735-1773)
‖
Thomas Baynard (1763-1805)
Sarah (Sally) Calder (1760-?)
‖
Archibald Calder Baynard (1798-1865)
Martha Sarah Chaplin (1805-1889)
‖
Benjamin Lawton Willingham (1825-1898)
Elizabeth Martha Baynard (1830-1887)
‖
Richard Furman Lawton (1841-1892)
Caroline (Carrie) Willingham (1852-1921)
‖
Furman Dargan Lawton (1877-1955)
Mary Elliott (May) Nottingham (1879-1966)
‖
Glover Futch Harrell
Carolyn Willingham Lawton

## THE GUTTENBERGER LINE

Johann Martin Guttenberger (1695-1765)
Katherine Susanna Steinfort (?-1784)

‖

Phillip Gerhart Guttenberger [I] (1746-1830)
Katharine Elizabeth Rogers (1732-1787)

‖

Johann Martin Guttenberger (1771-1821)
Margarite Juliana Diehl (1770-1841)

‖

Phillip Gerhart Guttenberger [II] (1799-1874)
Emily Antoinette Muse (1811-1887)

‖

John Jacob Nottingham (1850/51-1887)
Emily Jane Guttenberger (1852-1920)

‖

Furman Dargan Lawton (1877-1955)
Mary Elliott (May) Nottingham (1879-1966)

‖

Glover Futch Harrell
Carolyn Willingham Lawton

*THE HARRELL LINE*

Francis Harrell (?-1759)
Mary Benton
‖
Jacob Harrell (1716-1787)
?
‖
Levi Harrell [I] (1750-1806)
Elizabeth Holt (1782-1876)
‖
William Holt Harrell (1811-1895)
Sophia Hendley (1813-1879)
‖
Charles H. Harrell (1835-1912)
Mary Elizabeth McCoy (1835-1900)
‖
James Warren Harrell (1877-1959)
Ruby Coffee Harrell (1882-1967)
‖
Glover Futch Harrell
Carolyn Willingham Lawton

THE LAWTON LINE *(Number 1)*

William Lawton (1723-1757)
Mary Stone (Grimball) (c. 1720-1804)
||
Joseph Lawton (1753-1815)
Sarah Robert (1755-1839)
||
Benjamin Themistocles Dion Lawton (1782-1846)
Jane Mosse (1783-1857)
||
William Seabrook Lawton (1814?-1858)
Dorothea Furman (1820-1886)
||
Richard Furman Lawton (1841-1892)
Caroline (Carrie) Willingham (1853-1921)
||
Furman Dargan Lawton (1877-1955)
Mary Elliott (May) Nottingham (1879-1966)
||
Glover Futch Harrell
Carolyn Willingham Lawton

*THE LAWTON LINE (Number 2)*

William Lawton (1723-1757)
Mary Stone (Grimball) (c. 1720-1804)

||

Joseph Lawton (1753-1815)
Sarah Robert (1755-1839)

||

Benjamin Themistocles Dion Lawton (1782-1846)
Jane Mosse (1783-1857)

||

Thomas Henry Willingham [II] (1798-1862)
Phoebe Sarah Lawton (1808-1862)

||

Benjamin Lawton Willingham (1829-1898)
Elizabeth Martha Baynard (1830-1887)

||

Richard Furman Lawton (1841-1892)
Caroline (Carrie) Willingham (1853-1921)

||

Furman Dargan Lawton (1877-1955)
Mary Elliott (May) Nottingham (1879-1966)

||

Glover Futch Harrell
Carolyn Willingham Lawton

## THE MOSSE LINE

George Mosse (1742-1808)
Dorothy Phoebe Norton (1751-1808)
||
Benjamin Themistocles Dion Lawton (1782-1846)
Jane Mosse (1783-1857)
||
William Seabrook Lawton (1814?-1858)
Dorothea Furman (1820-1886)
||
Richard Furman Lawton (1841-1892)
Caroline (Carrie) Willingham (1853-1921)
||
Furman Dargan Lawton (1877-1955)
Mary Elliott (May) Nottingham (1879-1966)
||
Glover Futch Harrell
Carolyn Willingham Lawton

*THE NOTTINGHAM LINE*

Richard Nottingham [I] (1621-1692)
Elizabeth Hutton (c. 1630-?)

‖

Richard Nottingham [II] (1652-1728/29)
Mary Clark

‖

Jacob Nottingham [I] (?-1747)
Mary (last name unknown)

‖

Thomas Nottingham (c. 1730-1797)
Scarburgh

‖

Jacob Nottingham [II] (?-1809)
Bridget Brickhouse

‖

Smith B. Nottingham (1799-?)
Mary H. Elliott (1805-1859)

‖

John Jacob Nottingham (1830/31-1887)
Emily Jane (Emma) Guttenberger (1852-1920)

‖

Furman Dargan Lawton (1877-1955)
Mary (May) Elliott Nottingham (1879-1966)

‖

Glover Futch Harrell
Carolyn Willingham Lawton

## THE ROBERT LINE

Daniel Robert
Marie Huguent
‖
Pierre Robert [I] (1656-1715)
Jeanne Broye (1660-1717)
‖
Pierre Robert [II] (1675-1731)
Judith deBourdeau
‖
Jacques (James) Robert (1711-1774)
Sarah Jaudon (1719-1779)
‖
Joseph Lawton (1753-1815)
Sarah Robert (1755-1839)
‖
Benjamin Themistocles Dion Lawton (1782-1846)
Jane Mosse (1783-1857)
‖
William Seabrook Lawton (1814-1858)
Dorothea Furman (1820-1886)
‖
Richard Furman Lawton (1841-1892)
Caroline (Carrie) Willingham (1853-1921)
‖
Furman Dargan Lawton (1877-1955)
Mary Eliott (May) Nottingham (1879-1966)
‖
Glover Futch Harrell
Carolyn Willingham Lawton

## THE WILLINGHAM LINE

Joseph Willingham (?-1789)
Mary (Hodson) Roach
‖
Thomas Henry Willingham [I] (1772/3-c. 1798)
Sarah Chovin (1780-1825)
‖
Thomas Henry Willingham [II] (1798-1873)
Phoebe Sarah Lawton (1799-1872)
‖
Benjamin Lawton Willingham (1829-1898)
Elizabeth Martha Baynard (1830-1887)
‖
Richard Furman Lawton (1841-1892)
Caroline (Carrie) Willingham (1853-1921)
‖
Furman Dargan Lawton (1877-1955)
Mary Elliott (May) Nottingham (1879-1966)
‖
Glover Futch Harrell
Carolyn Willingham Lawton

## Section D
## Ancestor Charts

### ANCESTOR CHART NO. ___A___

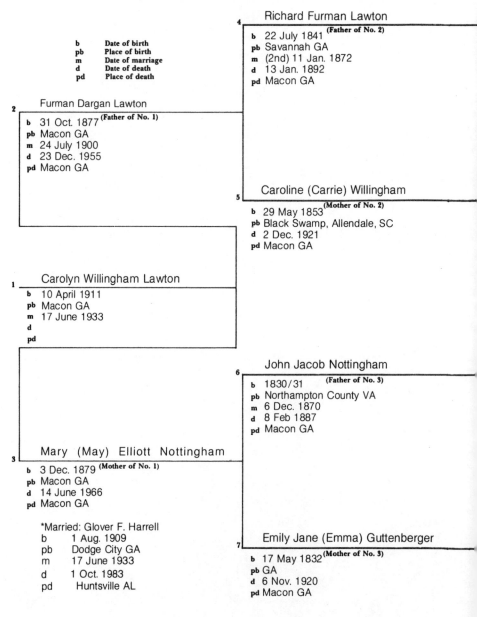

**b** Date of birth
**pb** Place of birth
**m** Date of marriage
**d** Date of death
**pd** Place of death

4 **Richard Furman Lawton** (Father of No. 2)
**b** 22 July 1841
**pb** Savannah GA
**m** (2nd) 11 Jan. 1872
**d** 13 Jan. 1892
**pd** Macon GA

2 **Furman Dargan Lawton** (Father of No. 1)
**b** 31 Oct. 1877
**pb** Macon GA
**m** 24 July 1900
**d** 23 Dec. 1955
**pd** Macon GA

5 **Caroline (Carrie) Willingham** (Mother of No. 2)
**b** 29 May 1853
**pb** Black Swamp, Allendale, SC
**d** 2 Dec. 1921
**pd** Macon GA

1 **Carolyn Willingham Lawton**
**b** 10 April 1911
**pb** Macon GA
**m** 17 June 1933
**d**
**pd**

6 **John Jacob Nottingham** (Father of No. 3)
**b** 1830/31
**pb** Northampton County VA
**m** 6 Dec. 1870
**d** 8 Feb 1887
**pd** Macon GA

3 **Mary (May) Elliott Nottingham** (Mother of No. 1)
**b** 3 Dec. 1879
**pb** Macon GA
**d** 14 June 1966
**pd** Macon GA

*Married: Glover F. Harrell
**b** 1 Aug. 1909
**pb** Dodge City GA
**m** 17 June 1933
**d** 1 Oct. 1983
**pd** Huntsville AL

7 **Emily Jane (Emma) Guttenberger** (Mother of No. 3)
**b** 17 May 1832
**pb** GA
**d** 6 Nov. 1920
**pd** Macon GA

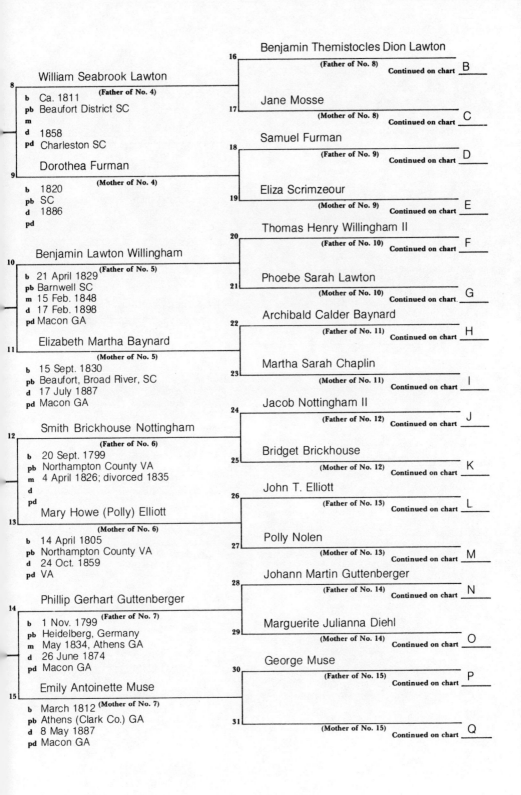

**8** William Seabrook Lawton *(Father of No. 4)*
b Ca. 1811
pb Beaufort District SC
m
d 1858
pd Charleston SC

**9** Dorothea Furman *(Mother of No. 4)*
b 1820
pb SC
d 1886
pd

**10** Benjamin Lawton Willingham *(Father of No. 5)*
b 21 April 1829
pb Barnwell SC
m 15 Feb. 1848
d 17 Feb. 1898
pd Macon GA

**11** Elizabeth Martha Baynard *(Mother of No. 5)*
b 15 Sept. 1830
pb Beaufort, Broad River, SC
d 17 July 1887
pd Macon GA

**12** Smith Brickhouse Nottingham *(Father of No. 6)*
b 20 Sept. 1799
pb Northampton County VA
m 4 April 1826; divorced 1835
d
pd

**13** Mary Howe (Polly) Elliott *(Mother of No. 6)*
b 14 April 1805
pb Northampton County VA
d 24 Oct. 1859
pd VA

**14** Phillip Gerhart Guttenberger *(Father of No. 7)*
b 1 Nov. 1799
pb Heidelberg, Germany
m May 1834, Athens GA
d 26 June 1874
pd Macon GA

**15** Emily Antoinette Muse *(Mother of No. 7)*
b March 1812
pb Athens (Clark Co.) GA
d 8 May 1887
pd Macon GA

**16** Benjamin Themistocles Dion Lawton *(Father of No. 8)* — Continued on chart **B**

**17** Jane Mosse *(Mother of No. 8)* — Continued on chart **C**

**18** Samuel Furman *(Father of No. 9)* — Continued on chart **D**

**19** Eliza Scrimzeour *(Mother of No. 9)* — Continued on chart **E**

**20** Thomas Henry Willingham II *(Father of No. 10)* — Continued on chart **F**

**21** Phoebe Sarah Lawton *(Mother of No. 10)* — Continued on chart **G**

**22** Archibald Calder Baynard *(Father of No. 11)* — Continued on chart **H**

**23** Martha Sarah Chaplin *(Mother of No. 11)* — Continued on chart **I**

**24** Jacob Nottingham II *(Father of No. 12)* — Continued on chart **J**

**25** Bridget Brickhouse *(Mother of No. 12)* — Continued on chart **K**

**26** John T. Elliott *(Father of No. 13)* — Continued on chart **L**

**27** Polly Nolen *(Mother of No. 13)* — Continued on chart **M**

**28** Johann Martin Guttenberger *(Father of No. 14)* — Continued on chart **N**

**29** Marguerite Julianna Diehl *(Mother of No. 14)* — Continued on chart **O**

**30** George Muse *(Father of No. 15)* — Continued on chart **P**

**31** *(Mother of No. 15)* — Continued on chart **Q**

# ANCESTOR CHART NO. __AA__

Person No. 1 on this chart is identical to person

No._____ on chart No._____

|   |   |
|---|---|
| b | Date of birth |
| pb | Place of birth |
| m | Date of marriage |
| d | Date of death |
| pd | Place of death |

### Charles H. Harrell

4

**(Father of No. 2)**
b   May 1835
pb  Pulaski County GA
m  6 Feb. 1861
d   15 March 1912
pd  Dodge County GA

### James Warren Harrell

2

**(Father of No. 1)**
b   16 March 1877
pb  Dodge County GA
m  8 Jan. 1899
d   21 March 1959
pd  Jacksonville FL
    Buried Eastman GA
    Dodge County

### Mary Elizabeth McCoy

5

**(Mother of No. 2)**
b   6 Feb. 1835
pb  Telfair County GA
d   13 Nov. 1900
pd  Dodge County GA

### Glover Futch Harrell

1

b   1 Aug. 1909
pb  Dodge County GA
m  17 June 1933
d   1 Oct. 1983
pd  Huntsville AL

### Andrew Jackson Coffee

6

**(Father of No. 3)**
b   5 March 1860
pb  Pulaski County GA
m  28 April 1881
d   30 Dec. 1916
pd  Rhine, Dodge County GA

### Ruby Coffee

3

**(Mother of No. 1)**
b   25 May 1882
pb  Dodge County GA
d   24 May 1967
pd  Fitzgerald GA
    Buried Lumber City GA
    Telfair County GA

### Mary Caroline Futch

7

**(Mother of No. 3)**
b   19 Jan. 1881
pb  Telfair County GA
d   24 Dec. 1934
pd  Fitzgerald GA
    Buried Rhine GA

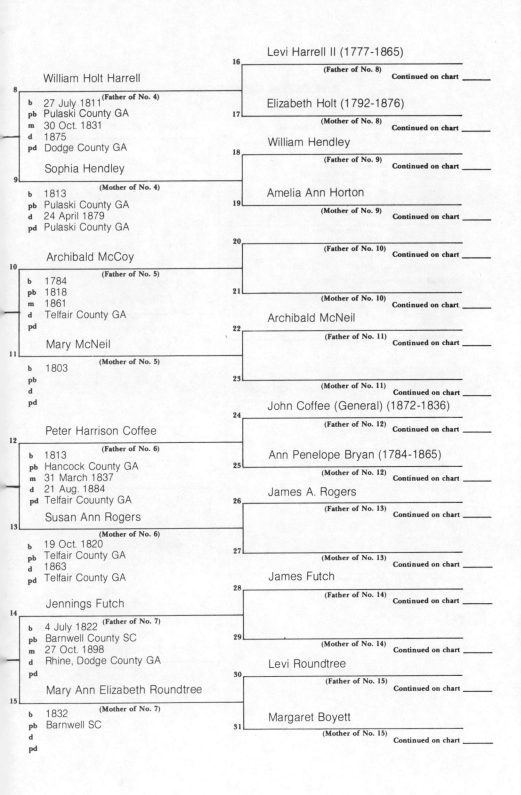

**William Holt Harrell**

8
                (Father of No. 4)
b   27 July 1811
pb  Pulaski County GA
m  30 Oct. 1831
d   1875
pd  Dodge County GA

**Sophia Hendley**

9
          (Mother of No. 4)
b   1813
pb  Pulaski County GA
d   24 April 1879
pd  Pulaski County GA

**Archibald McCoy**

10
          (Father of No. 5)
b   1784
pb  1818
m  1861
d   Telfair County GA
pd

**Mary McNeil**

11
          (Mother of No. 5)
b   1803
pb
d
pd

**Peter Harrison Coffee**

12
          (Father of No. 6)
b   1813
pb  Hancock County GA
m  31 March 1837
d   21 Aug. 1884
pd  Telfair Couunty GA

**Susan Ann Rogers**

13
          (Mother of No. 6)
b   19 Oct. 1820
pb  Telfair County GA
d   1863
pd  Telfair County GA

**Jennings Futch**

14
          (Father of No. 7)
b   4 July 1822
pb  Barnwell County SC
m  27 Oct. 1898
d   Rhine, Dodge County GA
pd

**Mary Ann Elizabeth Roundtree**

15
          (Mother of No. 7)
b   1832
pb  Barnwell SC
d
pd

16  **Levi Harrell II (1777-1865)**
        (Father of No. 8)    Continued on chart _____

17  **Elizabeth Holt (1792-1876)**
        (Mother of No. 8)    Continued on chart _____

18  **William Hendley**
        (Father of No. 9)    Continued on chart _____

19  **Amelia Ann Horton**
        (Mother of No. 9)    Continued on chart _____

20
        (Father of No. 10)    Continued on chart _____

21
        (Mother of No. 10)    Continued on chart. _____

22  **Archibald McNeil**
        (Father of No. 11)    Continued on chart _____

23
        (Mother of No. 11)    Continued on chart _____

24  **John Coffee (General) (1872-1836)**
        (Father of No. 12)    Continued on chart _____

25  **Ann Penelope Bryan (1784-1865)**
        (Mother of No. 12)    Continued on chart _____

26  **James A. Rogers**
        (Father of No. 13)    Continued on chart _____

27
        (Mother of No. 13)    Continued on chart _____

28  **James Futch**
        (Father of No. 14)    Continued on chart _____

29
        (Mother of No. 14)    Continued on chart _____

30  **Levi Roundtree**
        (Father of No. 15)    Continued on chart _____

31  **Margaret Boyett**
        (Mother of No. 15)    Continued on chart _____

# ANCESTOR CHART NO. __B__

Person No. 1 on this chart is identical to person
No.__16__ on chart No.__A__

| | |
|---|---|
| **b** | Date of birth |
| **pb** | Place of birth |
| **m** | Date of marriage |
| **d** | Date of death |
| **pd** | Place of death |

**4** William Lawton ("Capt.")
*(Father of No. 2)*
- **b** before 1724
- **pb** Cheshire County England
- **m** will proved 8 Dec. 1757
- **d** Edisto Island SC
- **pd** Came to Edisto Island before 1737

**2** Joseph Lawton
*(Father of No. 1)*
- **b** 18 Oct. 1755
- **pb** Edisto Island SC
- **m** 18 March 1773
- **d** 5 March 1815
- **pd** Mulberry Grove Plantation
  Robertville SC
  St. Peter's Parish

**5** Mary Stone (Grimball) Lawton
*(Mother of No. 2)*
- **b** St. Peter's Parish
- **pb**
- **d** d. Jan. 1804 (was then
- **pd** Mrs. Samuel Fickling)

**1** Benjamin Themistocles Dion Lawton
- **b** 22 Dec. 1782
- **pb** St. Peter's Parish SC
- **m** (1) 26 June 1803
- **d** 18 April 1846
- **pd** Albany GA

**6** Jacques (James) Robert
*(Father of No. 3)*
- **b** 3 April 1711
- **pb**
- **m** (2nd) 26 Aug. 1735
- **d** Nov. 1774
- **pd** Yamassee SC

**3** Sarah Robert
*(Mother of No. 1)*
- **b** 6 Feb. 1755
- **pb** Santee SC
- **d** 6 Oct. 1839
- **pd** Robertville SC

**7** Sarah Jaudon
*(Mother of No. 3)*
- **b** 24 Sept. 1719
- **pb**
- **d** 26 Apr. 1779
- **pd**

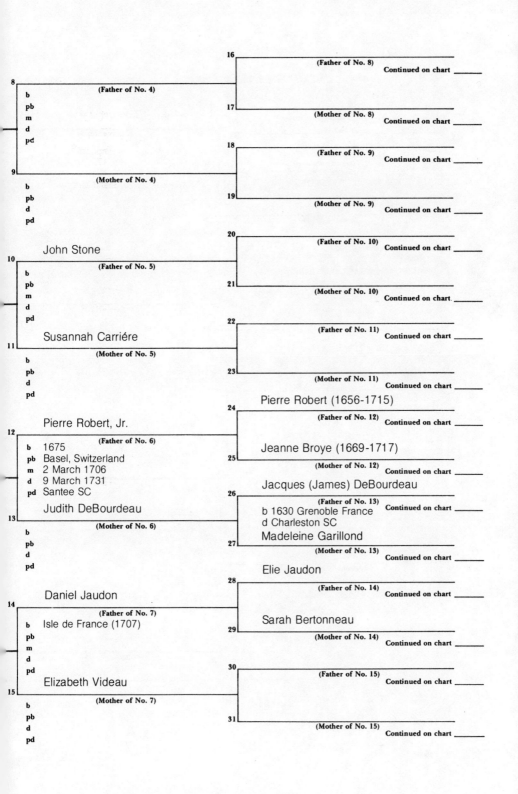

**16**
(Father of No. 8)
Continued on chart _____

**8**
(Father of No. 4)
b
pb
m
d
pd

**17**
(Mother of No. 8)
Continued on chart _____

**18**
(Father of No. 9)
Continued on chart _____

**9**
(Mother of No. 4)
b
pb
d
pd

**19**
(Mother of No. 9)
Continued on chart _____

**20**
(Father of No. 10)
Continued on chart _____

John Stone

**10**
(Father of No. 5)
b
pb
m
d
pd

**21**
(Mother of No. 10)
Continued on chart _____

Susannah Carriére

**22**
(Father of No. 11)
Continued on chart _____

**11**
(Mother of No. 5)
b
pb
d
pd

**23**
(Mother of No. 11)
Continued on chart _____

Pierre Robert (1656-1715)

**24**
(Father of No. 12)
Continued on chart _____

Pierre Robert, Jr.

**12**
(Father of No. 6)
b   1675
pb  Basel, Switzerland
m   2 March 1706
d   9 March 1731
pd  Santee SC

Jeanne Broye (1669-1717)

**25**
(Mother of No. 12)
Continued on chart _____

Jacques (James) DeBourdeau

**26**
(Father of No. 13)
b 1630 Grenoble France
d Charleston SC
Continued on chart _____

Judith DeBourdeau

**13**
(Mother of No. 6)
b
pb
d
pd

Madeleine Garillond

**27**
(Mother of No. 13)
Continued on chart _____

Elie Jaudon

**28**
(Father of No. 14)
Continued on chart _____

Daniel Jaudon

**14**
(Father of No. 7)
b   Isle de France (1707)
pb
m
d
pd

Sarah Bertonneau

**29**
(Mother of No. 14)
Continued on chart _____

**30**
(Father of No. 15)
Continued on chart _____

Elizabeth Videau

**15**
(Mother of No. 7)
b
pb
d
pd

**31**
(Mother of No. 15)
Continued on chart _____

# ANCESTOR CHART NO. __C__

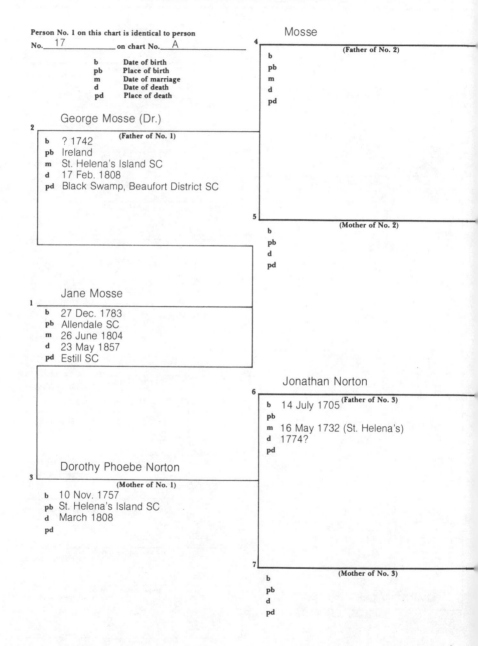

Person No. 1 on this chart is identical to person
No.___17_____ on chart No.___A_____

| | |
|---|---|
| b | Date of birth |
| pb | Place of birth |
| m | Date of marriage |
| d | Date of death |
| pd | Place of death |

**4**
Mosse
(Father of No. 2)
b
pb
m
d
pd

**2**
George Mosse (Dr.)
(Father of No. 1)
b   ? 1742
pb   Ireland
m   St. Helena's Island SC
d   17 Feb. 1808
pd   Black Swamp, Beaufort District SC

**5**
(Mother of No. 2)
b
pb
d
pd

**1**
Jane Mosse
b   27 Dec. 1783
pb   Allendale SC
m   26 June 1804
d   23 May 1857
pd   Estill SC

**6**
Jonathan Norton
(Father of No. 3)
b   14 July 1705
pb
m   16 May 1732 (St. Helena's)
d   1774?
pd

**3**
Dorothy Phoebe Norton
(Mother of No. 1)
b   10 Nov. 1757
pb   St. Helena's Island SC
d   March 1808
pd

**7**
(Mother of No. 3)
b
pb
d
pd

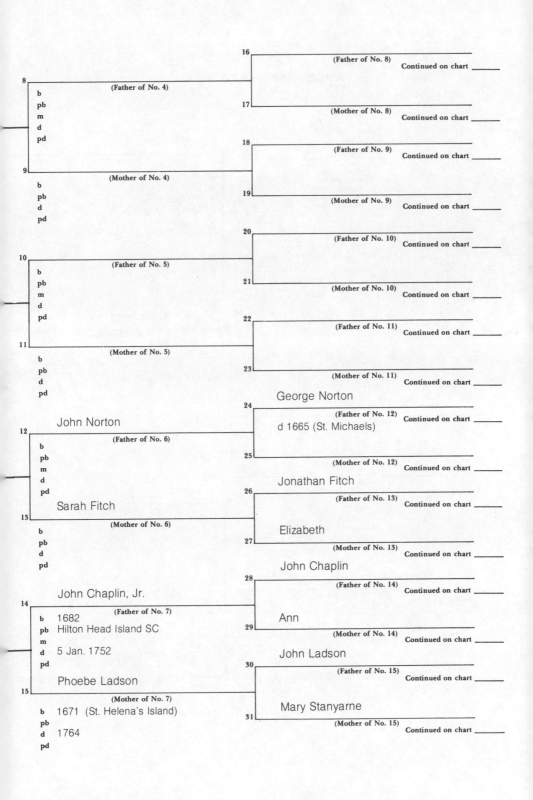

16
(Father of No. 8)
Continued on chart _____

8
(Father of No. 4)
b
pb
m
d
pd

17
(Mother of No. 8)
Continued on chart _____

18
(Father of No. 9)
Continued on chart _____

9
(Mother of No. 4)
b
pb
d
pd

19
(Mother of No. 9)
Continued on chart _____

20
(Father of No. 10)
Continued on chart _____

10
(Father of No. 5)
b
pb
m
d
pd

21
(Mother of No. 10)
Continued on chart _____

22
(Father of No. 11)
Continued on chart _____

11
(Mother of No. 5)
b
pb
d
pd

23
(Mother of No. 11)
Continued on chart _____

George Norton
24
(Father of No. 12)
Continued on chart _____
d 1665 (St. Michaels)

John Norton
12
(Father of No. 6)
b
pb
m
d
pd

25
(Mother of No. 12)
Continued on chart _____

Sarah Fitch
Jonathan Fitch
26
(Father of No. 13)
Continued on chart _____

13
(Mother of No. 6)
b
pb
d
pd

Elizabeth
27
(Mother of No. 13)
Continued on chart _____

John Chaplin
28
(Father of No. 14)
Continued on chart _____

John Chaplin, Jr.
14
(Father of No. 7)
b    1682
pb   Hilton Head Island SC
m
d    5 Jan. 1752
pd

Ann
29
(Mother of No. 14)
Continued on chart _____

John Ladson
30
(Father of No. 15)
Continued on chart _____

Phoebe Ladson
15
(Mother of No. 7)
b    1671  (St. Helena's Island)
pb
d    1764
pd

Mary Stanyarne
31
(Mother of No. 15)
Continued on chart _____

# ANCESTOR CHART NO. __D__

Person No. 1 on this chart is identical to person
No.___18_____ on chart No.___A_____

| | |
|---|---|
| **b** | Date of birth |
| **pb** | Place of birth |
| **m** | Date of marriage |
| **d** | Date of death |
| **pd** | Place of death |

**4** Wood Furman (Judge)

(Father of No. 2)
- **b** 15 Oct. 1712
- **pb** Newtown Long Island NY
- **m** 20 April 1742
- **d** 10 Feb. 1783
- **pd** Sumter County SC

**2** Richard Furman

(Father of No. 1)
- **b** 9 Oct. 1755
- **pb** Esopus NY
- **m** (2nd) 5 May 1789
- **d** 26 Aug. 1825
- **pd** Charleston SC

**5** Rachel Brodhead

(Mother of No. 2)
- **b** 28 Jan. 1722
- **pb** Long Island NY
- **d** 1795
- **pd** Sumter County SC

**1** Samuel Furman*

- **b** 27 March 1792
- **pb** SC
- **m** 5 May 1814
- **d** 1877
- **pd** SC

**6** Burn

(Father of No. 3)
- **b**
- **pb**
- **m**
- **d**
- **pd**

**3** Dorothea Marie Burn

(Mother of No. 1)
- **b** 17 March 1774
- **pb** Charleston SC
- **d** 1819
- **pd** Charleston SC

*Married Eliza Scrimzeour

**7**
(Mother of No. 3)
- **b**
- **pb**
- **d**
- **pd**

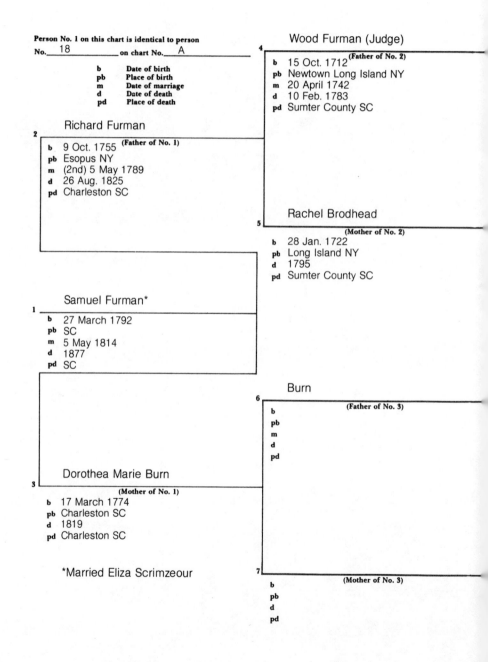

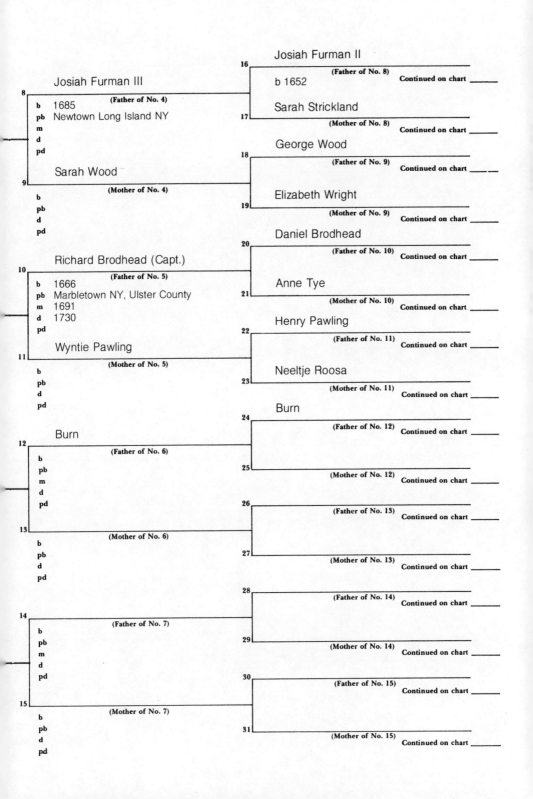

**8** Josiah Furman III
**(Father of No. 4)**
b 1685
pb Newtown Long Island NY
m
d
pd

**9** Sarah Wood
**(Mother of No. 4)**
b
pb
d
pd

**10** Richard Brodhead (Capt.)
**(Father of No. 5)**
b 1666
pb Marbletown NY, Ulster County
m 1691
d 1730
pd

**11** Wyntie Pawling
**(Mother of No. 5)**
b
pb
d
pd

**12** Burn
**(Father of No. 6)**
b
pb
m
d
pd

**13**
**(Mother of No. 6)**
b
pb
d
pd

**14**
**(Father of No. 7)**
b
pb
m
d
pd

**15**
**(Mother of No. 7)**
b
pb
d
pd

**16** Josiah Furman II
**(Father of No. 8)**
b 1652
Continued on chart _____

**17** Sarah Strickland
**(Mother of No. 8)**
Continued on chart _____

**18** George Wood
**(Father of No. 9)**
Continued on chart _____

**19** Elizabeth Wright
**(Mother of No. 9)**
Continued on chart _____

**20** Daniel Brodhead
**(Father of No. 10)**
Continued on chart _____

**21** Anne Tye
**(Mother of No. 10)**
Continued on chart _____

**22** Henry Pawling
**(Father of No. 11)**
Continued on chart _____

**23** Neeltje Roosa
**(Mother of No. 11)**
Continued on chart _____

**24** Burn
**(Father of No. 12)**
Continued on chart _____

**25**
**(Mother of No. 12)**
Continued on chart _____

**26**
**(Father of No. 13)**
Continued on chart _____

**27**
**(Mother of No. 13)**
Continued on chart _____

**28**
**(Father of No. 14)**
Continued on chart _____

**29**
**(Mother of No. 14)**
Continued on chart _____

**30**
**(Father of No. 15)**
Continued on chart _____

**31**
**(Mother of No. 15)**
Continued on chart _____

# ANCESTOR CHART NO. __D-1__

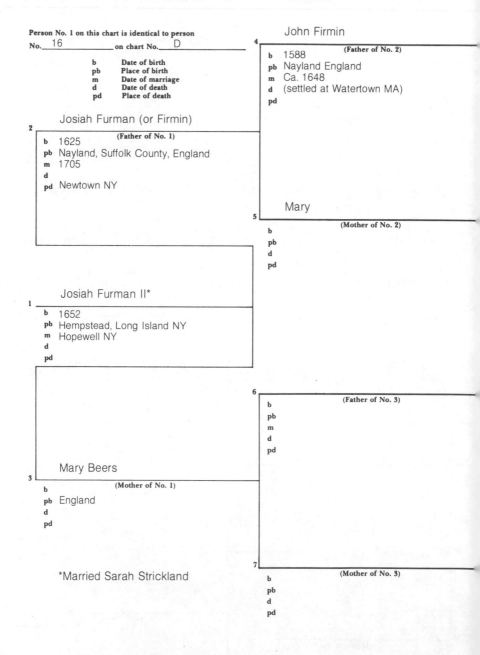

Person No. 1 on this chart is identical to person
No.__16_____ on chart No.___D_____

| | |
|---|---|
| b | Date of birth |
| pb | Place of birth |
| m | Date of marriage |
| d | Date of death |
| pd | Place of death |

**4**     John Firmin

(Father of No. 2)

b   1588
pb  Nayland England
m   Ca. 1648
d   (settled at Watertown MA)
pd

**2**   Josiah Furman (or Firmin)

(Father of No. 1)

b   1625
pb  Nayland, Suffolk County, England
m   1705
d
pd  Newtown NY

**5**    Mary

(Mother of No. 2)

b
pb
d
pd

**1**   Josiah Furman II*

b   1652
pb  Hempstead, Long Island NY
m   Hopewell NY
d
pd

**6**

(Father of No. 3)

b
pb
m
d
pd

**3**   Mary Beers

(Mother of No. 1)

b
pb  England
d
pd

*Married Sarah Strickland

**7**

(Mother of No. 3)

b
pb
d
pd

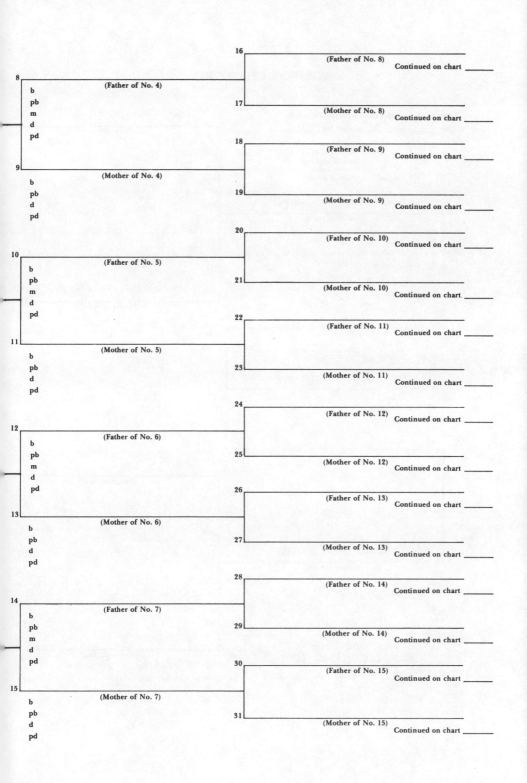

8
b
pb
m
d
pd
(Father of No. 4)

9
b
pb
d
pd
(Mother of No. 4)

10
b
pb
m
d
pd
(Father of No. 5)

11
b
pb
d
pd
(Mother of No. 5)

12
b
pb
m
d
pd
(Father of No. 6)

13
b
pb
d
pd
(Mother of No. 6)

14
b
pb
m
d
pd
(Father of No. 7)

15
b
pb
d
pd
(Mother of No. 7)

16
(Father of No. 8)
Continued on chart _____

17
(Mother of No. 8)
Continued on chart _____

18
(Father of No. 9)
Continued on chart _____

19
(Mother of No. 9)
Continued on chart _____

20
(Father of No. 10)
Continued on chart _____

21
(Mother of No. 10)
Continued on chart _____

22
(Father of No. 11)
Continued on chart _____

23
(Mother of No. 11)
Continued on chart _____

24
(Father of No. 12)
Continued on chart _____

25
(Mother of No. 12)
Continued on chart _____

26
(Father of No. 13)
Continued on chart _____

27
(Mother of No. 13)
Continued on chart _____

28
(Father of No. 14)
Continued on chart _____

29
(Mother of No. 14)
Continued on chart _____

30
(Father of No. 15)
Continued on chart _____

31
(Mother of No. 15)
Continued on chart _____

# ANCESTOR CHART NO. __F__

Person No. 1 on this chart is identical to person

No.__20__ on chart No.__A__

b      Date of birth
pb     Place of birth
m      Date of marriage
d      Date of death
pd     Place of death

**4**   Joseph Willingham
(Father of No. 2)
b   settled about 1771 on Myrtle Hill
pb   Santee SC
m   (2nd) ca, 1771
d   Ca. 1789
pd

**2**   Thomas Henry Willingham I
(Father of No. 1)
b   2 Jan. 1772-3
pb   Settled on Sullivan Island
m   St. James Parish SC ca. 1796
d   after 20 Feb. 1799
pd

**5**   Mary Hodson (widow Roach)
(Mother of No. 2)
b
pb
d
pd

**1**   *Thomas Henry Willingham II
b   23 Dec. 1798
pb   Santee SC
m   13 Nov. 1823
d   7 July 1783
pd   Allendale SC

**6**   Charles Chovine
(Father of No. 3)
b   1763
pb
m
d
pd

**3**   Sarah Chovine (or Chovin)
(Mother of No. 1)
b   7 Aug. 1780
pb
d   30 Dec. 1823
pd

m   Phoebe Sarah Lawton
b   7 July 1808
d   4 Feb. 1862

**7**   Sarah Guerin
(Mother of No. 3)
b   10 July 1763
pb
d
pd

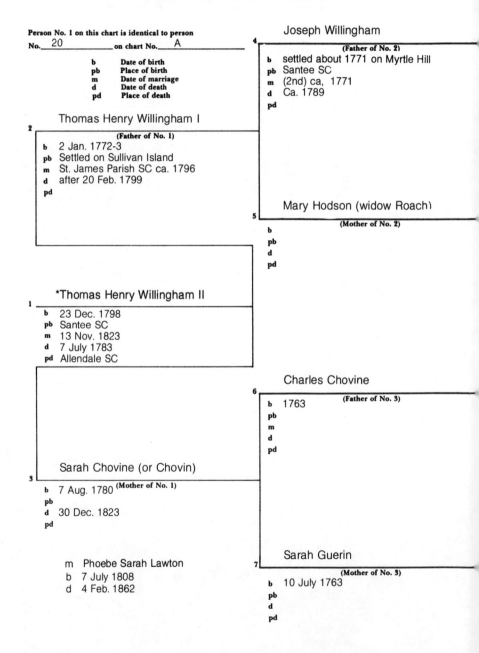

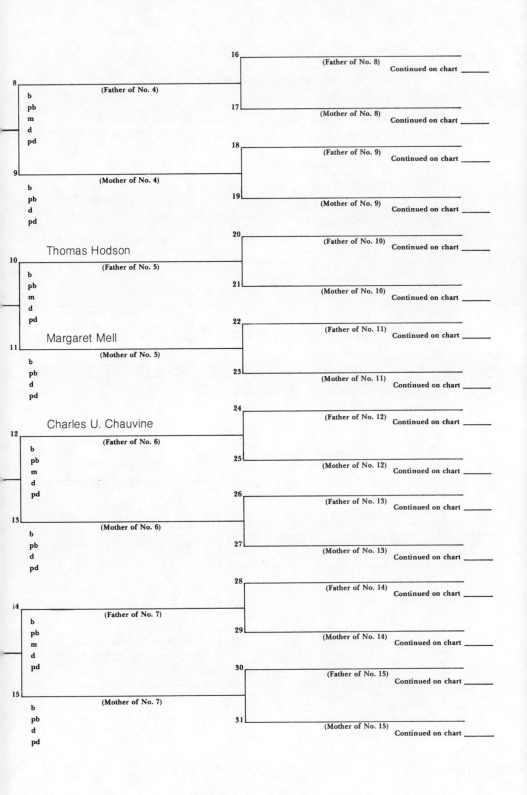

16
(Father of No. 8)
Continued on chart _____

8
(Father of No. 4)
b
pb
m
d
pd

17
(Mother of No. 8)
Continued on chart _____

18
(Father of No. 9)
Continued on chart _____

9
(Mother of No. 4)
b
pb
d
pd

19
(Mother of No. 9)
Continued on chart _____

20
(Father of No. 10)
Continued on chart _____

Thomas Hodson

10
(Father of No. 5)
b
pb
m
d
pd

21
(Mother of No. 10)
Continued on chart _____

22
(Father of No. 11)
Continued on chart _____

Margaret Mell

11
(Mother of No. 5)
b
pb
d
pd

23
(Mother of No. 11)
Continued on chart _____

24
(Father of No. 12)
Continued on chart _____

Charles U. Chauvine

12
(Father of No. 6)
b
pb
m
d
pd

25
(Mother of No. 12)
Continued on chart _____

26
(Father of No. 13)
Continued on chart _____

13
(Mother of No. 6)
b
pb
d
pd

27
(Mother of No. 13)
Continued on chart _____

28
(Father of No. 14)
Continued on chart _____

14
(Father of No. 7)
b
pb
m
d
pd

29
(Mother of No. 14)
Continued on chart _____

30
(Father of No. 15)
Continued on chart _____

15
(Mother of No. 7)
b
pb
d
pd

31
(Mother of No. 15)
Continued on chart _____

# ANCESTOR CHART NO. __G__

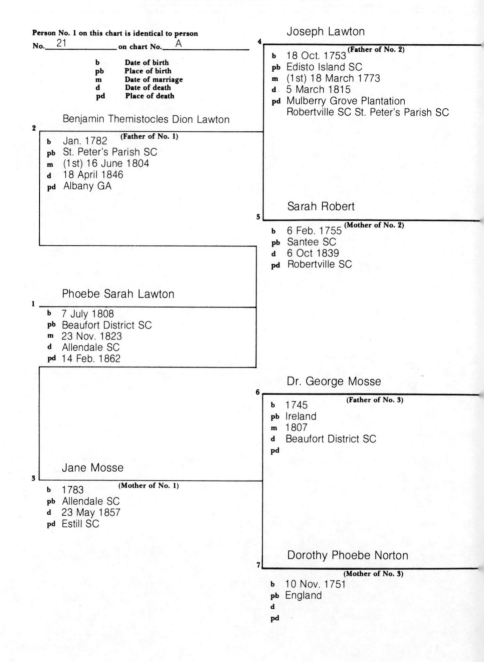

Person No. 1 on this chart is identical to person
No. __21__ _____ on chart No.__A__ _____

| | |
|---|---|
| b | Date of birth |
| pb | Place of birth |
| m | Date of marriage |
| d | Date of death |
| pd | Place of death |

**4** Joseph Lawton
    (Father of No. 2)
b 18 Oct. 1753
pb Edisto Island SC
m (1st) 18 March 1773
d. 5 March 1815
pd Mulberry Grove Plantation
    Robertville SC St. Peter's Parish SC

**2** Benjamin Themistocles Dion Lawton
    (Father of No. 1)
b Jan. 1782
pb St. Peter's Parish SC
m (1st) 16 June 1804
d 18 April 1846
pd Albany GA

**5** Sarah Robert
    (Mother of No. 2)
b 6 Feb. 1755
pb Santee SC
d 6 Oct 1839
pd Robertville SC

**1** Phoebe Sarah Lawton
b 7 July 1808
pb Beaufort District SC
m 23 Nov. 1823
d Allendale SC
pd 14 Feb. 1862

**6** Dr. George Mosse
    (Father of No. 3)
b 1745
pb Ireland
m 1807
d Beaufort District SC
pd

**3** Jane Mosse
    (Mother of No. 1)
b 1783
pb Allendale SC
d 23 May 1857
pd Estill SC

**7** Dorothy Phoebe Norton
    (Mother of No. 3)
b 10 Nov. 1751
pb England
d
pd

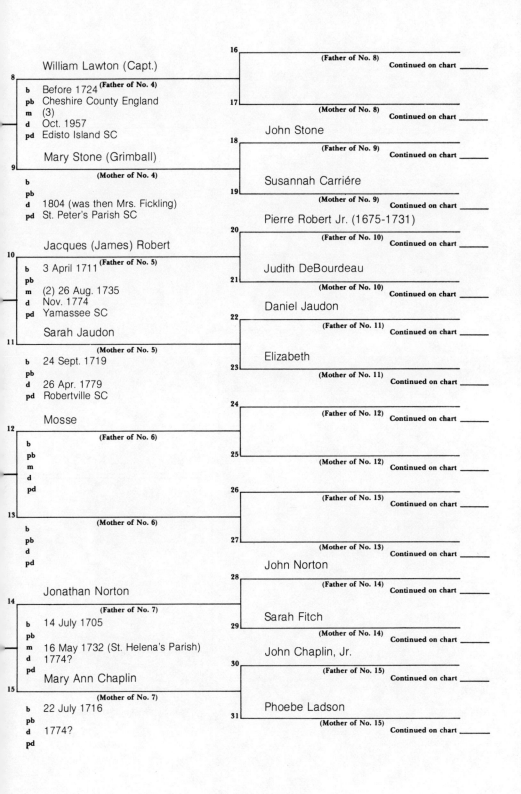

**William Lawton (Capt.)**

8

**(Father of No. 4)**
- b    Before 1724
- pb   Cheshire County England
- m    (3)
- d    Oct. 1957
- pd   Edisto Island SC

**Mary Stone (Grimball)**

9

**(Mother of No. 4)**
- b
- pb
- d    1804 (was then Mrs. Fickling)
- pd   St. Peter's Parish SC

**Jacques (James) Robert**

10

**(Father of No. 5)**
- b    3 April 1711
- pb
- m    (2) 26 Aug. 1735
- d    Nov. 1774
- pd   Yamassee SC

**Sarah Jaudon**

11

**(Mother of No. 5)**
- b    24 Sept. 1719
- pb
- d    26 Apr. 1779
- pd   Robertville SC

**Mosse**

12

**(Father of No. 6)**
- b
- pb
- m
- d
- pd

13

**(Mother of No. 6)**
- b
- pb
- d
- pd

**Jonathan Norton**

14

**(Father of No. 7)**
- b    14 July 1705
- pb
- m    16 May 1732 (St. Helena's Parish)
- d    1774?
- pd

**Mary Ann Chaplin**

15

**(Mother of No. 7)**
- b    22 July 1716
- pb
- d    1774?
- pd

16   **(Father of No. 8)**   Continued on chart _____

17   **(Mother of No. 8)**   Continued on chart _____

**John Stone**

18   **(Father of No. 9)**   Continued on chart _____

**Susannah Carriére**

19   **(Mother of No. 9)**   Continued on chart _____

**Pierre Robert Jr. (1675-1731)**

20   **(Father of No. 10)**   Continued on chart _____

**Judith DeBourdeau**

21   **(Mother of No. 10)**   Continued on chart _____

**Daniel Jaudon**

22   **(Father of No. 11)**   Continued on chart _____

**Elizabeth**

23   **(Mother of No. 11)**   Continued on chart _____

24   **(Father of No. 12)**   Continued on chart _____

25   **(Mother of No. 12)**   Continued on chart _____

26   **(Father of No. 13)**   Continued on chart _____

27   **(Mother of No. 13)**   Continued on chart _____

**John Norton**

28   **(Father of No. 14)**   Continued on chart _____

**Sarah Fitch**

29   **(Mother of No. 14)**   Continued on chart _____

**John Chaplin, Jr.**

30   **(Father of No. 15)**   Continued on chart _____

**Phoebe Ladson**

31   **(Mother of No. 15)**   Continued on chart _____

# ANCESTOR CHART NO. __H__

Person No. 1 on this chart is identical to person

No.__22__ on chart No.__A__

| | |
|---|---|
| b | Date of birth |
| pb | Place of birth |
| m | Date of marriage |
| d | Date of death |
| pd | Place of death |

4 **William Baynard**
(Father of No. 2)
b 1732
pb Edisto Island SC
m 1 Feb 1753
d 5 Jan. 1773
pd St. Helena's Parish
Beaufort SC

2 **Thomas Baynard**
(Father of No. 1)
b 1763
pb Edisto Island SC
m 6 July 1784
d 5 July 1805
pd

5 **Elizabeth Ann Grimball**
(Mother of No. 2)
b
pb Edisto Island 1735?
d 1773
pd

1 **Archibald Calder Baynard**
b 1798, Edisto Island SC
pb Edisto Island
m Nov. 1821
d 1865
pd Beaufort SC

6 **Archibald John Calder**
(Father of No. 3)
b
pb
m
d before 12 Dec. 1766
pd

3 **Sarah (Sally) Calder**
(Mother of No. 1)
b after 1760, and before 1766
pb
d
pd

7 **Sarah Bailey Eberson**
(Mother of No. 3)
b
pb
d
pd

(widow of Benjamin Splatt)

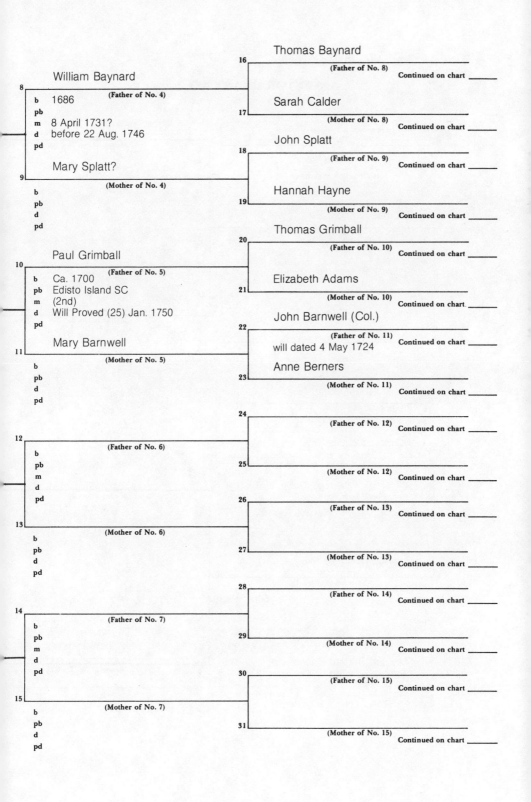

**8**

William Baynard

(Father of No. 4)

b   1686
pb
m   8 April 1731?
d   before 22 Aug. 1746
pd

**9**

Mary Splatt?

(Mother of No. 4)

b
pb
d
pd

**10**

Paul Grimball

(Father of No. 5)

b   Ca. 1700
pb  Edisto Island SC
m   (2nd)
d   Will Proved (25) Jan. 1750
pd

**11**

Mary Barnwell

(Mother of No. 5)

b
pb
d
pd

**12**

(Father of No. 6)

b
pb
m
d
pd

**13**

(Mother of No. 6)

b
pb
d
pd

**14**

(Father of No. 7)

b
pb
m
d
pd

**15**

(Mother of No. 7)

b
pb
d
pd

**16** Thomas Baynard

(Father of No. 8)          Continued on chart _____

**17** Sarah Calder

(Mother of No. 8)          Continued on chart _____

**18** John Splatt

(Father of No. 9)          Continued on chart _____

**19** Hannah Hayne

(Mother of No. 9)          Continued on chart _____

**20** Thomas Grimball

(Father of No. 10)         Continued on chart _____

**21** Elizabeth Adams

(Mother of No. 10)         Continued on chart. _____

**22** John Barnwell (Col.)

(Father of No. 11)         Continued on chart _____
will dated 4 May 1724

**23** Anne Berners

(Mother of No. 11)         Continued on chart _____

**24**

(Father of No. 12)         Continued on chart _____

**25**

(Mother of No. 12)         Continued on chart _____

**26**

(Father of No. 13)         Continued on chart _____

**27**

(Mother of No. 13)         Continued on chart _____

**28**

(Father of No. 14)         Continued on chart _____

**29**

(Mother of No. 14)         Continued on chart _____

**30**

(Father of No. 15)         Continued on chart _____

**31**

(Mother of No. 15)         Continued on chart _____

# ANCESTOR CHART NO. ___J___

Person No. 1 on this chart is identical to person

No. __24__ on chart No. __A__

| | |
|---|---|
| b | Date of birth |
| pb | Place of birth |
| m | Date of marriage |
| d | Date of death |
| pd | Place of death |

**4** Jacob Notthingham I

(Father of No. 2)
b
pb
m
d
pd

**2** Thomas Nottingham

(Father of No. 1)
b  Ca. 1730
pb
m
d  10 July 1797 (will proved)
pd

**5** Mary

(Mother of No. 2)
b
pb
d
pd

**1** Jacob Notthingham II*

b  26 Jan. 1794
pb  Northampton County VA
m
d  will proved 26 Jan. 1809
pd

**6**
(Father of No. 3)
b
pb
m
d
pd

**3** Scarburgh

(Mother of No. 1)
b  after 1797
pb
d
pd

*Married Bridget Brickhouse
on 20 Jan. 1794

**7**
(Mother of No. 3)
b
pb
d
pd

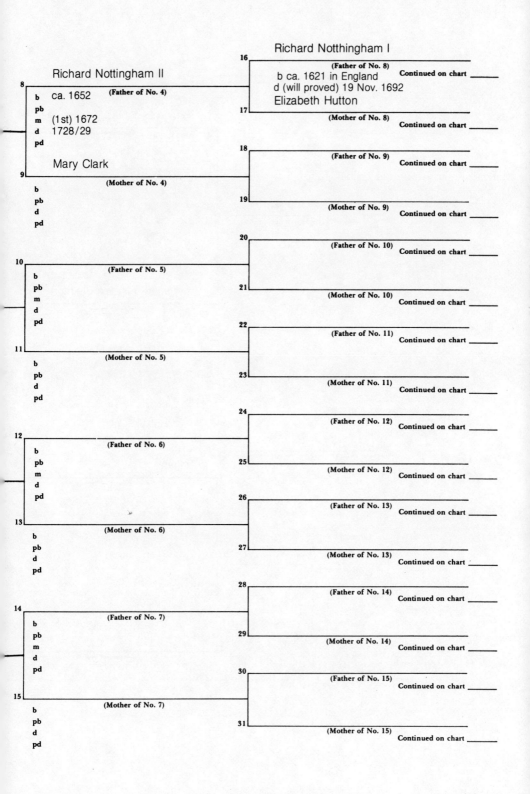

**Richard Nottingham II** (Father of No. 4)

8
- b ca. 1652
- pb
- m (1st) 1672
- d 1728/29
- pd

**Mary Clark** (Mother of No. 4)

9
- b
- pb
- d
- pd

**Richard Notthingham I** (Father of No. 8)

16
- b ca. 1621 in England
- d (will proved) 19 Nov. 1692

Continued on chart _____

**Elizabeth Hutton** (Mother of No. 8)

17

Continued on chart _____

18 (Father of No. 9)

Continued on chart _____

19 (Mother of No. 9)

Continued on chart _____

10 (Father of No. 5)
- b
- pb
- m
- d
- pd

11 (Mother of No. 5)
- b
- pb
- d
- pd

20 (Father of No. 10)

Continued on chart _____

21 (Mother of No. 10)

Continued on chart _____

22 (Father of No. 11)

Continued on chart _____

23 (Mother of No. 11)

Continued on chart _____

12 (Father of No. 6)
- b
- pb
- m
- d
- pd

13 (Mother of No. 6)
- b
- pb
- d
- pd

24 (Father of No. 12)

Continued on chart _____

25 (Mother of No. 12)

Continued on chart _____

26 (Father of No. 13)

Continued on chart _____

27 (Mother of No. 13)

Continued on chart _____

14 (Father of No. 7)
- b
- pb
- m
- d
- pd

15 (Mother of No. 7)
- b
- pb
- d
- pd

28 (Father of No. 14)

Continued on chart _____

29 (Mother of No. 14)

Continued on chart _____

30 (Father of No. 15)

Continued on chart _____

31 (Mother of No. 15)

Continued on chart _____

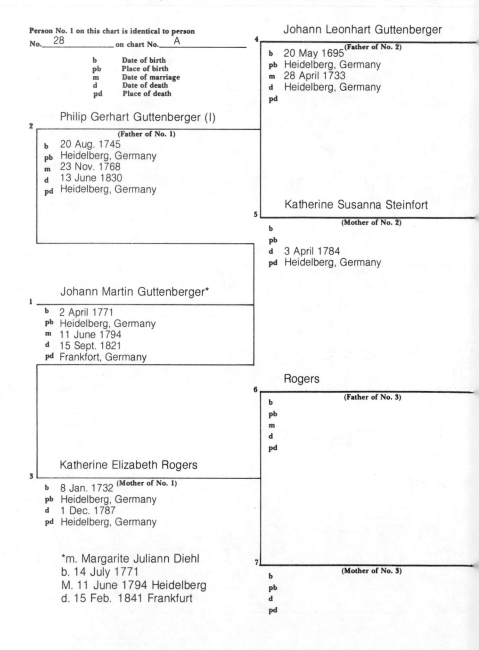

Person No. 1 on this chart is identical to person
No.___28___ on chart No.___A___

| | |
|---|---|
| b | Date of birth |
| pb | Place of birth |
| m | Date of marriage |
| d | Date of death |
| pd | Place of death |

4
### Johann Leonhart Guttenberger
(Father of No. 2)
b  20 May 1695
pb  Heidelberg, Germany
m  28 April 1733
d  Heidelberg, Germany
pd

2
### Philip Gerhart Guttenberger (I)
(Father of No. 1)
b  20 Aug. 1745
pb  Heidelberg, Germany
m  23 Nov. 1768
d  13 June 1830
pd  Heidelberg, Germany

5
### Katherine Susanna Steinfort
(Mother of No. 2)
b
pb
d  3 April 1784
pd  Heidelberg, Germany

1
### Johann Martin Guttenberger*
b  2 April 1771
pb  Heidelberg, Germany
m  11 June 1794
d  15 Sept. 1821
pd  Frankfort, Germany

6
### Rogers
(Father of No. 3)
b
pb
m
d
pd

3
### Katherine Elizabeth Rogers
(Mother of No. 1)
b  8 Jan. 1732
pb  Heidelberg, Germany
d  1 Dec. 1787
pd  Heidelberg, Germany

*m. Margarite Juliann Diehl
b. 14 July 1771
M. 11 June 1794 Heidelberg
d. 15 Feb. 1841 Frankfurt

7
(Mother of No. 3)
b
pb
d
pd

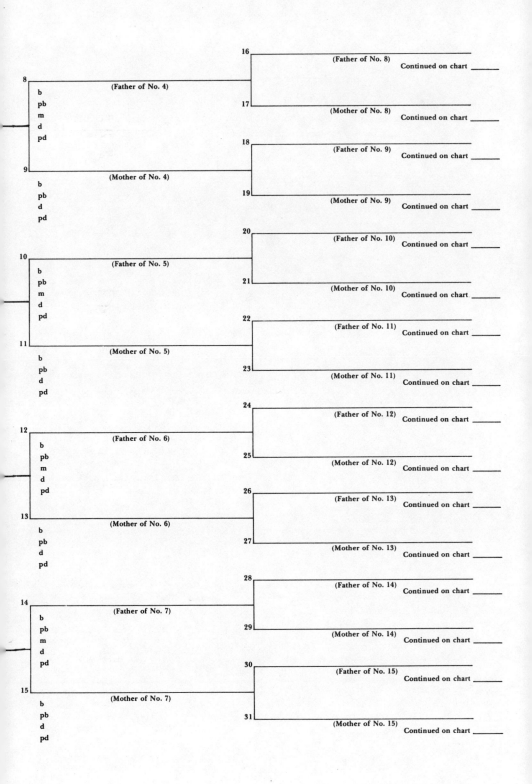

8
b
pb
m
d
pd
(Father of No. 4)

9
b
pb
d
pd
(Mother of No. 4)

10
b
pb
m
d
pd
(Father of No. 5)

11
b
pb
d
pd
(Mother of No. 5)

12
b
pb
m
d
pd
(Father of No. 6)

13
b
pb
d
pd
(Mother of No. 6)

14
b
pb
m
d
pd
(Father of No. 7)

15
b
pb
d
pd
(Mother of No. 7)

16
(Father of No. 8)
Continued on chart _____

17
(Mother of No. 8)
Continued on chart _____

18
(Father of No. 9)
Continued on chart _____

19
(Mother of No. 9)
Continued on chart _____

20
(Father of No. 10)
Continued on chart _____

21
(Mother of No. 10)
Continued on chart _____

22
(Father of No. 11)
Continued on chart _____

23
(Mother of No. 11)
Continued on chart _____

24
(Father of No. 12)
Continued on chart _____

25
(Mother of No. 12)
Continued on chart _____

26
(Father of No. 13)
Continued on chart _____

27
(Mother of No. 13)
Continued on chart _____

28
(Father of No. 14)
Continued on chart _____

29
(Mother of No. 14)
Continued on chart _____

30
(Father of No. 15)
Continued on chart _____

31
(Mother of No. 15)
Continued on chart _____

# GLOSSARY

## 1. Barnwell

John Barnwell (1671-1724) Head of Household

*Barnwell/Berners/Grimball* (England, SC) John Barnwell (1671-1724), m. Anne Berners. Children: Margaret (m. John Whitmarsh), Nathaniel (m. Mary Gibbs), Anne (m. Thomas Stanyarn), Mary (m. Paul Grimball [II]), John (m. Martha Chaplin), possibly two other children. See Barnwell and Grimball Lines and Ancestor Charts A, B, G, H, and H-5. CP/GHS, MD/SCL, M/OFC, SCDA, WL/SC.

## 2. Baynard

Thomas Baynard (1763-1805) Head of Household

*Baynard/Calder/Grimball* (SC) Thomas Baynard (1763-May 7, 1805), son of William and Elizabeth Ann Grimball Baynard; m. Sarah (Sally) Calder, d. of John Calder. Children of Thomas and Elizabeth Baynard: John, Thomas, Sarah Calder (m. Henry Bailey), Ephriam Mikell, Archibald Calder (m. Martha Sarah Chaplin), and William Edings (m. Catherine Adelaide Scott). See Baynard and Grimball Lines and Ancestor Charts A, B, H, and H-5. CP/GHS, MD/SCL, M/OFC, RCO/SC, SCDA, SCHS, WL/SC.

Archibald Calder Baynard (1798-1865) Head of Household
Baynard/Chaplin/Willingham/Lawton (SC, GA) Archibald Calder Baynard (1798-
1865), m. Nov. 1, 1821, Martha Sarah Chaplin, d. of Benjamin Chaplin.
Their children: Archibald Calder (Jr.) (m. Julia Howard), Thomas Stapleton
(m. Sara Caroline DeTreville Ellis), Sara (m. Dr. James Stoney Lawton), Ju-
lianna Sophia (m. 1st Rev. Wilson Edward Hall, m. 2nd Stephen Gratton
Ellis), and the three youngest daughters of Martha Sarah and Archibald
Calder Baynard married three Willingham brothers, sons of Phoebe Sarah
Lawton and Thomas Henry Willingham [II] as follows: Cecelia Matilda (m.
Thomas Henry Willingham [III]), Elizabeth Martha (m. Benjamin Lawton
Willingham), and Florence Margaret (m. Winborn Joseph Willingham). See
Baynard and Willingham Lines and Ancestor Charts, Lawton Lines #1 and
#2, and Ancestor Charts A, B, F, H, H-5. A/MU, GHR/WML, CO/BCG,
MD/SCL, M/OFC, PCR/BCG, SCDA, WL/SC, WR.

### 3. Furman

Richard Furman (1755-1825) Head of Household
Furman/Haynsworth/Burr/Brodhead (England, NY, SC) Richard Furman (Oct. 1,
1755-Aug. 15, 1825), son of Wood and Rachel Brodhead Furman. The two
wives of Richard Furman: m. 1st Elizabeth Haynsworth, children: Rachel,
Wood, and Richard (d. early); m. 2nd Dorothea Marie Burn, children: Rich-
ard [II], Samuel (1792-1877) (m. Eliza A. Scrimzeour), John Gano (d. early),
Josiah B., Charles Manning, Dorothea Marie, Henry Hart, Sarah Susanna,
John Gano [II], Thomas Fuller, James Clement, Anne Eliza, William D. See
Furman Line and Lawton Lines #1 and #2, and Ancestor Charts A, D, D-
1. BHC/FUL, FFSC, GHR/WML, MD/SCL, M/OFC, SCDA, SCHS.

Samuel Furman (1792-1877) Head of Household
Furman/Scrimzeour/ Lawton (SC, GA, Scotland), Samuel Furman (March 27,
1792-1877), son of Richard and Dorothea Marie Burn Furman, m. Eliza A.
Scrimzeour (May 5, 1814), children: Mary Scrimzeour, Richard [III], Samuel
[II], Eliza Scrimzeour, Julia, John, Dorothea (m. William Seabrook Lawton
[1714/15-1858]), William. See Furman Line and Lawton Lines #1 and #2,
and Ancestor Charts A, D, and D-1. BHC/FUL, GHR/WML, GHS, M/
OFC, SCDA, SCHS.

### 4. Guttenberger

Phillip Gerhart Guttenberger (1799-1874) Head of Household
Guttenberger/Muse/Diehl (Germany, France, GA) Phillip Guttenberger (Nov. 1,
1799-June 26, 1874), son of Johann Martin and Marguerite Julianna Diehl

Guttenberger. Phillip Guttenberger m. Emily Antoinette Muse, May 1834. Her father: George Muse. Children of Emily Muse and Phillip Gutttenberger: Ferdinand Alexander (m. Sarah Nottingham), Francesca (m. Erastus Hanger Link), Louisa (Loulie) (m. Thomas Hunt), Charles W. (m. 1st Laura Daniel, m. 2nd Emma Peacock), Julia Helene (Jule) (m. Clark Davis), Emily Jane (Emma) (m. John Jacob Nottingham). See Guttenberger and Nottingham Lines, and Ancestor Charts A, J, and N. GDAH, GHR/WML, HF/ WC, CO/BCG, PCR/BCG.

### 5. Harrell

Glover Futch Harrell (1909-1983) Head of Household
Harrell/Lawton/Coffee/Nottingham (GA) Glover Harrell (Aug. 1, 1909-Oct. 1, 1983), son of James Warren and Ruby Coffee Harrell, m. Carolyn Willingham Lawton (April 10, 1911- ) on June 17, 1933, d. of Furman Dargan and Mary Elliott (May) Nottingham Lawton. Children of Carolyn Lawton and Glover Harrell: Mary Elliott (m. Charles Edward Reeves), and Carolyn Coffee (Lyn) (m. James Vincent Foley). See Harrell and Lawton Lines #1 and #2, and Ancestor Charts AA through N. A/MU, GDAH, GHR/WML, HF/WC, CO/BCG, M/OFC, PCR/BCG, SC/MGHC.

### 6. Lawton

William Lawton (1724?-1757) Head of Household
Lawton/Clark/Winborn/Stone (England, SC) The three wives of William Lawton (b. before 1724-d. Oct. 9, 1757): m. 1st Mary Clark, children: Josiah, William [II], Jeremiah, Sarah (m. John Seabrook); William Lawton m. 2nd d. of Thomas Winborn, children: Winborn, Mary; William Lawton m. 3rd Mary Stone (the widow Grimball), child: Joseph (b. Oct. 18, 1753-d. March 5, 1815). Joseph's mother, Mary Stone Grimball Lawton (b. c. 1720-d. 1803), m. Samuel Fickling after William Lawton's death. See Lawton Lines #1 and #2, and Ancestor Charts A, B, and G. SCL, CPCR, MD/SCL, M/OFC, SCDA, SCHS.

Joseph Lawton (1753-1815) Head of Household
Lawton/Robert/Jaudon (SC) Joseph Lawton (Oct. 18, 1733-March 5, 1815) m. Sarah Robert (1755-1839), d. of Jacques (James) and Sarah Jaudon Robert. Sons of Joseph and Sarah Robert Lawton: William Henry (1775-1827) (m. Catherine Maner); Joseph James (1777-1859) (m. Phoebe Mosse); Benjamin Themistocles Dion (1782-1846) (m. Jane Mosse); Alexander James (1790-1876) (m. Martha Mosse); Winborn Asa (1793-1878) (m. 1st Mary Cater Rhodes, m. 2nd Lucindra Landrum). Daughters of Joseph and Sarah Robert Lawton:

Thirza (1787-1811) (m. Thomas Polhill); Charlotte Anne (1785-1852) (m. cousin James Jehu Robert). The three Mosse sisters (Phoebe, Jane, and Martha) m. the three Lawton brothers (Joseph James, Benjamin T. D., and Alexander James). See George Mosse Family Group Record, Lawton Lines #1 and #2, and Ancestor Charts A, B, G, H. M/OFC, FFSC, HSSC, WR, SHC/ UNC, SCDA, SCHS, CPCR, MD/SCL.

Benjamin Themistocles Dion Lawton (1782-1846) Head of Household

*Lawton/Mosse/Robert/Norton* (SC, GA) Benjamin Themistocles Dion Lawton (Dec. 22, 1782-Apr. 18, 1846), fourth child and third son of Joseph and Sarah Robert Lawton; m. Jane Mosse (Dec. 17, 1783-May 22, 1857), d. of Dr. George and Dorothy Phoebe Norton Mosse. Children of Benjamin and Jane Mosse Lawton: Robert Themistocles Dion (m. Harriet Charlotte Singleton), Alexander Benjamin (m. 1st Elizabeth Brisbane, m. 2nd Mary Cater Rhodes), William Seabrook (m. Dorothea Furman), Winborn Joseph (m. 1st Harriet Sarah Jordan, m. 2nd Sarah Lewis), James Stoney (m. Sarah C. Baynard), Thirza, Anna, Phoebe Sarah (m. Thomas Henry Willingham [II]), Martha (m. Benjamin James Jaudon), Charlotte Esther (m. Edward H. Peeples), Mary Elizabeth (m. Theodore D. Mathews). See Lawton Lines #1 and #2, and Robert and Mosse Lines; also see Ancestor Charts A, B, C, and G. M/OFC, FFSC, HSSC, WR, SHC/UNC, SCDA, SCHS, CPCR.

Alexander James Lawton (1790-1876) Head of Household

*Lawton/Mosse/Robert/Norton* (SC, GA) Alexander James Lawton (Nov. 21, 1790-Apr. 8, 1876), sixth child and fourth son of Joseph and Sarah Robert Lawton; m. Martha Mosse (Sept. 5, 1788-July 1836), d. of Dr. George and Phoebe Norton Mosse. Children of Alexander James and Martha Mosse Lawton: Adeline E. (m. Joseph T. Robert), Catherine B., George Mosse (m. Mary E. Lewis), Dr. William Seabrook (m. Elizabeth Jones), [General] Alexander Robert (m. Sarah Gilbert Alexander), Amanda (m. Jonathan Miller), Edward Payson (m. Evelina Loyer Davant). See Robert, Mosse, and Lawton Lines #1 and #2, and Ancestor Charts, A, B, C, and G. M/OFC, FFSC, HSSC, WR, SHC/UNC, SCDA, SCHS, CPCR.

William Seabrook Lawton (1814/15-1858) Head of Household

*Lawton/Furman/Mosse/Scrimzeour* (SC, GA) William Seabrook Lawton (1814/15-Sept. 14, 1858) m. Dorothea Furman (April 24, 1820-Dec. 2, 1886). Her parents, Samuel Furman and Eliza Scrimzeour. William and Dorothea Furman Lawton's children: John Marshall, Richard Furman (July 22, 1841-Jan. 13, 1892) (m. 1st Elizabeth McLeod, m. 2nd Caroline [Carrie] Willingham), Agnes (m. John F. Cargile), Benjamin A., Samuel, James Stoney (m. Mrs. Bessie Smith), Robert, Wilhemina, Samuel (2nd—his older brother, Samuel 1st, had died before Samuel 2nd was born). Five of the nine children of Wil-

liam S. and Dorothea Furman Lawton died young. See Furman Line and Lawton Lines #1 and #2, and Ancestor Charts A, B, C, D. DAC, M/OFC,
SCDA, SCHM, GHS, MD/SCL, BHC/FUL, WR.

Richard Furman Lawton (1841-1892) Head of Household
*Lawton/Willingham/Furman/Baynard* (SC, GA) Richard Furman Lawton (July 22,
1841-Jan. 13, 1892); his first wife Elizabeth McLeod; his second wife Caroline
(Carrie) Willingham (May 29, 1853-Dec. 2, 1921). Her parents: Benjamin
Lawton Willingham and Elizabeth Martha Baynard Willingham. Children of
Carrie Willingham and Richard Furman Lawton: Elizabeth (m. 1st George
C. Johnson, m. 2nd William Gorman), Robert, Furman Dargan Lawton
(Oct. 31, 1877-Dec. 23, 1955) (m. May Nottingham), Corinne (m. Robert
Green Jordan), Calder Baynard (m. Mary Nunnally), Richard Furman [II]
(m. Mattie Chappell), Osgood Pierce (m. Gladys Taylor), Walter Terrell (m.
Lucille Ray), Caroline (m. 1st Albert T. Vaughn, m. 2nd Dr. McLaughlin,
m. 3rd Johnson). See Lawton Lines #1 and #2 and Ancestor Charts A, B,
D, F, G, H. M/OFC, WR, GHR/WML, PCR/BC, BHC/FUL A/MU, SC/
MGHC, PCR/BC, VMHB/VHS, WR.

Furman Dargan Lawton (1877-1955) Head of Household
*Lawton/Willingham/Nottingham/Guttenberger* (GA) Furman Dargan Lawton (Oct.
31, 1877-Dec. 23, 1955), his parents Carrie Willingham and Richard Furman
Lawton, his wife Mary Elliott (May) Nottingham (Dec. 3, 1879-Apr. 29,
1966). May Nottingham's parents: Emily Jane (Emma) Guttenberger and
John Jacob Nottingham. Children of May Nottingham and Furman Dargan
Lawton: Furman and Dorothea (both died young), Emily Elizabeth, Carolyn
Willingham (m. Glover Futch Harrell), Elliott Nottingham (m. 1st Margaret
Bond, children: Emily, Russell; m. 2nd Sarah Sue Holbrook). Children of
Carolyn L. and Glover F. Harrell: Mary Elliott and Carolyn (Lyn) Coffee. See
Lawton Lines #1 and #2, and Ancestor Charts A, B, D, F, G, J, N. M/OFC,
GDAH, GHS, GHR/WML, HF/WC, MD/SCL, SCDA, CB/NCV, CC/
NCV, DB/NCV, WB/NCV, CO/BCG.

### 7. Mosse

George Mosse (1742-1808) Head of Household
*Mosse/Norton/Chaplin* (Ireland, SC, GA) Dr. George Mosse (1742-Feb. 17, 1808),
educated as a physician in Ireland, m. (2nd) Dorothy Phoebe Norton, d. of
Jonathan and Mary Ann Chaplin Norton. Children of George and Dorothy
Phoebe Norton Mosse: Esther Marie (Hettie) (m. 1st Pat McKenzie; m. 2nd
Prof. Terrence Hughes), Elizabeth (m. James Stoney), Phoebe (Sibby) (m. Jo-
seph James Lawton), Jane (m. Benjamin Themistocles Dion Lawton), Mary

Anne (m. Rev. Adam Fowler Brisbane), Martha (m. Alexander James Law-
ton), Sarah (m. Robert Godfrey Norton). See Joseph Lawton Family Group
Record and Mosse Line, Lawton Lines #1 and #2, and Ancestor Charts A,
B, and C. CPCR, MD/SCL, M/OFC, SCDA, SCHM, SCHS, WL/SC.


## 8. Nottingham

Smith B[rickhouse] Nottingham (1799-1835) Head of Household
*Nottingham/Elliott/Brickhouse/Nolen* (VA) Smith B. Nottingham (Sept. 20, 1799-
Divorced 1835), son of Jacob and Bridget Brickhouse Nottingham; m. Mary
(Polly) Howe Elliott Apr. 4, 1826, d. of John and Polly Nolen Elliott. Children
of Mary (Polly) and Smith Nottingham: Leonard, Mary, Frances (all died as
infants), John Jacob (m. Emily Jane [Emma] Guttenberger, May 17, 1852), and
Martha Ann (unmarried). See Nottingham and Guttenberger Lines and
Ancestor Charts A and J. CB/NCV, CC/NCV, DB/NCV, GDAH, GHR/
WML, HF/WC, VHS, VMHB, WB/NCV. VMHB, WB/NCV.

John Jacob Nottingham (1830/31-1887) Head of Household
*Nottingham/Guttenberger/Elliott/Muse* (VA, GA) John Jacob Nottingham (1830/31-
Feb. 8, 1887), son of Smith B. and Mary (Polly) Elliott Nottingham; m. Emily
Jane (Emma) Guttenberger on Dec. 6, 1870, d. of Phillip G. and Emily An-
toinette Muse Guttenberger. Children of Emily Jane (Emma) and John Jacob
Nottingham: Julia Lee (m. Thomas F. Cook, Gen. Stonewall Jackson) ( no
children), Mary Elliott (May) (m. Furman Dargan Lawton), John Jacob [II].
See Lawton Lines #1 and #2, Nottingham and Guttenberger Lines, and
Ancestor Charts A, J, and N. DB/NCV, GHR, WML, HL/WC, CB/NCV
CC/NCV, CO/BCG, DB/NCV, M/OFC, PCR/BCG, SC/MCHC, VHS,
VMHB, WB/NCV.


## 9. Robert

Pierre Robert [II] (1675-1731) Head of Household
*Robert/Broye/LeGrande/deBourdeau* (Switzerland, SC) Pierre Robert [II] (1675-March
9, 1731). His parents: Pierre [I] and Jean Broye Robert (1655-1715). The two
wives of Pierre Robert [II]: m. 1st Anne Marie Louise LeGrande, child: Pierre
[III]; m. 2nd Judith deBourdeau. Children of Pierre [II] and Judith:
Jacques (m. Sarah Jaudon), Elizabeth (m. Elias Jaudon, b. of Sarah), Made-
laine (m. 1st Archibald Hamilton, m. 2nd William Gough). See Robert
Line, Lawton Lines #1 and #2, and Ancestor Charts A, B, G. M/OFC,
HSSC, MD/SCL, SCDA.

Jacques (James) Robert (1711-1774) Head of Household
*Robert/Jaudon/deBourdeaux/Lawton* (SC) Jacques (James) Robert (Apr. 3, 1711-Nov.
1774), son of Pierre [II] and Judith deBourdeaux Robert. Jacques m. Sarah Jaudon (Sept. 24, 1719- Apr. 26, 1779), d. of Elizabeth Videaul and Daniel Jaudon. Sarah Jaudon and Jacques Robert's children: James, Capt. Peter (m. Anne Grimball), John (m. Elizabeth Dixon), Elias (m. Mary Rue), Sarah (m. Joseph Lawton), and Judith (m. 1st John Audebert; 2nd John Cheney; 3rd John Callahan). See Robert Line, Lawton Lines #1 and #2, and Ancestor Charts A, B, C, and G. M/OFC, FFSC, HSSC, WR, SCDA, SCHS, CPCR.

## 10. Willingham

Thomas Henry Willingham [II] (1799-1872) Head of Household *Willingham/Lawton/Chovin/Mosse/Baynard* (SC, GA) Thomas Henry Willingham [II] (Dec. 23, 1799-July 7, 1872), only child of Sarah Chovin and Thomas Henry Willingham [I]. Thomas [II] m. Phoebe Sarah Lawton (July 7, 1808-Feb. 4, 1861), d. of Jane Mosse and Benjamin Themistocles Dion Lawton. Children of Phoebe Sarah and Thomas Willingham [II]: Thomas Henry [III] (m. Cecelia Matilda Baynard), Benjamin Lawton (m. Elizabeth Martha Baynard), Anna Cornelia (m. Broadus Estes), Edward George (m. 1st Anna Cornelia Kirk; m. 2nd Mary Peeples), William Alexander (m. Emma Dews), John Calhoun (m. 1st Sarah Lawton; m. 2nd Gillette Bibb), Robert Josiah (d. at 18), Winborn Joseph (m. Florence Margaret Baynard), Sarah (m. 1st S. C. Bryan; m. 2nd George Rhodes), Mary Phoebe (m. Thomas O. Lawton), and Belle (m. W. J. Wood). See Willingham, Lawton, Mosse, and Baynard Linear Charts, and Ancestor Charts A, B, C, F, G, H. GDAH, GHR, WML, MD/SCL, M/OFC, SCDA, SC/MGHA, WR.

Benjamin Lawton Willingham (1829-1898) Head of Household
*Willingham/Baynard/Lawton/Chaplin* (SC, GA) Benjamin Lawton Willingham (Apr. 21, 1829-Feb. 17, 1898), son of Phoebe Sarah Lawton and Thomas Henry Willingham [II]; m. Elizabeth Martha Baynard (Sept. 15, 1830-July 17, 1887), d. of Martha Sarah Chaplin and Archibald Calder Baynard. The eighteen children of Elizabeth Martha Baynard and Benjamin Lawton Willingham: Phoebe Sarah (m. Charles E. Malone), Thomas Henry [IV] (m. Frances [Fannie] Harper Wright), Calder Baynard (m. Lila Ross), Caroline (Carrie) (m. Richard Furman Lawton), Robert Josiah (m. Sarah Cornelle Bacon), Martha Harriet (unmarried), Osgood Pierce (m. Ida Thorpe), Cecilia (Telie) (m. William S. Payne), Elizabeth (Lizzie) (m. Walter T. Johnston), Edward John (m. Eula Felton), Broadus Estes (m. Annie Lewis Rushin), Jose-

phine Mary (d. young), George Milton (d. at 7), Paul Dargan (m. Sarah [Sally] Cleveland), Ernest Pringle (m. Pauline Lewis), Lou Belle (d. young), Benjamin Brooks (m. Wilson Shelton), Alice Cobb (d. young). See Willingham and Baynard Lines, and Lawton Lines #1 and #2. Also see Ancestor Charts A, B, C, F, G, H. A/MU, GDAH, GHR/WML, GHS, CO/BCG, MD/SCL, M/OFC, PCR/BCG, SCDA, SC/MGHC, SCHA, WL/SC, WR.

# BIBLIOGRAPHY

## Books

Akers, Samuel Luttrell. *The First Hundred Years of Wesleyan College*. Savannah GA: Beehive Press, 1976.

Allen, Frederick Lewis. *The Big Change: America Transforms Itself, 1900-1950*. New York: Harper & Row, 1952.

Andrist, Ralph K., ed. *The American Heritage History of the 20's & 30's*. New York: American Heritage Publishing Company, 1970.

Barnwell, Stephen B. *The Story of an American Family*. Milwaukee WI: Marquette Publishing Company, 1969.

Barrett, John G. *Sherman's March Through the Carolinas*. Chapel Hill: University of North Carolina Press, 1956.

Batts, H. Lewis. *History of the First Baptist Church of Christ of Macon, Georgia, 1826-1928*. N.p.

Beard, Charles A., and Mary R. Beard. *The Rise of American Civilization*. Volumes one and two. New York: Macmillan Co., 1961.

Beer, Thomas. *The Mauve Decade*. New York: Alfred A. Knopf, 1926.

British Council, eds. *British Life and Thought*. Freeport NY: Books for Libraries Press, 1941.

Brooks, Robert Preston. *The University of Georgia Under Sixteen Administrations, 1785-1955*. Athens GA: University of Georgia Press, 1956.

Bruce, Philip Alexander. *The Social Life of Virginia in the Seventeenth Century*. New York: Ungar Publishing Co.

Cady, Edwin H. *The American Poets (1800-1900)*. Glenview IL: Scott, Foresman and Company.

Candler, Alan D. and Clement A. Evans. *Cyclopedia of Georgia*. Atlanta GA: State Historical Association, 1906.

Carse, Robert. *Ports of Call, the Great Colonial Seaports*. New York: Charles Scribner's Sons, 1967.

Carter, Hodding. *Southern Legacy*. Baton Rouge: Louisiana State University Press, 1950.

Castel, Albert. *The Presidency of Andrew Johnson*. Lawrence KS: Regents Press of Kansas, 1979.

Catton, Bruce and William B. Catton. *The Bold and Magnificent Dream*. Garden City NY: Doubleday & Company, Inc., 1978.

Chalmers, S. Murray. *Names in South Carolina*. Columbia SC: University of South Carolina Press.

Channing, Steven A. *Crisis of Fear: Secession in South Carolina*. New York: W. W. Norton & Company, Inc., 1974.

*Christian Index. History of the Baptists in Georgia*. Atlanta: James P. Harrison and Co., 1881.

Churchill, Winston S. *The Age of Revolution*. New York: Dodd, Mead & Company, 1964.

Clark, Thomas D. and Albert D. Kirwan. *The South Since Appomattox*. New York: Oxford University Press, 1967.

Clemens, William Montgomery. *North and South Carolina Marriage from the Earliest Colonial Days*. New York: E. P. Dutton, 1927.

Coles, Robert. *Farewell to the South*. Boston: Little, Brown and Company, 1972.

_____. *Flannery O'Connor's South*. Baton Rouge: Louisiana State University Press, 1980.

Conway, Alan. *The Reconstruction of Georgia*. Minneapolis: University of Minnesota Press, 1966.

Cook, Harvey T. *A Biography of Richard Furman*. Greenville SC: *Baptist Courier* Job Rooms, 1918.

Copeland, Melvin Thomas. *The Cotton Manufacturing Industries of the United States*. New York: Augustus M. Kelley, Publishers, 1911. Reprint, 1966.

Côté, Richard N. *Local and Family History in South Carolina: A Bibliography*. Easley SC: Southern Historical Press, 1981.

Coulter, E. Merton. *Georgia, A Short History*. Chapel Hill NC: University of North Carolina Press, 1933.

Craven, Avery. *The Coming of the Civil War*. New York: Charles Scribner's Sons, 1942.

Craven, Wesley Frank. *The Southern Colonies in the Seventeenth Century, 1607-1689*. Baton Rouge: Louisiana State University Press, 1949.

_____. *The Colonies in Transition*. Evanston IL and London: Harper & Row, 1968.

Cumming, W. P. *The Southeast in Early Maps*. Princeton NJ: Princeton University Press, 1962.

Dabbs, James McBride. *Who Speaks for the South?* New York: Funk & Wagnalls Company, Inc., 1964.

Dalcho, Frederick. *Historical Account of the Protestant Episcopal Church in South Carolina*. N.p. Charleston, 1820.

Daniels, Jonathan. *The Time Between the Wars: From the Jazz Age and the Depression to Pearl Harbor*. Garden City NY: Doubleday & Company, Inc., 1966.

Daughters of the American Colonists. *Lineage Book, National Society of the Daughters of the American Colonists*. Compiled by Alice C. Hendricks. Volume seven. Washington: Judd and Detweiler, Inc., 1946.

Davidson, Chalmers Gaston. *The Last Foray, The South Carolina Planters of 1860: A Sociological Study*. Columbia SC: University of South Carolina Press, 1971.

Davis, Burke. *Sherman's March*. New York: Random House, 1980.

Dennett, John Richard, *The South as It Is: 1865-1866*. New York: The Viking Press, 1965.

*Directory of the City of Macon and Business Advertiser,* A. Macon GA: John C. Judson and Co., 1890-1891.

Dobb, William E. *The Cotton Kingdom*. New York: United States Publishers, 1919.

DuBose, Samuel and Frederick A. Porcher. *History of the Huguenots*. Columbia SC: R. L. Bryan Co., 1972.

Easterby, J. H. *The South Carolina Rice Plantation as Revealed in the Papers of Robert F. W. Allston*. Chicago: University of Chicago Press, 1945.

Eaton, Clement. *The Growth of Southern Civilization, 1790-1860*. New York: Harper & Row, 1961.

——————. *The Mind of the Old South*. Baton Rouge: Louisiana State University Press, 1967.

Edgar, Walter B., ed. *Biographical Directory of the South Carolina House of Representatives*. Volume One: *Session Lists, 1692-1973*. Columbia SC: University of South Carolina Press, 1973.

Ervin, Sara Sullivan. *South Carolinians in the Revolution*. Baltimore: Genealogical Publishing Company, 1965.

Ezell, John Samuel. *The South Since 1865*. Norman OK: University of Oklahoma Press, 1978.

Fancher, Betsy. *The Lost Legacy of Georgia's Golden Isles*. New York: Doubleday & Company, Inc., 1971.

Faulkner, Harold Underwood. *American Political & Social History*. Seventh edition. New York: Appleton Century Co., Inc., 1957.

Faunt, J. R. and E. B. Reynold, eds. *Biographical Directory of the Senate of the State of South Carolina, 1776-1964*. Columbia SC: South Carolina Department of Archives, 1964.

Fleming, Thomas. *1776: Year of Illusions*. New York: W. W. Norton & Company, Inc., 1975.

Furman, James D. *The Furman Legend*. Greenville SC: Keys Printing Co., 1878.

Gerster, Patrick and Nicholas Cords, eds. *Myth and Southern History*. New York: Rand McNally College Publishing Co., 1974.

Goff, Frederick R. *The Permanence of Johann Gutenberg*. Austin: University of Texas, 1970.

Green, E. B. *Provincial America, 1670-1740*. New York and London: Harper and Brothers, 1905.

Hammond, M. G. *The Cotton Industry: An Essay in American Economic History*. New York: The Macmillan Company, 1897.

Harden, William. *A History of Savannah and South Georgia*. Atlanta: Lewis Publishing Co., 1913.

Hasell, Annie Baynard Simons. *Baynard, An Ancient Family Bearing Arms*. Columbia SC: R. L. Bryan Co., 1972.

Haynsworth, Hugh Charles. *Haynsworth, Furman and Allied Families*. Sumter SC: Osteen Publishing Co., 1942.

Helmbold, F. Wilbur. *Tracing Your Ancestry*. Birmingham AL: Oxmoor House, Inc., 1976.

Heyman, C. David. *American Aristocracy, The Lives and Times of James Russell, Amy and Robert Lowell*. New York: Dodd, Mead, & Company, 1980.

Hirsch, Arthur Henry. *The Huguenots of Colonial South Carolina*. Durham NC: Duke University Press, 1928. Reprint, Archon Books, 1962.

*History of the Baptist Denomination in Georgia*. Atlanta: Jos. P. Harrison and Co., 1881.

Howe, George. *History of the Presbyterian Church in South Carolina*. Volume One. South Carolina: Columbia and Chapman Publishers, 1870.

Hudson, Charles. *The Southeastern Indians*. Knoxville: University of Tennessee Press, 1976.

Jenkins, Alan. *The Thirties*. New York: Stein and Day, Publishers, 1976.

Jensen, Merrill. *The Founding of a Nation: A History of the American Revolution, 1763-1776*. New York: Oxford University Press, 1968.

Johnson, Allen. *Dictionary of American Biography*. New York: Scribner's, 1827.

Johnson, Gerald W. *The Wasted Land*. Chapel Hill: University of North Carolina Press, 1938.

Johnston, Coy K. *Two Centuries of Lawtonville Baptists, 1775-1975*. Estill SC: Historical Committee of Lawtonville Baptist Church, 1974.

Jones, Charles C., Jr. *History of Georgia*. Syracuse NY: D. Mason and Company, 1890.

Jones, James Pickett. *Yankee Blitzkrieg: Wilson's Raid through Alabama and Georgia*. Athens: University of Georgia Press, 1976.

King, Joe M. *A History of South Carolina Baptists*. General Board of the South Carolina Baptist Convention, 1964.

King, Richard H. *A Southern Renaissance. The Cultural Awakening of the South, 1930-1955*. New York and Oxford: Oxford University Press, 1980.

Kirby, Jack Temple. *Darkness at the Dawning*. Philadelphia: J. P. Lippincott Co., 1972.

Lambdin, Augusta, ed. *History of Lamar County*. Barnesville GA: The Barnesville News-Gazette, 1932.

Lamont, D. S., ed. *War of the Rebellion. Official Records of the Union and Confederate Armies.* Series 1, part 1. Washington DC: Government Printing Office, 1895.

Lane, Mills B., ed. *William T. Sherman.* Savannah: The Beehive Press, 1974.

Lanier, Sidney. *Poems and Letters.* Introduction by Charles R. Anderson. Baltimore: The Johns Hopkins Press, 1969.

——————————. *Poems of Sidney Lanier.* Athens: University of Georgia Press, 1916.

Lawton, Alexania E. and Minnie Reeves Wilson. *Allendale on the Savannah.* Bomberg SC: Bomberg Herald Printers, 1970.

Lawton, Edward P. *A Saga of the South.* Fort Myers Beach FL: The Island Press, 1965.

Linton, Calvin D. *The Bicentennial Almanac.* Nashville TN: Thomas Nelson, Inc., 1976.

Lord, Walter. *The Good Years from 1900 to the First World War.* New York, Evanston, & London: Harper & Row, 1960.

Luckie, George C., ed. *Georgia—a Guide to its Towns and Countryside.* Atlanta: Tupper and Love, 1940.

McClothlin, W. M. *Baptist Beginnings in Education: A History of Furman University.* Nashville TN: Sunday School Board of the Southern Baptist Convention, 1926.

McCrady, Edward. *The History of South Carolina under the Proprietary Government, 1670-1719.* New York: Macmillan Company, 1897.

——————————. *The History of South Carolina Under the Royal Government, 1719-1776.* New York: Macmillan Company, 1901.

McDonald, Forrest. *E Pluribus Unum. The Formation of the American Republic, 1776-1790.* Boston: Houghton Mifflin Company, 1965.

McKay, John J., Nelle Edwards Smith, and Spencer B. King, Jr., eds. *Macon's Architectural and Historical Heritage.* Macon GA: The Middle Georgia Historical Society, Publishers, 1972.

*Macon Guide, a WPA Project.* Macon GA: J. W. Burke Co., 1939.

Mann, Golo. *The History of Germany Since 1789.* New York: Frederick A. Praeger, 1968.

Martin, Harold W. *Georgia: A Bicentennial History.* New York: W. W. Norton & Company, Inc., 1977.

Massey, Mary Elizabeth. *Refugee Life in the Confederacy.* Baton Rouge: Louisiana State University Press, 1964.

Meriwether, Robert L. *The Expansion of South Carolina.* Kingsport TN: Southern Publishers, Inc., 1940.

Miller, Annie Elizabeth. *Our Family Circle.* Macon GA: J. W. Burke Co., 1931. Reprint. Linden TN: Continental Book Co., 1975. Corrections and additions by Robert E. H. Peeples.

Mills, Robert. *Mills' Atlas of South Carolina: An Atlas of the Districts of South Carolina in 1825.* Reprint. Lexington SC: Sand Lapper Store, 1979.

Mitchell, Broadus. *The Rise of Cotton Mills in the South.* New York: DaCapo Press, 1968.

Montgomery, Sir Robert. *A Discourse Concerning the Designed Establishment of a New Colony to the South of Carolina in the Most Delightful Country of the Universe*. London: 1717. Reprint. Atlanta: Cherokee Publishing Co., 1964.

Montgomery, Sir Robert and John Barnwell. *The Most Delightful Golden Islands . . .* London: 1717. Reprint. Atlanta: Cherokee Publishing Company, 1969.

Montrose, Lynn. *The Reluctant Rebels: The Story of the Continental Congress, 1774-1789*. New York: Barnes & Noble, Inc., 1970.

Morris, Richard and James Woodress. *Voices from America's Past. Backwoods Democracy to World Power*. Volume Two. New York: E. P. Dutton & Co., Inc., 1961.

Morris, Willie. *North Toward Home*. New York: Houghton Mifflin Co., 1967.

Munsell, Frank and Thomas Patrick Hughes. *American Ancestry: Giving Name and Descent, in the Male Line, of Americans whose Ancestors Settled in the United States Previous to the Declaration of Independence, A.D. 1776*. Twelve volumes. Albany NY: Joel Munsell's Sons, 1887-1889.

Norton, Mary Beth. *Liberty's Daughters: The American Revolutionary Experience of American Women*. Boston: Little, Brown and Company, 1980.

Nottingham, Carolyn Walker. *History of Upson County, Georgia*. Vidalia GA: Genealogical Reprints, 1969.

Nottingham, Stratton. *Marriage License Bonds of Northampton County, Virginia*. Baltimore: Genealogical Publishing Co., 1974.

O'Brien, Michael. *The Idea of the American South, 1920-1941*. Baltimore: The Johns Hopkins University Press, 1979.

Parks, Edd Winfield. *Sidney Lanier: The Man, The Poet, The Critic*. Athens: University of Georgia Press, 1968.

Payne, Calder Willingham. *Descendants of Benjamin Lawton Willingham and Elizabeth Martha Baynard*. Macon GA: Published by the author, 1975.

Phillips, Ulrich B. *Life and Labor in the Old South*. Boston: Little, Brown & Company, 1929.

Pierce, Neal R. *The Deep South States of America*. New York W. W. Norton and Co., Inc.

Pole, J. R. *Paths to the American Past*. New York: Oxford University Press, 1979.

Pound, Jerome B. *Memoirs of Jerome B. Pound*. N.p. 1949.

Powell, Lawrence N. *New Masters*. New Haven: Yale University Press, 1980.

Readers Digest Association, ed. *Family Encyclopedia of American History*. Pleasantville NY: Reader's Digest, 1957.

Reynolds, E. B., and J. R. Faunt, eds. *Biographical Directory of the State of South Carolina, 1776-1964*. Columbia SC: Department of Archives, 1964.

Roark, James L. *Masters Without Slaves: Southern Planters in Civil War and Reconstruction*. New York: W. W. Norton and Co., 1977.

Romasco, Albert U. *The Poverty of Abundance: Hoover, the Nation and Depression*. New York: Oxford University Press, 1965.

Rose, Willie Lee. *Slavery and Freedom*. New York: Oxford University Press, 1982.

Rubin, Louis D[ecimus], ed. *The American South, Portrait of a Culture*. Baton Rouge: Louisiana State University Press, 1980.

Salley, Alexander S., ed. *Journal of the Grand Council of South Carolina*, August 25, 1671—June 24, 1680. Columbia SC: South Carolina Historical Commission, 1907.

——————. *Minutes of the Vestry of St. Helena's Parish, South Carolina, 1726-1812*. Columbia SC: N.p., 1919.

Salley, Alexander S. *Warrants for Lands in South Carolina, 1672-1711*. Columbia SC: University of South Carolina Press, 1910.

Sandburg, Carl. *Abraham Lincoln, War Years*. Volume six. New York: Charles Scribner's Sons, 1939.

——————. *Storm over the Land: A Profile of the Civil War*. New York: Harcourt, Brace & World, Inc., 1939.

Savage, Henry, Jr. *River of the Carolinas. The Santee*. New York: Rinehart & Company, 1956.

Sherwood, Adiel. *Gazetteer of Georgia: A Particular Description of the State*. N.p. Fourth edition, 1860.

Simkins, Francis Butler and Robert Hilliard Woody. *South Carolina During Reconstruction*. Gloucester MA: Peter Smith Co., 1966.

Sirmans, M. Eugene. *Colonial South Carolina: A Political History*. Chapel Hill: University of North Carolina Press, 1966.

Snell, John L. and Hans A. Schmitt. *The Democratic Movement in Germany*. Chapel Hill: University of North Carolina Press, 1976.

Snell, Tee Loftin. *The Wild Shores: America's Beginning*. Washington DC: National Geographic Society, 1974.

Somer, Robert. *The Southern States Since the War, 1870-1871*. University AL: The University of Alabama Press, 1965.

Stokes, Thomas L. *The Savannah*. New York: Rhinehart & Co., Inc., 1951.

Stoney, Samuel Gaillard. *Plantations of the Carolina Low Country*. Charleston: The Carolina Art Association, 1955.

Stowe, Eugenia. *Yesterday at Tift*. Doraville GA: Foote and Davis, 1969.

Sullivan, Mark. *Our Times: The United States, 1900-1925*. Volumes two and four. New York: Charles Scribner's Sons, 1936, 1932.

Taylor, Rosser H. *Ante-Bellum South Carolina: A Social and Cultural History*. Chapel Hill: University of North Carolina Press, 1942.

Taylor, William R. *Cavalier and Yankee: The Old South and American National Character*. New York: George Braziller, 1961.

Thomas, Gordon and Max Morganwitts. *The Day the Bubble Burst: A Social History of the Wall Street Crash of 1929*. Garden City NY: Doubleday & Company, Inc., 1979.

Thompson, Ernest Trice. *Presbyterians in the South*. Volume one. Richmond VA: John Knox Press, 1963.

Thorp, Willard. *A Southern Reader*. New York: Alfred A. Knopf, 1955.

Townsend, Leah. *South Carolina Baptists.* Florence SC: 1935. Reprint. Baltimore: Genealogical Publishing Co., Inc., 1974.

Tuchman, Barbara W. *The Guns of August.* New York: Macmillan Company, 1962.

——————. *The Proud Tower: A Portrait of the World Before the War, 1890-1914.* New York: Macmillan Company, 1966.

Tupper, H. A., ed. *History of the First Baptist Church of Charleston, 1683-1883.* Baltimore: R. H. Woodward & Co., 1889.

Tyler, Lyon and Lewis Gardner. *Encyclopedia of Virginia Biography.* Volume five. N.p., 1915.

Virkus, Frederick Adam. *The Abridged Compendium of American Genealogy: First Families of America. A Genealogical Encyclopedia of the United States.* Seven volumes. Chicago: F. A. Virkus, 1925-1942.

Weeden, Howard. *Songs of the Old South.* New York: Doubleday, Page and Company, 1901.

Wertenbaker, Thomas J. *The Shaping of Colonial Virginia.* New York: Russell & Russell, 1910.

Whitelaw, Ralph T. *Virginia's Eastern Shore: A History of Northampton and Accomack Counties.* Volume one. Richmond: Virginia Historical Society, 1951.

Wiley, Benn Irvin. *Confederate Women.* Westport CT: Greenwood Press, 1975.

Willingham, Elizabeth Walton. *Life of Robert Josiah Willingham.* Nashville TN: Sunday School Board of the Southern Baptist Convention, 1917.

Woodman, Harold D. *King Cotton and His Retainers.* Lexington: University of Kentucky Press, 1968.

Woodward, C. Vann, ed. *Mary Chesnut's Civil War.* New Haven: Yale University Press, 1981.

Wright, Louis B. *South Carolina: A History.* New York: W. W. Norton & Company, Inc., 1976.

Young, Ida, Julius Gholson, and Clara Nelle Hargrove. *History of Macon, Georgia.* Macon: Lyon, Marshall and Brooks, 1950.

## Journal Articles

Boardman, Hollis. "The French Huguenots." *Transactions of the Huguenot Society of South Carolina* 80 (1975): 65-69.

Cuttino, J. P. "The Huguenots in History." *Transactions of the Huguenot Society of South Carolina* 68 (1963): 1-7.

Davidson, Donald. "Preface to Decision." *Sewanee Review* 53 (1945): 394-412.

First Baptist Church. "Historical Sketch of the First Baptist Church, Charleston, Est. 1682." Charleston SC: published by the church. 4 pp.

Greene, A. "The Political Crisis." *DeBow's Review* 1 (1886).

Harrell, Carolyn L. "Susan Myrick—Conservationist." *Southern Agriculturist* (1950): 22, 42, 43.

Lawton, Thomas O., Jr. "Captain William Lawton: 18th Century Planter of Edisto." *South Carolina Historical Magazine* 40 (1959): 86-93.

Murray, Chalmers S. "Edisto Island and its Place Names." In Claude H. Neuffer, ed., *Names in South Carolina*. 1967. Reprint. Spartanburg SC: Reprint Company, 1976.

Peeples, Robert E. H. "A Grimball Plantation Journal." *Transactions of the Huguenot Society of South Carolina* (1982): 64-69.

_____, ed. "The Memoirs of Benjamin Spicer Stafford." *Transactions of the Huguenot Society of South Carolina* 84 (1979): 100-105.

Ravenel, Daniel. "Historical Sketch of the Huguenot Congregations of South Carolina." *Transactions of the Huguenot Society of South Carolina* 7 (1900): 31-33.

Records of the Clerk's Office. "List of Tithables in Northampton, Virginia, August 1666." *Virginia Historical Magazine* 10: 195.

Salley, Alexander S., ed. "Abstracts from Records of the Court of Ordinary." *South Carolina Historical and Genealogical Magazine* 11 (1910): 54-55.

_____. "John Barnwell, Tuscarora Jack." *South Carolina Historical and Genealogical Magazine* 2 (1901): 46-53.

_____. "Records Kept by Colonel Isaac Hayne." *South Carolina Historical and Genealogical Magazine* 11 (1910): 93.

_____. "The Tuscarora Expedition: Letters of Colonel John Barnwell." *South Carolina Historical and Genealogical Magazine* 9 (1908): 28-54.

Schneider, Keith. "The Citadel." *Southern World* 3 (March/April 1981): 44-49.

South Carolina Militia, Captain Blake's Company. "Revolutionary Records." *South Carolina Historical and Genealogical Magazine* 5 (1904): 19.

Webber, Mabel C. "Grimball of Edisto Island." *South Carolina Historical and Genealogical Magazine* 23 (1922): 1-7, 39-45.


## Newspapers

*Christian Index*, August 7, 1863.

*Courier*, April 5, 1808, Charleston SC.

*Georgia Journal*, October 29, 1851; November 5, 1851.

*Georgia Messenger*, December 13, 1838, Macon GA.

*Georgia Telegraph*, August 31, 1850; October 21, 1851; January 31, 1852; September 14, 1858; May 8, 1887.

*Macon Daily Telegraph*, July 18, 1887, Macon GA.

*Macon News*, November 15, 1959, Macon GA.

*Macon Telegraph*, January 21, 1861; July 4, 1865; February 8, 1887; July 26, 1900; February 24, 1911; April 2, 1911; January 4, 1919; March 9, 1926, Macon GA.

*Macon Telegraph and News*, July 19, 1964; August 30, 1964, Macon GA.

*Observer*, July 30, 1948, Macon GA.

*Times*, April 4, 1808, Charleston SC.

## Letters

Furman, Richard. Letters, 1755-1825. MD/SCL.

Grimball, Thomas. Journal. Cunningham Papers, GHS/Savannah GA.

Lawton, Alexander James. Plantation Diary, 1810-1840. SHC/UNC.

Lawton, Capt. B. W. to Col. C. I. Colcock, March 2, 1863. Lawton Papers, MD/SCL.

Lawton, Furman Dargan to Mary (May) Nottingham, April 17; June 14, 20, 27; July 6, 11, 14, 16—1900.

Lawton, Sarah Alexander to Adeline Lawton Robert, December 30, 1860. SHC/UNC.

Lawton, Sarah Robert to Winborn Joseph Lawton, July 23, 1825. Lawton Papers, MD/SCL.

Lawton, Thomas Oregon to Anne Willingham Willis, 1941. Lawton Papers, MD/SCL.

Lawton, William M. to editors of the *New York Journal of Commerce*, July 17, 1869; William M. Lawton to Robert Mure, July 19, 1869; William M. Lawton to James R. Sparkman, August 2, 1869. Sparkman Papers, SHC/UNC.

Lawton, Winborn Asa to Winborn B. Lawton, September 7, 1854. MD/SCL.

Robert, W. H. to A. R. Lawton, June 11, 1895. Lawton Papers, MD/SCL.

Watson, Henry, Jr., to Dr. John H. Parrish, August 9, 1861. Henry Watson Papers, Duke University Library, Durham NC.

## Public Records

Account Book, 1778, SCDA.

Auditor General, SCDA.

Book of Royal Grants, SCDA.

Cash Book, 1777-1779, SCDA.

Chancery Causes Determined, 1831-1842, Cause #8, divorce petition dated December 3, 1834, CC/NCV.

College Catalogs and Commencement Programs, Historical Room, Wesleyan College, Macon GA.

Confederate Roster Books, J. J. Nottingham, Troop D, 43rd Battalion, Virginia Cavalry, CSA, Partisan Rangers, Mosby's Regiment.

Court Records, 1882 Term, Bibb County GA.

Deed Book 4, 1657, Northampton County VA.

Deed Book 78, Land Purchase, November 19, 1895, Bibb County, Macon GA.

Deed Book M, Abstract of Title of Property of Phillip G. Guttenberger, June 24, 1854, Vineville, Bibb County, Macon GA.

Grantors and Grantees Deed Index, 1632-1732, DB/NCV.

Guttenberger Historical File, Wesleyan College Library, Macon GA.

Inventory Book, 1756-1758, CPCR.

Inventory Estate of Captain William Lawton, 1756, CPCR.

Land Records, South Carolina Memorials, 1731-1776, SCDA.

Minutes of the Court of Ordinary, 1896, Bibb County, Macon GA.

Moore, ed., Records of the Secretary of the Province, 1694-1705, SCDA.

Plot Book 6, August 13, 1756, SCDA.

Plot Book 10, May 10, 1768, SCDA.

Probate Court, 1889 Term, Bibb County, Macon GA.

South Carolina Historical Society Collections.

South Carolina Land Grants, SCDA.

Thirtieth Report of the Central of Georgia Railroad and Banking Company of Georgia, December 1, 1895.

Treasury Journal, 1778-1787, SCDA.

Virginia Census, 1850, Northampton County VA.

Virginia Historical Register, 1848-1849.

Will Book, 1740-1747, CPCR.

Will Book, 1760-1784, CPCR.

Will Book, 1767-1771, CPCR.

Will Book, 1832, Northampton County VA.

Will Book, Records of the Court of Ordinary, 1696, South Carolina, SCDA.

Will of Martha Nottingham, November Term, 1896, PCR/BCG.

Will of Joseph Lawton, November 16, 1811, MD/SCDL.

Will of Richard Furman, vol. F, WB/SCDA.

Will of Pierre Robert [II], Will Book, 1731-1827, Office of the Probate Judge, Charleston SC.

Willingham Cotton Mills Account Books, 1899-1922, SC/MGHS.

# INDEX

family policy concerning, 167, 191; meetings to discuss, 193; Jefferson Davis on, 89; John Calhoun defends, 124; Richard Furman on, 28-29; William Brisbane's changing views on, 125

Slaves: act banning importation of, 167; boom in, 120-21; Brisbane frees his, 125; church attendance of, 28-29; cotton production by, 129-30, 162-63; disappear from Grimball plantation, 41; duties of masters to, 28; economic importance of, 205-206, 212-13; employment of former, 144, 155-56, 158; on flight to Georgia, 133-34; on Gravel Hill Plantation, 124-28; housing of, 131; Joseph Lawton's attitude toward, 162; moved to Robertville, 69, 101, 105, 108, 111, 120; obtain freedom, 134, 138, 212; rice produced by, 121-22, 156, 157; Sarah Lawton manages, 173, 183, 185, 189; sharecropping of former, 215-17, 228; silk production of, 162; trade in, 128; treatment of, 128; Willingham ownership of, 130

Small pox, 207

Smaw, Daniel G., 105-106; guardian of Mary Elliott Nottingham, 106, 108

Smaw, Mrs. Daniel G. (Nancy Elliott), 105, 108, 111, 113

Smith, Thomas: on Fundamental Constitution Committee, 41

Society of the Cincinnati, 16

Society Hill, Peedee SC, 19-20

Society for Promoting Christian Knowledge and Practice, 18

Soldiers Relief Fund, 90-91

Solomon, Colonel Edward S.: field report of, 136; on march through SC, 136

Somers, Robert: describes the town, 140; visits Macon in 1870, 139

Southell, Governor Seth (1690-1691), 42, 61

South Carolina, state of: becomes royal colony, 53; Calhoun's advocacy of, 124; cotton production booms in, 129; during Revolutionary War, 15, 21; the elected Assembly of, 68; first Legislative Assembly, 13; first state to secede, 89-90; General Assembly of, 173; House of Representatives of, 178; land grants, 11; secession convention, 207; Sherman's march through, 133-34; Willingham and Lawton planters in, 182, 184, 185, 208

South Carolina Agricultural and Mechanical Society, 217

South Carolina College, 174

Southern Baptist Theological Seminary, 143

Southern Central Agricultural Association: in Macon, 194; convention of, 194-95

Spanish American War, 227

Stateburg SC: described, 12, 32: Furman returns to, 16; plantation at, 19, 32

States' rights, 193

Stephens, Alexander Hamilton, 202

Stone, Captain William, 99

Suffolk County, England, 9

Sullivans Island SC, 119; Moultrie defends, 161; Thomas Willingham [I] settles on, 121-22

Sumter SC, 189

Sumter, General Thomas (1734-1832), 17, 69; organizes Claremont Society, 17; as senator, 17

Taft, William Howard (1857-1930), 246

Tallulah Falls GA, 75-77, 88

Taylor, Zachary (1784-1850), 191-92

Thackeray, William Makepeace (1811-1863), 188

Thomaston GA, 143

Thompson, Rebecca Virginia. See Nottingham, Mrs. Custis Bell

Tift College, 219

Tobacco: improved methods of processing, 104; marketing, 155-56; planters, 99

Toombs, Robert (1810-1885), 220

Transpine, 168-69, 196, 212; plantings at, 171; Sarah Robert Lawton dies at, 177; summer house built at, 174

Trott, Nicholas (chief justice), 49

Tuscarora Indian War, 51-53

Tuscarora Jack. See Barnwell, John

Uhink, John H., 81

University of Georgia, 73-74, 143

University of Maryland, 31

University of Heidelberg, 72-73

University of Virginia, 176

Verstille, Charlotte, 176-77

Verstille, Tristram, 176; and his wife, Rebecca, 176

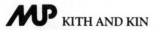 KITH AND KIN

Designed by Margaret Jordan Brown

Composition by MUP Composition Department

Production Specifications:
    text paper-60 pound Warren's Olde Style
    endpapers-Multicolor Adobe Dove Gray
    cover-(on .088 boards) Holliston Kingston Natural Finish
        35481
    dust jacket-Multicolor Adobe Dove Gray. Printed in two colors,
        PMS 168 and black

Printing (offset lithography) by Omnipress of Macon, Inc.,
    Macon, Georgia

Binding by John H. Dekker and Sons, Inc.,
    Grand Rapids, Michigan

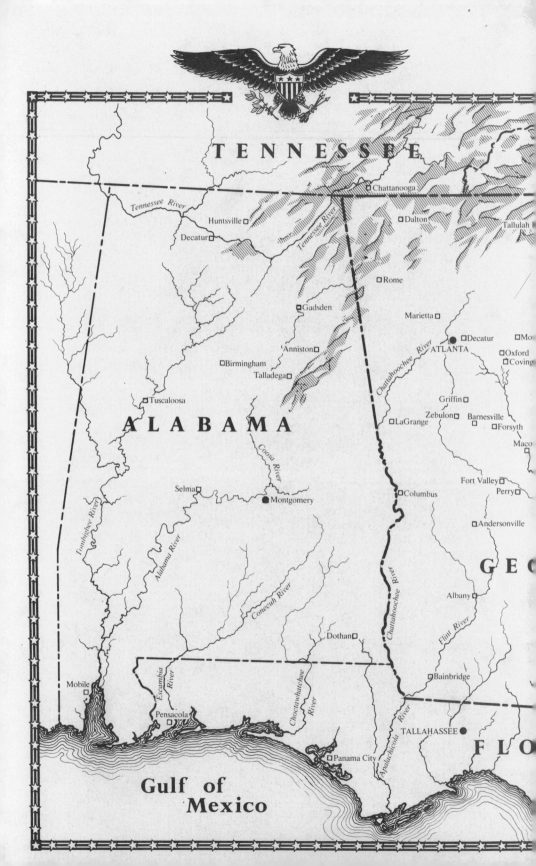